# CHEMICALLY ENHANCED BUTCH

For Aiden,

Queer ♡'s,

Ty Bo Yule

TY BO YULE

# CHEMICALLY ENHANCED BUTCH

WISE INK

MINNEAPOLIS

This is a work of creative non-fiction. All of the events in this memoir are as true as the author's memory will allow. Some timelines have been elided for the sake of brevity. Some names and identifying details have been changed to protect the identities of certain parties. The views and opinions in this story are solely those of the author. The author in no way represents any company, corporation, or brand mentioned herein.

ISBN 13: 978-1-63489-343-5

Library of Congress Catalog Number: 2020907316
Printed in the United States of America
First Printing: 2020

24  23  22  21  20          5    4    3    2    1

Cover design by Zoe Norvell
Interior design by Patrick Maloney
Author photo by Sayge Carroll


Wise Ink Creative Publishing
807 Broadway St NE
Suite 46
Minneapolis, MN, 55413

For my parents, the most powerful wizards I know,
who gave me shine.

For my wife, who loves me and gave me home.

# PREFACE

A number of my favorite people helped me edit this book. I am grateful to have had a smart millennial among them. They go by they/them pronouns and told me I sounded like a grumpy, irrelevant turd in a number of places and also told me I should change some of my language or explain why I didn't. Here is that then.

My language, especially when written, strives to be intentional. I never want to hurt anyone's feelings and I am usually aware of which buttons I push. I put this story in the world because it is my dream to talk to people about complex social power matrices all the time forever and ever. So as not to foreclose those potential conversations, let me begin by telling you how much I love sissies and vaginas. I really do. Using "wuss" and "pussy" as insults was fashionable in the last century. It would have been inauthentic and anachronistic to retrofit my character with a political consciousness. I have almost exclusively directed those words at pomposity in my lifetime, not femininity. Can a butch posture without a trace of internalized misogyny? Would anybody think they were hot if they never postured? Good questions. Let's talk about them.

Next, I am squarely Gen X. I am almost exactly the same age as the modern LGBT movement. It is possible I was conceived during the first Pride march, because of magic destiny, not my parents' awareness. Queer identities and perceptions have changed as dramatically for the movement as they have for me in our lifetimes, and it's been a messy journey for both of us. The language surrounding identity in my story reflects either the era in which it was expressed or my character's own naïveté.

When I was born, feminists were explaining to the world that gender is merely a social construct. In the last two decades, a good number of my friends have told me that they were born in the wrong body, which necessitates a more essentialist theory of gender. I think both can be true simultaneously, so I can try to be a good feminist as well as transmasculine and we can all stop fighting now.

I think identity formation and cultural competence begin in the same way and at the same time as language acquisition. During my twenty-year quest for a bachelor's degree, I was serendipitously introduced to Noam Chomsky's theory of universal grammar. It supposes that babies are born with a hard-wired capacity to absorb and assimilate the basic rules of grammar in their native language as opposed to learning merely through mimicry. Mimicry doesn't account for spontaneous variance of the rules.

Shockingly, I was not the first to expand the implications of Chomsky's theory. Spoken language is only one aspect of effective communication. It is equally important to internalize all the appropriate power relationships in one's native culture. These power relationships exist during every interaction witnessed by a baby, and can involve every combination of gender, age, race, class, abilities, and formality of circumstances. It's a lot to take in, so children are often forgiven for speaking to everyone with the same lack of deference. Propriety is like vocabulary, the arcane protocols of which can only be accumulated through experience. Gender is more like grammar. It's a fundamental set of rules that inform every other interaction. A child's ability to learn new languages starts to diminish by the time they're five. Most kids' gender deviance is evident by that age as well. Nobody does gender wrong. Kids know the rules. What if some kids just understand themselves creatively within the matrix of the power relationships they have to work with? By the time they're five, they can't unlearn their identity any more than they can unlearn their own language. Then they just have to deal with the fact that everybody else thinks they got it wrong for the rest of their life. The adversity they feel comes from the anxiety of not being able to play or win with the rules they've been given.

Gender was not the only subject of confusion for me. I was born into a completely homogenous, white, working-/middle-class culture. I didn't understand that anything else existed. I did not have a formative interaction with a person of color until I was nine. I did not know other people didn't have as much stability as I had until I was ten. I try to be truthful about my journey as an individual navigating new experiences. I did not start questioning the foundations of my cultural assumptions until I moved away from home to the big city. My work to dismantle dominant, conservative norms regarding gender, class, race, and beauty continues. I have tried to be honest about both productive and problematic behavior in my history.

Finally, it has been suggested that my treatment of my own sexual trauma was glib. I have always used humor to overcome discomfort. That is the way it was processed at the time, and perhaps the way I'm still processing it. My use of humor is not intended to minimize the pain of others, or even my own.

Let's talk about our flaws and triumphs together. Let's laugh about how ridiculous and sexy and tragic and powerful it is to be different.

# CHAPTER ONE

# MA AND ME

"Are you going to stop dressing like a gas station attendant now?" This wasn't the first time my mother had asked me that. We'd been fighting about my appearance since the seventies, a decade that still employed gas station attendants.

"I thought the point of this was for you to blend in now," she said.

"What do you think I'm going to wear now? Did you think I would start dressing like Dad? Do you see any Dockers and golf shirts around you?" I asked.

"You don't have to wear golf shirts, but you could look normal. I just thought you could look clean now that you're going to Harvard. You know, just blend a little."

"Where do you blend, ma? Out to lunch in Palm Springs? Seriously, where do you and Dad blend?" I replied.

We were getting louder. People at the Mexican fusion restaurant were staring. We paid our bill and spilled onto Mass Ave. We were yelling now. My mother was hurling the word *blend* at me like it was a spell and she was a well-dressed Disney villainess conjuring the dark magic of suburbs everywhere to permanently fuse a light-blue Oxford button-up to my skin. She was so mad, she didn't even care that the muggles in Cambridge could see the green laser beams shooting from her eyes.

At forty-one, I still could do nothing to stem the shame of knowing I was a cliché: an overprivileged, underachieving urban queer, with all the fashion that implies. But I'd gotten into Harvard, which I did solely to impress my parents and avoid this ongoing conflict. My best defense in the moment was, "They let me in *because* I'm weird, Ma. People think I'm cool."

"What people?" she asked.

She did have a point.

Earlier that day, my mother and I were sitting in my small room in Brookline. She was visiting during my second semester at Harvard Divinity School. Part of her still didn't believe I'd gotten in, so she seemed relieved people at school recognized me. There was an atmosphere of giddiness and trepidation around us, as if Harvard might call any second to tell us they'd discovered their error and would appreciate it if we left quietly.

I'd warned my mother over the phone that I had something to tell her. We'd gone to breakfast at the Busy Bee Café across the street, where the waitresses were all over fifty, had real Boston accents, and wore brightly colored running shoes. Our waitress was just telling Mom what a nice boy I was when I started to fall apart over my eggs, so we went back to my room.

"You know I've always been sorta masculine, pretty awkward as a girl?" I was sitting by the window, staring at my hands, starting to tear up.

"Yes." Her voice firm, letting me know she was ready.

I'd been having this conversation with my mother in my head for weeks, not caring that passing strangers could see my lips moving. But the well-crafted, assertive essay I'd perfected during this exercise fell out of my mouth as a stuttering monologue about our long history of fighting about my clothes.

"Remember when we had to go shopping for a prom dress

for me? And even you thought I looked ridiculous? Remember how attached I was to that army fatigue jacket in junior high?" I don't know where I was going with this preface, but my mom figured it out. I was about to remind her she'd always suggested a tunic as a unisex option for formal wear, but I thought I looked terrible in tunics, when she stopped me.

"You want to do what Benny did?" Benny, my best friend back in Minneapolis, had started taking testosterone to become a man a couple of years before this.

"Yes" was all I could get out. I couldn't look at her.

She sighed. "Oh, thank god. I thought you were going to tell me something important."

I stopped crying and stared at her. In the silence that followed, my eyebrows affected befuddlement, then anger, and then I started laughing. So did my mom. We both laughed that laugh of venting lifelong, mutual anxiety that only the two of us share. It went on for quite some time.

"Well, you always did suck at being a girl," she offered in lieu of some time-consuming, gratuitous gesture of sentimentality. "Should we go do your laundry now?"

# CHAPTER TWO

# CAPTAIN AWESOME

My parents possess a special mortal magic. They have faults, just not the ones most people have. No other child would have thrived better with them. And no other parents would have succeeded where some may feel they failed.

Mom was hot and Dad was a stud. They didn't grow into the aging beauty and ex–football hero, sitting around, drinking, retelling stories of their glory days, wondering what happened. They find that kind of slovenly nostalgia uncomfortable. Mom was Twiggy, not Sandra Dee. Dad turned down a dozen athletic scholarships to get away from people who bored him. Both preferred hard work to adoration. Mom needed to be more than arm candy, and Dad needed someone who could keep up with him. Neither could have tolerated anyone else. They relied on each other's competence and will. In the summer of 1969, my alphas were united, destined to be more than underestimated, working-class middle children from a small Midwestern town. They both gave me the very best of their genes. The sum of which made a giant, handsome girl unicorn that scared the shit out of everyone.

During a Minnesota blizzard in January of 1970, after making prenatal preparations to not be too needy, I emerged at nine pounds with a full head of hair. Mom found some lady down the street with between six and twelve children to take care of me so she could return to her serving job ten days after giving birth. Dad worked at a gas station while finishing college. Mom waited tables and helped Dad finish college.

When I was two years old, and forty-five pounds, my favorite TV show was *The Sonny & Cher Comedy Hour*. The best part was when Sonny and Cher would close the show by bringing Chastity out for their final number. Chastity and I are the same age. I thought I was cuter than Chastity. I just knew I would make a better famous TV child. I used to carry a picture of Cher with me wherever I went. I'd torn it out of a *TV Guide*. I told my day-care providers that I was actually Sonny and Cher's child and just on loan to my parents. They must have told my folks, who must have thought it was cute. My parents started calling me Tara Bono, which was quickly shortened to just Bo. The nickname has endured along with the story my entire life.

We moved to Iowa from Minnesota when my dad took a job as a salesman for a freight company. We often threw parties at our house for my dad's bosses, coworkers, and customers. My parents and I worked as a team, impressing and captivating other families. I thought we were shiny. We sometimes felt like a shark family. I especially loved when I found the look of cautious amusement on an adult's face when I'd said something too witty for my age. Unfortunately, I was often tasked with entertaining clients' children at these functions.

My parents knew I found kids-only time tedious, but they didn't know I was a wizard from ancient times. I led the other children on expeditions into the woods behind our house to show them where undiscovered ancient burial grounds were. I warned them about the witch that lived deep in the woods. I would protect my less-magical cohort from imagined dangers. Also, I sincerely believed I could move objects with my mind. It was obvious to me I wasn't like other human children.

My mother held the same suspicion, but she had high hopes that school would reveal my potential as a pack leader. I entered kindergarten at seventy-five pounds and nearly a foot taller than any of my classmates. I could also read and write and understand basic arithmetic. All this had been a source of pride at home, but then some apprehension at the thought of me joining an institutionalized peer group.

Public education is mainly about conformity with sporadic opportunities for competition. (Competition was later banned in the nineties.) Both teachers and fellow students were relentlessly thrilled by circumstances that reaffirmed societal standards of uniformity and mediocrity. In contests of strength, agility, and intellect, I won. This did not make me popular, but it did give me an outsider power in my social group. I was occasionally called upon to vanquish an enemy at recess or help with homework. Mostly, I spent my recesses alone, until I was needed. I was Ferdinand the Bull instead of a bully.

Teachers didn't help my integration. They routinely set me in a corner with my own work. They all suggested to my mom that I be skipped ahead one or two grades. Mom thought it more important for me to have extra time to hone my social skills, to fit in. This is her area of expertise, though she has never striven to be in the middle of the pack. I'm pretty sure she could see me next to the other kids. I think, in her own way, she was trying to protect me by completely denying there was anything unusual about me.

I did have a certain longing to be liked and popular. I was funny right away. Big kids sometimes get that gift. I wasn't ugly and I didn't pick my nose, but my peers and I had difficulty deciding whether I was a boy or a girl. I was a confusing blend of the two or something else entirely. Children understand gender intuitively, in the same way they understand their native language. By the time a kid is five, they have grasped the general rules of grammar and gender. They just don't have the experience yet to know what to do with irregular verbs.

This is the age when slumber parties are all-inclusive. If a female classmate had a birthday, all the other girls in her class were invited. At these functions, I was to sleep by the door and protect us from intruders and ghosts. I was terrified of ghosts, but protecting girls seemed to be my job, so I sacked up. When playing house or Dukes of Hazzard or Charlie's Angels, it was always assumed I would play the dad or Bo Duke. Although with Charlie's Angels, whether I would play Sabrina or Bosley depended on how many girls we had. No one thought this was weird, though we never ran the casting by the grown-ups.

With the boys, I was a fun object of physical spectacle. As an ally, I assured victory. As a foe, my defeat required strategic collaboration. Boys repeatedly invented a game just for me. It was basically to see how many boys it would take to tackle me, or how many I could drag. I always took dares. During PE, I was always team captain or first chosen. Boys teased me, but their nicknames always referenced my size and strength, like Tarzan, or Mothra, or T-Rex. I was secretly proud of my status, as it confirmed my inner identity as a future superhero whose unique qualities would save the world someday.

If I could've remained that singular combination of David Cassidy and She-Ra, perhaps I would've been happy. None of us knew what to do with me when girls and boys interacted with each other in a girl/boy kind of way. Girls were naturally drawn to me. There was something about my tomboy charisma they found endearing. Logic trumped these feelings in mixed company. Boys would occasionally get little crushes on me in the way they do before puberty. Their attraction would only last a few hours or days, though, usually until they worked out in their head that if the other boys found out, they would feel kinda gay (even before they knew what that meant).

I was more invested in the girls' perceptions of me. It was not uncommon for the prettiest or most popular girl in class to develop an intimate bond with me. So as not to diminish her status, our connection was always cultivated in private. I lived for these one-on-one enchanted bubbles of interdimensional, interarchetypal sorcery. In proximity to the larger social arena, I would follow at a distance, or lurk around corners like a crazy stalker. I spun these precious infatuations into epic story lines, quietly played out incessantly, during my considerable hours spent alone in trees or under bleachers.

Rebecca Johnson started this lifelong theme in the first grade. She was the prettiest, littlest, most popular girl in class. She would confide in me. I would carry stuff for her. I protected her from all the boys. She was the first in an interminable line of pretty straight girls to utter those six soul-crushing words to me. "I wish you were a boy." These girls have always stopped playing happily-ever-after long before I'm ready. Then I am left to my hours, perfecting a triumphant scenario where they regret their hasty dismissal of me, but it's too late. Either I die, or I am a pirate king who is best friends with Cher.

Human children are not unlike puppies. They tussle and flirt and shove each other, settling into a complex and self-evident power structure. I was an alpha before I was a boy, genetically unsurprising. At some point, masculinity emerged as a by-product of my well-rounded competence and my

utter inability to do anything cute. The only thing I couldn't
do that boys could do was be one. At the time, I didn't think
I ought to be something other than what I was, which was
more like a wise Pegasus who knew kung fu. There were numerous circumstances where it wasn't confusing to anyone
that little alpha girls were attracted to me, and boys deferred
to me. Then there were those occasions where the fact that
I was a girl with long hair would emerge from the mist and
startle everyone, like they'd been dozing off and now wondered where the fuck I'd come from. These carefully avoided
but inevitable circumstances would often inspire long fits of
convulsed tittering and fidgety self-awareness, as well as remind me that everyone is dumb and stupid and dumb and I
hate everyone.

Like that time Mom tried to help when it was my turn for
show-and-tell. We'd gone to some carnival. I'd won a doll for
knocking something down with a ball. I was excited about
winning a prize for doing something sporty. My mother was
excited that it was my turn for show-and-tell. She suggested I
take my prize doll for the occasion. I knew this was a terrible
idea, but I didn't know how to tell her that.

We began that morning using a system my mother had perfected so she could get to work on time. She would set a tray of
food by my bed and then go shower. Food was the only thing I
liked more than sleep. By the time she was dressed, I was done
eating. I'm a slow eater. Then she'd usually come into my room
and yell at me to stop playing with my Legos and get dressed.
But since it was show-and-tell day, she picked out a cute dress
for me to wear and put ribbons in my hair. *A doll and a dress?
This is going to be bad.* Technically, it should work to put a little
girl in a dress and have her publicly display a doll. I even had
long hair, because Cher. But I could sense anxiety coming from
her as well, like deep down she also knew she was putting a

tutu on a bulldog. We proceeded through our daily routine of awkwardness and conflict. She handed me my doll and put me in the car.

I must've hidden the doll and probably myself until it was time. When Mrs. Hansen called me up with my dumb doll, I could barely move. She looked nervous too. I walked to the front of the class, my least favorite place, but before I got out my story about how I knocked down the thing with the thing, all of the boys shat themselves laughing at me. The girls were giggling too, but with a look of discomfort like, "Oooh, I thought we were clear about you not doing things that we do." I ran out of the room crying.

I felt betrayed, but I really couldn't blame the other kids. The illusion I'd created with my classmates would not stand up to grown-up interference. Kids were not going to let me be a girl, and they knew I wasn't a boy. That liminal space that allowed me full access to my secret magic superpowers meant that I had, at some point, agreed to maintain distance from conventional categories. Grown-ups saw me as an awkward, large girl who needed extra help being feminine. Kids saw their captain in a dress, with a doll. I also hated being bad at anything, even things I did not want to do, even being a girl. The doll went in the trash. I sat against the lockers and cried. At six, I did not have the language of Judith Butler's queer performance theory to aid me, nor did any of my elfin clan come to find me in that hallway. I was just mad. Then there was disappointing Mom, the worst thing of all.

Adding my mother's gaze into this social paradox was something I tried to avoid. How could I explain to her that I was sort of famous and kind of in charge, when I never had any friends over? How could I explain that my T-shirts and Toughskins made everyone more comfortable? When it was just the two of us, she never cared that I wasn't girly. She didn't care for the more bubbly or frail female stereotypes in general. She was my best friend, and I think I may have been hers. Why did I have to go to school? But she knew I was going to have to make it as a girl. From her own experience, she believed cute fashion and conversational enthusiasm were required for social achievement. I knew I would never be able to assimilate my mother's gender example. We already wore almost the same size clothes. I just kept my mouth shut.

# CHAPTER THREE

# THE MOTHER-FUCKING KING

What was clear to me at an early age was that I would have to either find the portal to the nether realm where I was long-lost Amazon royalty or be as cool as my dad.

These are equally difficult quests. My dad's masculinity was effortless and exalted. And for most of my life, it just pissed me off.

My dad has a way of walking that tells the rest of the species that he doesn't lose. It's not some cocky strut that invites competition. It's more of an elegant saunter that conveys that one should not even bother. I practiced that walk every time I was aware of myself as a child.

And he always won, at everything.

Legend has it, he won the down payment for our first house in a card game. He taught me gin at an early age. "This is your card, right here," he would say at the beginning of a hand, while tucking the card in his glasses above his nose. The card would stay perched there, until he used his final discard to show me the card I'd been waiting for. I wanted his voodoo. It was my birthright.

"Keep your glove up," he told me during our first game of catch as I was wiping the blood from my nose.

"K, Dad."

He let me be a batgirl for his slow-pitch softball team,

which meant I got to wear boys' clothes and perform a task usually reserved for boys. I think he was unaware of and un- interested in my failures as a girl. Watching my dad, with a cigarette hanging out of his mouth and a beer by his foot, play shortstop with his supernatural hand-eye coordination, I had high hopes that could be my destiny if I trained hard enough.

He took me hunting once and let me shoot his shotgun. My fingers barely reached the trigger when the stock was on my shoulder. He stood behind me, but I told him to move be- cause I could do it myself. I ended up on my ass with a sweet bruise on my shoulder. He laughed and lit another cigarette. "How was that for you?"

"Pretty fun, Dad." I laughed, scared he was disappointed.

Hanging out with my dad always felt like auditioning for a secret guild of infallibility. If I could be just like him, I would wield the power of confidence and indifference against the petty preoccupations of mere mortals. Most importantly, my mother would stop bothering me about my outfits. Dad was the only person as strong as Mom. He was the only one who could win arguments with her.

He traveled all the time because of his job. One-on-one time with him was a special occasion. This only added to my anxiety about impressing him. My dad excels at playful, ver- bal roughhousing and challenging one's insecurities. He does not baby or flatter. He conditions through sarcasm and im- provisational belligerence. He does not believe in letting any- one win, even young children. Inevitably, no matter what we were doing or how much fun I was having, I would succumb to my frustration at not being as good as him and have some sort of fit. Then I would spend long hours envisioning my eventual triumph or possible scenarios where I might save my parents from imminent doom.

My dad never hesitated to teach me "boy" things. He

wasn't trained for anything else. He assumes everyone is capable until they prove otherwise. He was my role model, but I saw him too infrequently for him to be my mentor. I always thought he might understand how I felt at school. Other people seemed to annoy him too. But I never talked to him about it. I wavered between proud underdog determination and indignant defeat when it came to trying to emulate my father. I could never figure out how I was going to get other people to treat me like they treated my dad. Nobody ever put him in a dress and told him to smile.

It seemed like girls were always supposed to be worried about everything, and my dad just wasn't. I started feeling like my considerable efforts to mimic ease and confidence were in the same category as wearing boy's clothes. Both were strongly discouraged if the ambiguous boundary confining innocent "dress-up" was crossed. I felt a little angry at my dad for getting to be him. When he was home, Mom wouldn't make pancakes for dinner, and she wouldn't play Supremes albums while we were getting ready in the morning.

There must be some other world where I shall be king.

CHAPTER FOUR

# FIGURE IT OUT, GRASSHOPPER

I went to a new school for third and fourth grades when we moved to our new house. I didn't understand why my mom insisted that I keep going to school. I felt capable of continuing my education on my own. I experienced the same interpersonal dynamics with kids at my new school, which I would've preferred to avoid. Smear the Queer was only fun until the boys realized the Queer kept winning. Girls didn't find me an appropriate wingman for their fledgling efforts at flirting with the boys, since most of them were scared of me. I started spending a great deal of time with the school nurse. I think I even developed the ability to willfully raise my body temperature. She was maternally patient with my mutinous hypochondria. My mom always worked full-time, and kids really can't understand what chaos they create when all they want is to go home. Mom always bought nice Christmas presents for the school nurse.

I also began to see the cracks in the façade of authority that adults who were not my parents claimed over children. How could they hope to compete with the double-barreled fortitude I experienced at home? My folks weren't disciplinarians, they just had high expectations. My mother had made them clear as a toddler, when we were in a department store and I decided to throw my one and only temper tantrum. I'd seen other children doing it. My mother simply behaved as if she didn't know whose child I was and left. As I got older, if other adults tried to correct my behavior by treating me like a child, I tended to return the gesture. I started spending some time in the corner for reasons that were not purely academic.

My teachers tried to channel my potential by testing me for a gifted program, but I thought this boy Tom, who was in the gifted program, was a pompous dick. He was always talking about being gifted like he was special, but he was just a wuss. I didn't want to be in the same club as Tom, so I threw the test. To get me out of the classroom, they let me spend extra time in the library.

This was the beginning of the special secret training montage that began repeating itself in my head for the rest of my life. If I was never going to become either my mom or my dad, I needed to prepare for my encounter with the parallel universe where I would be like Caine in *Kung Fu* and wander alone through the country, fighting injustice and sleeping in caves. I wouldn't allow myself to read frivolous children's novels. I read Edith Hamilton's *Mythology* and books on Native American culture. I was sure there was a wisdom in the world that would make me stoic and spooky. Really, it was the only destiny that made sense with my obviously superior fairy genes.

I'd also just seen the 1976 Olympics, when Bruce Jenner won the decathlon, so I began my clandestine Olympic training behind the gym during recess. There must be a reason I was so much bigger and stronger than anyone else my age. Surely it must be that I would be the first girl to win the gold medal in the Olympic decathlon . . . or weight lifting, maybe, like that big Russian dude.

Leather Tuscadero from *Happy Days* was also a big influence, so I got my hair cut for the first time into a shag just like hers. I remember consciously deciding to sever ties with Cher, which was terrifying since it meant symbolically taking a step away from my mother. I fainted off the barber's chair, but recovered to feel cool. Mystic-athlete-tough-girl is a complex identity for third grade, but I'd been backed into a corner. Besides, I was totally nailing it.

My mom and I were still close. I was watching her identity manifest as well. She was a young mother who took pride in her appearance and the tidy tastefulness of her house. She loved her job. She worked for the State of Iowa as an administrative assistant. It was her first opportunity to wear professional clothes and dazzle people with her organizational skills and shining work ethic. Her job resulted in my first brief contact with lesbians.

Pat and Barb. I'm pretty sure lesbians were only allowed one syllable for their name in the seventies. Both had short, salt-and-pepper hair. Barb was bigger and wore overalls with no bra. Pat's fashion was slightly crisper, and she wore glasses. I had no idea what they were. I just knew I should be near them.

Mom and I went to an amusement park with them one day. I spent the whole day holding Barb's hand, hoping she would take me to whatever distant land she'd come from. I think my mom had a crush on Pat. There was probably something extraordinarily appealing to my mom about shared household chores and an absence of masculine entitlement. This was just a brief brush with an alternative reality for both of us, however.

Saturdays were spent doing household chores. When my dad was home, his buddies gathered at the house in the morning before golf or after hunting. I learned to make eggs for them. It was my job to listen for the rattle of my dad's beer can on the table, signaling me to fetch him another. These cocky displays somehow seemed charming coming from him, while also fostering my seething defiance. That was his gift to me. Mom would clean everything and run all the errands in time to make dinner. She always looked flawless.

Sundays were family day, which meant my mom and me. She'd tried taking me to church for a period, putting me in Sunday school. I couldn't imagine a nightmare worse than spending another day of the week away from my mom, with other children, in a learning environment that seemed even more childish and singsongy than regular school. After the fourth consecutive Sunday of being hauled out of services to come get me, Mom decided God would understand if we spent Sundays going to museums and movies and playing games.

My parents and I reserved temperament control for required tasks. They went to work, and I went to school. They got promotions, and I got As. I would've rather gotten a job to pay for all the food I ate. The higher frequencies of my personality were discouraged in front of people with a simple, firm hand on my thigh, as if our superpowers were a secret. Around others, I watched my parents soften their edges. They didn't want to overwhelm or scare outsiders. When it was just the three of us, it was okay to let our wolf nature show. This setting always had the potential to erupt into a yelling contest of wills, like canines barking at each other in a loving, primal way. Our magnitude was better left within our triad. The uninitiated didn't stand a chance.

My dad worked with a guy named Rich. His wife, Patty, took care of me after school and during the summer while my mom was at work. She was a stay-at-home mom because she was Catholic. This was new to me. She had a daughter my age and another, two years younger. I liked them a lot, but I loved Patty. Patty had soft features and wore comfortable clothes, and I could always make her laugh. She made us macaroni and cheese and always gave me extra. When I was "rambunctious," like pulling their trampoline next to their second-story balcony, she would just roll her eyes and laugh and give me more food. It was the "boys will be boys" affirmation I'd never known I wanted so badly. One summer night, there was a tornado warning. I was over at Patty's. Rich wasn't home and my mother was still at work. Not only did Patty and her girls give the rest of their dinner to me because they were too nervous to eat, but they also told me they were glad I was there to protect them. I was nine years old. It might still be one of the proudest days of my life.

"We're moving to California," my dad announced at the beginning of fourth grade. Dad had gotten promoted several times, and they were putting him in charge of his own trucking terminal in Southern California.

It seemed like a grand adventure, but I had responsibilities in Iowa. Would Patty be okay without me? My mother was also not sure about leaving the relative respect she'd found. My dad left for California for a few months to find a place to live and get settled. I sensed tension in their relationship, but when Dad came home to get us, Mom consolidated all her apprehension into commitment. I was nervous but pretty excited. Perhaps things would be different in California. To a kid from the Midwest, before the internet or even cable TV, California was just Disneyland and the beach.

We packed the moving truck and spent our last night in Iowa with Patty and Rich. When we were pulling out of the driveway in the morning, I saw Patty in the doorway waving to me as I watched through the back window. I could see her crying, and I was too. She was the only adult who had been able to see me. She had been my fairy godmother.

We turned a corner. I turned around and stopped crying as soon as we got on the freeway.

# CHAPTER FIVE

# PIT STOP ON TOM SAWYER'S ISLAND

Dad rented a house with a pool in a place called Whittier, California. Instead of a garage, we had a pool-house, which was a lot like a secret pirate lair. My parents got me a dog because they felt guilty for moving me. I picked out an enormous Great Dane named Blue.

Mom and I went to Disneyland immediately. Back then, they had Tom Sawyer's Island. That was where I wanted to live. It was an isolated, wooded part of Disneyland with forts and rock formations and ropes and ladders and secret passages. It really was the most magical place on Earth. That island was a backdrop for my daydreams for years.

Los Angeles smelled bigger. The sun was closer. I set out to explore my new surroundings. There were so many more people here. They were different too. They looked at me differently, like I wasn't supposed to be wandering down Whittier Boulevard by myself. It was the first time I was white. It was the first time I was small. There were other worlds.

My last two months of fourth grade were spent at a school where I was one of the only kids who spoke English as my first language. I wasn't just ahead in my normal way. I don't remember a single person from that school.

Mom was also emerging from our Midwestern bubble. Jogging was just becoming a trend. With no job, Mom put on a pair of my sneakers and started running around the baseball field next to my school. There was no local chapter of the Welcome Wagon, and no one played bridge in Southern California. I think she tried to make cookies and introduce herself to some neighbors. Most of them didn't answer their doors. Our initial California experiment was not destined to last long. It was confusing and unsuccessful. The dog went back to the pound after a couple weeks.

Our home was broken into, and my folks said there were "drug dealers" living on our block. I hadn't anticipated our superpowers would not work here. How could this nice house with a swimming pool be in a bad neighborhood? Aren't all public schools supposed to be the same? Why are the neighbors looking at us like that when we wave and smile?

My folks decided on a do-over. After less than a year in Whittier, we moved to Huntington Beach. Our new condo was only ten blocks from the ocean! I could walk. My parents still believed that ten-year-olds should be allowed to wander unaccompanied until dinner time.

CHAPTER SIX

# CALIFORNIA DREAMING

A few things happened that year in Huntington Beach. I got my first group of friends. I got my period. And I got my first taste of being bad.

The kids at my new school seemed tough or like they knew they were cool because they lived by the beach. They cursed a lot more and were better at insults. I kept to myself and tried to look intimidating. PE always established my athleticism quickly and possible uses for my size. It took a moment for the boys to reconcile having a ringer on their dodgeball team with my blossoming bustline. And then, at some point, I found myself heading up a wee girl gang.

Roberta, Graciela, Penelope, and me. Roberta was a little heavy. Graciela was one of the only Latina kids at the school. Penelope was small and hyperactive. And I was still me. All four of us were naturally forced to the fringe of the pre-pubescent social matrix of fifth grade. We formed a secret club. I was elected bodyguard, probably at my own insistence. This was my first experience with a misfit alliance. There was a new special power in that simple solidarity. It was a whisper of my superhero future. It was also just nice to have someone to eat lunch with.

It was the first time I brought friends home since the age of enforced slumber party gender integration. My gated condominium complex was conveniently located across the street from school and had the added benefit of a web of small swimming pools throughout the development, connected by partially wooded walking paths. Hardly anyone used the little pools, since there was a large central pool with a clubhouse. Their relative isolation made them ideal locations for top-secret meetings and for our group to comfortably don swimwear.

My mom seemed excited to make us snacks and give us games to play and even take us on outings. She was always eager to support any interest I showed in being social. Except then one night, at dinner, she joked to my dad, "Bo always makes friends with the fat kids or the Mexican kids. She doesn't like the normal kids."

*Jesus fuck, aren't you ever happy with anything I do? I finally have some friends. Haven't you been in my ass my whole life about making friends?* I thought. I didn't say anything that night, but then she said it again to a group of my dad's coworkers and their wives at our house. She said it like she was proud of my social work with the less fortunate or something.

"Who do you think talks to me, Ma? What's wrong with my friends? They're nice and they're smart. Who do you want me to bring home?" I asked.

"I just think if you stopped wearing your surf clothes, and combed your hair once in a while, your life could be a lot easier," she said.

"K, Ma. Gotta go."

I always knew what she meant by *easier*. It looked something like being a kid in an Oscar Meyer wiener commercial. The part where she blamed me for all my social difficulties became increasingly irritating, though. I was conflicted. My folks had worked hard to find their way into the middle class, and they were very supportive. I felt guilty for being unable to obtain this easy life my mother and father worked to provide for me, like I was letting the family down and being a spoiled brat. But Mom also implied my friends were losers, and I just didn't want to be a winner. Had she really missed the memo? The social elite of my numerous grade schools had made my outsider status repeatedly clear. It would not be remedied by pegged jeans and cowl-necks. I did not know how to giggle or have a smaller ass.

I started spending more time at Roberta's house. Robbie and I had the most in common. Plus, she had two older sisters that I thought were totally rad. I quickly developed a big crush on the middle sister, Terri. I was captivated by her teenage wisdom and woes. Also, Robbie's house was messy, and she, her mom, and her sisters were all fleshy. It was fascinating. My clothes and my size didn't cause anxiety in this house. When I was there, growing angrier at my mother's and the world's expectations of my improbable normality, I started to feel embarrassed about my relative privilege. I didn't want Robbie and her sisters to come to my house and see how hot my mom was or how tidy and tastefully decorated our house was. That was not tough or cool or empathetic in any way. I did not want my dad quizzing or teasing my friends. As the spawn of the dominant paradigm, it was my duty to provide a buffer for the untrained and less experienced disenfranchised of the world. This is how messy little liberal underachievers are born.

I hid who I was with my friends from my parents, and I hid who I was at home from my friends. Donning appropriate identities really is a superpower. All of my façades were finished with an extra salty, preteen "fuck you" veneer. My required worlds were sometimes exhausting, though, so I often took some me-time to remember that I was destined for glory.

There was an empty lot a few blocks from the ocean with a lone eucalyptus tree. I had to jump to reach the lowest branch, then walk up the trunk high enough to swing my legs over. From there, it was an easy scramble up the next few branches. To get to my branch, though, I had to stand up and lean out over a pretty good fall to catch myself on my destination. Then it was a jump to wrap my legs around the lower part of the branch and shimmy up to the crook that was mine. It was the perfect branch, with a back and footrest.

Shrouded by foliage, high above human gaze, I would spend hours imagining my tragic death, followed by the tear-filled funeral where my parents would finally see my potential. Or I'd fantasize about beating and humiliating Robbie's older sister's dickhead boyfriend. I most enjoyed daydreams where nearly everyone else died in some cataclysmic global catastrophe and I was left to lead the ragtag remnants in a just utopia. I just knew I would ultimately be a misunderstood loner in a more substantial adult way. I prepared for my future hermitage poeticizing the skin-like embrace of eucalyptus bark.

But I knew I also needed to continue training for my destiny as a famous person who is amazing at everything.

Ocean adventures feel far different than Midwestern woods expeditions. The warm, hazy smell of sea and smog makes everything seem more exotic. The sight of the ocean intensifies the sensation that you're continually in a movie. There was a bike path along the beach that went the entire length of Orange County. I had a beach cruiser. I would ride north to the Queen Mary in Long Beach or south to Laguna Beach. Both destinations were well outside my jurisdiction and required all day for the round trip. The mixture of transgression and exhaustion was electrifying. This was the year I started lying to my parents.

I swam in the ocean a lot. I had a boogie board as well. Huntington Beach was the location of the OP National

Surfing Championships. Perhaps I could be a famous surfer. The actual surfers on that stretch of beach were pretty mean, though. They used to shout, "Harpoon the whale," at me frequently. This brings me to my size again.

I had been a really big kid. I was solid and thick. I'd already developed a few curves and grown a few hairs. Two weeks into fifth grade, I got my period for the first time, at school. I was wearing white painter's pants. My teacher mercifully let me go home. My mother didn't believe me when I called her at work. This was long before hormones in milk made menstruation at ten common. It shouldn't have been surprising to either of us, considering my body's enthusiasm for rapid maturity. This made my little curves and hairs seem like a bigger deal. I was already over five feet tall and weighed about a hundred and fifty pounds. I looked a lot older than I was.

My baby fat became a cause for concern for my mother. Until this development, she still had hope my stockiness would streamline with puberty. "Fat people are lazy and unsuccessful, and they are not of our people" was the general fear I sensed from my mother. I hadn't been round, exactly, but I was a bigger gal. I was not shaped like the bikini-clad teenage girls the surfers did not yell mean things at on the beach. But I was not shaped like a boy. I was shaped like a teenage girl with low self-esteem. I was shaped like a target.

When I wasn't in my tree or trekking across the globe, I wandered, like a sad antelope straying from the herd, down to the pier. At the beginning of the eighties, Huntington Beach wasn't yet gentrified or especially affluent. It was a scruffy little beach town. Congregating at the pier were all the characters one might expect of a slightly seedy oceanside hamlet. Along with the tanned and toned were the homeless and eccentric. There was the old guy with pinwheels in his sun hat and an authentic peg leg. There was a couple of Hell's

Angels who liked to fish there. There were a few aging hippie guys living in vans. And there was a whole variety of people doing a whole lot of drugs by the Green Burrito under the pier. The lonely and the disassociated have always been able to see me. It's as if they were welcoming me home. I didn't understand everything I saw. I had zero street smarts. I was open to learning. I enjoyed listening to bizarre and incoherent monologues. I had no struggles with my body or my fashion here. People talked to me like I was allowed to be there, so I kept coming back. I became an auxiliary character and was greeted warmly when I returned. It felt very special and secret. I needed more material for my tough-guy persona, but it was also where I was objectified as a girl for the first time.

I wore board shorts and men's OP beach shirts and Vans. To the surfers hanging out in the sun, I was invisible. Under the pier, in the shadow, I was a focal point. A young girl, by herself, unafraid. Occasionally, an aging surfer or delivery guy for the taqueria would approach me. The conversation would often lead to their van. (Creepy dudes honestly do always have vans at their disposal.) I learned that balls smell terrible, and that nothing promising ever happened in a van that smelled like balls. I would always get freaked out before it went *too* far. Luckily, I was always allowed to leave. I would feel a little shame. But I also discovered the stirrings of a new kind of power. Perhaps this was the way pretty girls felt at school. Except those girls never came down here by themselves. Maybe this was something cooler. I felt a little brave. I felt sort of grown-up. I felt like a spy.

I was ten. As an adult, if I were to encounter men leering at a girl that age, I would happily cave in their face with a bat. As that girl, I felt just as accountable as they were. I wasn't scared of them. I had a sense of control in those meetings. I was smarter than they were. It made me feel worldly and mysterious. Back at school, or at home, I had a secret. Those encounters were wholly separate from my life, connected to my daydreaming, but the vestiges of that power lingered in my everyday identities and reaffirmed my belief that I alone could endure anything to lead and protect the misfits of the world.

During this year, I was unaware that my father was also discovering how different life in Southern California was. He'd been put in charge of an enormous freight hub that handled distribution to most of the Southwest. His company hoped he could resolve some of their more long-standing labor issues. After he learned a number of teamsters working in his region were altering their time cards or stealing shipments, he fired dozens of them, because that's what you do in the Midwest when someone cheats or steals. Apparently, the rash of death threats my father received against himself and us reached a point of urgency. We moved to Arizona.

CHAPTER SEVEN

# JESUS WAS A NERD

Paradise Valley, Arizona, lacked all the seedy charm of a damp little beach town. It was a clean, older suburb of Phoenix with pleasant adobe bungalows and desert landscaping. In the summer, the heat can kill you. There are rattlesnakes, scorpions, and poisonous spiders. A friendly, neat suburban community feels a bit frivolous in this environment.

My school felt familiar. It was a well-funded, homogenous, midsized school. Sixth grade was my last year of elementary school, and the last year I would be the biggest, strongest kid in my class. I brought my beach mystique to my bright, tidy desert surroundings. I got custom black-and-yellow Vans that matched the new black-and-yellow BMX bike that my parents bought me because they'd moved me again.

The kids there were less cynical than their Huntington Beach counterparts. They were more easily impressed. They initially thought I was a teacher's aide. I was aloof for a while. I felt superior to the suburban fluff because of my extensive street experience. Kids asked me about California and the beach. The one nice thing about changing schools all the time is that you can just make shit up. I had them thinking I was some sort of surfing crime lord. The kids weren't just intimidated by my size; they actually thought I was tough and worldly. Sweet.

There was the inevitable ring of popular, pretty girls, headed up by Jessi Russo. Jessi had that aura of distant sadness that sometimes surrounds pretty girls. Even though they're popular, they have an angst that probably comes from being overly objectified from an early age and never really seen. Considering who my mother is, it isn't surprising I've always been sensitive to the special melancholy of pretty girls. I was tailor-made to be an animated woodland sidekick for forlorn Disney princesses, like a wide-eyed, empathetic cartoon bunny.

Because of my unique air of relative maturity and ongoing status as an outsider, I was a natural counselor. Jessi would bring me her woes surrounding her relationship with Rick Schumacher, a handsome blond lad whose prepubescent acne didn't tarnish his chiseled jawline. He had biceps and an Adam's apple, among the first to achieve these manly attributes.

Jessi and Rick were the "it" couple at Desert Cove Elementary. I could listen to Jessi relate Rick's shortcomings as a boyfriend for hours. I beat Rick arm-wrestling one day, in front of half the school, during recess. I made Jessi a mixtape. She even invited me to her house once. After a long session of my thoughtful insights and heartfelt reassurances, Jessi said to me, "It's funny, Tara, sometimes I kind of wish you were a boy."

After decades of practice with this particular scenario, I know that this portended the end of a mutually delusional intimacy with a pretty, straight girl. Long before I knew it was possible to date a girl, or even that I might want to, there was a temporary fairy-tale plausibility to my transcendent identity as a swashbuckling super pirate when I was close to a pretty girl. This identity is completely relational. It is only ever possible with a willing damsel in distress, and it is intoxicating. There has never been a damsel shortage in my life. And it never lasts. Pretty girls always come to the disappointing but practical realization that they have been participating in some kind of dark magic that is unsustainable and dangerous. Our relationship has taken place outside space and time. They get scared and I morph back into the Beast from the handsome prince. Princesses are always able to compartmentalize and move on. I, however, have a bottomless capacity for hardcore fantasy use. It usually takes me a few years to get over a few weeks of fanatical devotion.

Pretty girls are the only thing that has ever distracted me from my destiny as king defender of the weirdos. I had a pattern of neglecting misfits who were actually nice to me if, for a moment, it seemed possible I would get to play in the reindeer games and looked like I'd win. But some dippy woodsman always came along and stepped on my little bunny head, and the princess giggled off into the sunset with him. Then I was dumb and a dick. It's a sick, self-hating, delicious addiction, just like Charlie Brown trusting Lucy to hold that fucking football. Puberty only intensified my investment in this fruitless hobby. Good grief.

I never told my mom about my fantastical misadventures with playground royalty. I knew she would've disapproved of the breathless romanticism of the encounters. Neither of my parents had raised me to be enchanted with fantasy. I didn't understand what I was doing anyway. If I'd just had a hormonal urge to make out with girls or a clear longing to just be a boy, maybe we could've had a discussion. But I wanted to win. I wanted the rules of the game to be changed for me. I wanted what I was to be awesome enough. There was a cosmic injustice to my daily gender clusterfuck. My mystical glamouring abilities only had a temporary effect. I didn't belong in this world, and the fallout after each defeat was becoming ever more dramatic.

This is the age when you're incredibly indignant about your parents' expectations, but you want to meet them anyway. My parents were still the coolest people I knew. Dad had just gone in on buying a race horse, and his old friend and bookie from Iowa who'd come to visit us took me to the track and taught me how to handicap the horses. Everyone called him Bookie. Dad always showed me that we were more interesting than normal people.

I still wanted my mom to like me, even though we fought a lot and she couldn't see the magic me. I thought she knew a lot about music. She'd fantasized about being a doo-wop backup singer in college. She had the asymmetrical Diana Ross hair, but she was white and couldn't sing. She did love to dance. She taught me a few of the old sixties dances like the Pony and the Twist. These were our special fun times. My mother's regular record rotation included Diana Ross, Dolly Parton, Cher, Tina Turner, Barbara Streisand, and Bette Midler. Neither of us knew she was intuiting drag lineups at gay bars across America for the next three decades. She taught me the way of the gay all along. I think it would have been much easier for my mom to raise a gay boy. She had a natural respect for theatricality. I still have a tiny queen inside me that makes holiday appearances. During the years we lived in Phoenix, she took me to see Diana Ross, Michael Jackson's "Off the Wall" tour, and Tina Turner. I felt that I had an esoteric musical knowledge my suburban peers didn't seem to possess. I expanded on my mom's Motown fidelity with my personal cassette tape collection. I bought the Temptations and Four Tops' greatest hits along with additional Ike and Tina, and Aretha. It was the only music I had access to that provided a worthy opposition to Air Supply and Debbie Gibson. It had the authority of the previous generation. The performers were also Black. They still weren't a strong presence on mainstream TV or radio stations, and I still didn't know any, but I imagined they were equally disenchanted with suburban white culture. I thought I could understand how they felt. I also didn't know any of those nerds who somehow knew about punk rock or any other obscure counterculture music. Maybe they were only in John Hughes movies.

My Walkman provided a soundtrack while I hiked alone, like Jesus, under the relentless Arizona sun. If you've ever lived in the southwestern United States, you know that once you pass the condescending assertions of human development, you discover random, mysterious footpaths or roads to nowhere. I would follow these trails for as long as my batteries held out. I needed to continue my secret Jedi training, while practicing to be a lonely drifter with a past. Sometimes I would take my shoes off to see how far I could walk on the martyr-vetting, alien sunscape without modern protection. I reveled in the idea of dying where no one could find me.

The alchemy of the emotive music and desolate isolation was just what my preteen resignation to identity failure required to elevate my sense of future, eternal purpose. Perhaps I could live in a tent in the woods and blow up malls or get really good at the stock market because I was good at math. I could make rich people lose all their money and give it to poor people. I even called real estate agents in Sedona to ask about wooded acreage for sale, because that's how responsible, suburban preteen pirates plan their escapes. I figured I could afford the loan payments on a small parcel by working full-time at Burger King. I thought my folks would eventually be proud of my self-sufficiency and we could still spend holidays together.

I needed to be more of a badass. I knew I wasn't one. My mom had taught me not to litter or steal, and my dad taught me to be polite to old people. I just needed a portion of badass for the amalgam of awesome I was creating. I was eleven when I first stole a cigarette from my dad. It made me sick, but it was important to smoke. All badasses smoked, including my dad. I could get cigarettes from the nearby diner with the vending machine in the entry. I once brought them to school and had one in the far corner of the playground with a girl who was also a budding suburban hoodlum. Somebody snitched. It was quickly decided that I was the more culpable influence in the incident. I was the first student in the history of our principal's tenure to receive in-house suspension. I got it again for punching a kid who was picking on a smaller kid. And again for inciting a minor coup over the forced auditions for the sixth-grade production of *The Pirates of Penzance*. Elementary school suspension was pretty sweet. I didn't have to go to class, just sit in the office, do homework, and help the secretary with minor filing. She was nice.

Mom was most annoyed by the condescending phone calls she received from my principal, who was a caricature of elementary school principals. Mom thought I was too young to start smoking and too smart to get in trouble. She was convinced I was being targeted because of my appearance. She made me get a perm, the first of many in the eighties. "It'll just soften your features a little, make you seem more friendly."

"Why do you have to look stupid for people to like you?"

"You'll look cute. It'll be fun."

A perm, zits, and braces—must be time for junior high. Seventh grade wasn't that awful. I wasn't the biggest kid anymore, now merely the weirdest girl, and I'd cultivated a decent reputation for myself in sixth grade. Junior high had school teams, so I got to play softball and basketball for the school. I was the only seventh-grader in algebra. In eighth grade, I had to go to the high school for geometry, and I got to tutor a real senior cheerleader. I still wasn't like any of the other kids, but I was turning that into a successful sideshow. I got kicked out of class frequently. Mrs. Hubbard, the school counselor, and I became close during my classroom expulsions. I also hung out with the school janitor, Kit, during lunch sometimes. So I had friends.

I babysat for one of my dad's coworker's sons. He was a couple years younger and was in a wheelchair. He had cerebral palsy. For Halloween, he dressed as Big Bird and I pushed him around for trick-or-treating. For my costume, I'd found an old army fatigue jacket at a thrift store and wore it with a red bandana and mirrored aviator sunglasses. I looked a little like an extra from *The Deer Hunter*. People shoveled candy into our bag to get rid of us. I enjoyed the antagonism, so I started wearing that outfit to school every day. No one who came of age in the eighties should ever regret their fashion, but it was a little intense. Mom tried to put her foot down. I told her Jennifer Beals wore one just like it in *Flashdance*. She said when I looked like Jennifer Beals, I could have the coat back. We started fighting more about my weight. NutraSweet was invented and invaded our house.

*The Breakfast Club* distilled the number of possible archetypes for suburban, white youth to five. However, these five represented only the Major Arcana. One had to possess an early aptitude with eccentricity to occupy a subtype. I had elements of the Brain and the Athlete, but could never fully embody them because of the penis requirement. Obviously not Princess. Criminal and Basket Case can be gender-inclusive if you are committed. Combined, they allowed access to a special American classic that doesn't require overly feminine affectations. It's a minor character in the suburban landscape, but someone has to do it. To offset my spectacular heartbreak at not getting to be a junior high stud, but to also expand on my bad-girl theme, I became a bit of a slut.

The thing about being a pudgy, eerily masculine, junior high slut in a conservative suburb is that none of the boys you blow tell *anyone*. This simple fact produces feelings of deep dejection and heady power in exactly equal measures. I even groped around with some of the most popular boys in school. Getting people to want to have sex with me is one of my real superpowers. It's not that difficult in junior high, with boys. It happened surprisingly regularly but was always a one-time thing, and we just pretended it never happened. I was never sad that none of them really liked me. I have never seen myself with a boyfriend because then I would have to be a girlfriend, and how the hell does that work? It was a more complicated enticement involving a little puritanical shame, a profound lack of dignity, the sweet magic of dry-humping, and the rush of having control over boys: an auxiliary compulsion involving my hormones and blossoming self-loathing.

MTV came along and gave me Joan Jett and the Go-Go's. It also gave me AC/DC and Van Halen. Rock 'n' roll made me feel better, like I had a chance. AC/DC's "Problem Child" was obviously written just for me. I was certain I understood the intangible qualities necessary to be a Rocker *and* a Roller and that I was both. Rock 'n' roll really does corrupt the minds of youth. It teaches you how to say "fuck you" with your whole heart, and that was the most sensible spirituality available to me at the time. My new musical prophets helped elevate my solitary desert training missions into ecstatic anger dance rituals, during which the God of Defiance communed directly with me, calling me. It made me certain of my pivotal role in the coming revolution. It also gave me the perspective necessary to affirm that leg warmers and scrunchies really were lame.

My new music affiliations let me take another step away from my mom, which was still scary. I ran away every day, and I was always home in time for dinner. Mom would make me Crystal Light and microwave a Lean Cuisine for me. We would watch HBO together, when they used to show the same movies every day for months. We watched *The Best Little Whorehouse in Texas* about a hundred times. It made the idea of being a sex worker seem heroic and fun. I never had friends over, I didn't talk much, and I made another dinner when she wasn't looking.

Either because of my preteen angst, or our fat fights, or maybe my folks just wanting a parent vacation, in the summer before eighth grade, my folks sent me back to Huntington Beach to stay with Robbie and her sisters for a month.

It was a bold and unexpected move. Robbie, Terri, and I had stayed in touch, but it was still odd that Mom would let me go there by myself. Sometimes I thought my mom was hoping, just a little, that I would get kidnapped or run away. There was something about my appearance that disturbed her, existentially. It made no sense to her. We still loved each other very much, but we each had zealous, nationalistic allegiances to very different worlds. Her world was more practically located in the places we lived, where she was successful. My world was in a dark alley with Joan Jett and Annie Lennox and maybe Jodie Foster from *The Hotel New Hampshire,* hanging out on motorcycles talking about life or math or something. Maybe she was just trying to make me happy, or maybe I would join a cult for weird chubby people and she and my dad could start over. It's hard to say.

Right before I left, Mom tried to have "the talk" with me. She wasn't dumb. She knew I looked many years older than I was. She was also apparently familiar with the potential fat girl / slutty girl association. Our talk seemed to focus on how guys took advantage of girls with low self-esteem. I already relied on that. She didn't want me to end up pregnant, and she didn't want me to get any fatter. These were her concerns, considering I would be staying with three curvy sisters and a single mother who worked nights.

"Don't be a slut and don't be fat? That's the talk? Basically, do whatever you want, just don't make me look any worse than you already do? Is that it?"

"Sounds good. Call me when you get there."

I was so angry with her I didn't eat for a month.

# CHAPTER EIGHT

# WE ARE THE WEIRDOS, MISTER

I was excited to be back in California. Robbie, Terri, and JoAnne lived in the same house, a small beach rambler eight blocks from the ocean. Their mom worked nights as an ER nurse and slept during the day. Their house had a working-class, open-door, California casualness that was completely dissimilar to uptight, high-fenced, suburban propriety. People were always stopping by, sitting out on the stoop. Robbie was thirteen like me, Terri was fifteen, and JoAnne was eighteen. We could pretty much do whatever we wanted if it didn't cost much money or require a car. Teenage girls, when assembled in crews, especially in summer months, are powerful and have access to a special sorcery together.

I was emboldened by the chemistry we girls created in that house. Terri had a friend, Tammy, who spent most of her time at the house. Tammy was a tough, skinny blonde, with freckles. JoAnne also had a friend who hung out a lot. Suzette. I had never met anyone like Suzette. Suzette was a striking, confident eighteen-year-old with short-cropped black hair and intense dark eyes. The three sisters and we three friends frequently found ourselves on the back bedroom floor, in a messy, unsupervised house late at night together. We all smoked. We were all misfits. We controlled the secret summer forces with the volume of our laughter. We played "light as a feather, stiff as a board" and used a Ouija board to tell the future and talk to ghosts. Those things only work for teenage girls.

One night, Suzette introduced us to Truth Cards. Truth Cards is simply Truth or Dare without the dare. Four people play, each picking a suit. You go around the circle in turns, picking a card. The suit of the card you pick determines the person who must answer your question. I almost threw up when Suzette drew her first Truth Card and it was my suit. She stared straight at me and asked, "Have you ever thought about being a dyke?"

After an uncomfortable pause, I replied, "I don't know. What is that?" They all cackled. I was flush with shame. How could I not know what a dyke was? I'd been working so hard on my street smarts. How could I have missed this obviously important bit of lingo?

It seems impossible now to imagine a time when there was an utter lack of homo in American pop culture. Well, it was everywhere, but only through innuendo, and it was decidedly male. I had made it to the age of thirteen never once hearing the word *dyke*. None of my Arizona peers must have known it either. Somebody would have called me that by this time.

"A dyke is a lesbian. Have you ever thought about being a lesbian?" Suzette replied.

I honestly hadn't ever thought about it. I didn't really understand what that meant either. I knew it was bad, like there was something wrong with you, and maybe you had to go live somewhere else and not talk to your mom anymore. I was intrigued.

"I don't know," I said.

The cards went around the circle again. Suzette drew another one of my suit. This time, she asked, "What would you do if I kissed you right now?" This is easily in the top ten hottest moments in my entire life. All of the blood in my body divided itself into two parts: half to my face and half to my crotch. My stomach flew into the void it left. I almost passed out.

"Uh, I don't know," I said.

In all my years of obsessing over pretty girls, it had never occurred to me that maybe I wanted to kiss them. I certainly wouldn't have dared to imagine they would ever want to kiss me. I had just wanted to be their hero. In that moment, all I wanted was to kiss Suzette.

The rest of the girls sensed the tension and continued the game. I tried to play it off like I wasn't shattered into a million tiny, tingly pieces. I managed to share a twin bed with her that night and I waited, wide awake, half of the night, for her to kiss me. When I woke up, she was gone. I spent the entire day quizzing Robbie, Terri, and Tammy about my potential lesbianism. They assured me that I wasn't. I was relieved to hear that.

A week later, I went to a beach party and Suzette was there. I watched her walk away from the fire toward the water. I followed and found Suzette, staring into the ocean, by herself. She knew I had a terrible crush on her, and she knew how old I was. She turned and gave me one warm, soft kiss and planted a whole new world in my head.

In that same month, I also learned that I reacted violently to marijuana, by spending about five hours passed out on a strange man's bathroom floor. I had a threesome with JoAnne and the thirty-year-old guy who lived behind them and sold pot. And I helped super-glue a guy's balls to his legs because he was mean to Tammy, who I also had a crush on. The kissing a girl thing was by far the most important thing that happened to me that month and was thenceforth an integral component in my fantasy life.

My dad got free tickets to Disneyland through his work. Robbie, Terri, JoAnne, Tammy, and I all went toward the end of my visit. I still have pictures from that day. How is it possible that no one thought to tell me what a butchy baby bulldyke I was? There I am in my white cutoffs and Vans. I am wearing a yellow button-up men's shirt with the sleeves rolled up and a pack of Marlboro Reds in the pocket. I have a newsboy flat cap on, and I'm flexing for the camera. Astonishingly, it would be several more years before the lesbians and I crossed paths again.

When I got home, my mother was thrilled to see I had lost about twenty pounds. "I haven't eaten in a month," I said.

"Well, you look great." She went and got her camera. I still have that picture too.

At the start of eighth grade, I got a new crush on Amy, who lived on the block next to mine. She had hair kind of like Olivia Newton-John. She was a friend of my friend Gabby. Gabby and I had more in common, but I needed to obsessively make myself completely available to Amy at all times, just in case she needed to confide in me about her boyfriend, Billy, for hours. I did tell her about Suzette. Amy was Catholic. She assured me that whatever I felt would pass, because I wasn't a bad person.

That was the first time I imagined kissing a girl I had a crush on. I thought about that a lot. What else could I do with her? Penises are so uncomplicated and silly. What would I do with all her business down there? That thought was terrifying. I wanted to touch her boobs. I was pretty sure about that. Her boyfriend used to confide in me too. We'd strategize about how to win Amy's affections together. He let me smell his fingers once, after they made out.

I didn't realize that my father had been commuting to California the entire time, because teenagers are oblivious and selfish. I guess the teamsters had been appeased. At the end of eighth grade, we moved back to Huntington Beach. Mom was irritated with Dad for moving us again. I had been superficially successful at Shea Middle School. She disregarded the suspensions and boys' clothing to emphasize my perfect grades and my sports trophies. She noted I had also spent time with normal-looking (pretty) girls. She herself had another full-time job that she enjoyed because she was valued for her competence, even though she had probably been hired for her appearance.

But Dad made more money and had a broader scope of opportunity. Sometimes, he referred to us as "nonproducer number-one and number-two." He did it to irritate both of us, which worked, but I also got the impression that maybe he felt like his hard work and commitment to our family were underappreciated because he was never there and we could not see how hard he worked or how much he sacrificed. My mother had a stoic pride in severing ties like she thought that was her superpower as well as her burden. The resentment they both displayed toward the consequences of their own ambition sometimes felt like resentment toward my existence for making them do it in the first place. I tried not to make my feelings about moving all the time their problem. I'd even gotten a bit used to it and started counting on fresh starts. If you cultivate multiple fictional identities in one location for an extended period, especially if one of them is a public persona evaluated by adult expectations, there will always come the time they all get too close to one another. You start forgetting all the lies you've told to keep them separate, and the threat of multiple identity collision keeps you up at night thinking about dying or running. Three years in Arizona was the longest period I'd had to keep the con going. I was leaving with the star athlete and student, the wise and heroic companion of popular girls, the secret blow job queen, the tough-girl defender of the less popular, and the double-secret future me who would show them all.

# CHAPTER NINE

# Outlaw Prerequisites

I had a whole summer back in Huntington before high school started. The magic of the summer before was not to be repeated, which is commonly the case with the shiny golden times in your life. Robbie had a new group of friends, JoAnne and Terri were older and doing their own thing, Tammy moved, and I never saw Suzette again. The lot where my eucalyptus tree had been now had apartments on it. I naturally wandered back down to the pier.

I spent a couple weeks dating a Hell's Angel named Buzzy who lived with his mom. I met this kid Kenny who was actually my age and apparently only had one outfit: parachute pants and a Scorpions tour shirt. He introduced me to the back room of a corner store that had a pool table, a jukebox, and a cigarette vending machine. I spent the rest of the summer perfecting my bank shot with a smoke hanging from the corner of my mouth, listening to "Life in the Fast Lane" by the Eagles. I was pretty sure I was the coolest.

We moved back to the same condo complex. My dad's coworker Doyle lived there with his girlfriend, Jackie. It was 1984. Doyle had that Tom Selleck thing with his bushy mustache and thick, wavy dark hair. Jackie was six feet tall with long blond hair and high cheek bones, like an elite Charlie's Angel assassin. Jackie and Doyle got into fights because Doyle didn't want to get married. Jackie once set Doyle's expensive suits on fire in the living room and then took his alligator briefcase outside and threw it in the air while shooting it with a handgun. I had a huge crush on Jackie and was thrilled whenever I was invited over with my dad. The day security came because my dad, Doyle, and their friend Russ were shooting beer cans off the TV, they just ended up drinking whiskey with the security guard. My dad was like a rock star. Once again, he was the coolest person I knew. His cocky privilege was so annoying and everything I wanted so badly.

My mom seemed depressed for a while. She had to quit another job she liked. My dad and I spent most of our time out of the house. I'm sure she thought about running away too. She took up jogging again and engineered special adventures for us. We went for bike rides and played frisbee golf. She took me on my first camping trip, which I was grateful for because in all my fantasies of living in a tent by myself, I had never learned to pitch one. I think it was a long summer for my mom.

Huntington Beach High School was right next to our condo complex. My folks bought me a moped this time, which was especially cool because I wasn't legally allowed to ride it. It represented a new level of freedom even though it only went twenty miles per hour. Every day I drove it through a hole in the back fence to emerge next to the football stadium. I was well on my way to outlaw biker.

No one at this school gave a shit about my worldly affectations. The school was too big, and I was a freshman. Everybody knew way more than me about music and sex and drugs. I stayed quiet and tried to overhear what the cool kids were saying. I stuck to the nerd things I knew I was good at. I made the JV basketball team. I was sure the assistant coach was one of those lesbians. She was also my JV softball coach, and she palled around with some of the varsity players who also seemed like lesbians, but they never let me near their club.

I was in Model United Nations solely for the extra street cred. I made the only friend I remember of this year there, Sophia. She was really nice and smart. She was also Latina and pretty curvy, so I spent most of our time together away from my house. No need to involve my mother. I had real Mexican food for the first time and went to her Quinceañera. I was captivated by her big family with all her aunties who were nice to me and wanted me to eat more. I had seen things like that on TV but didn't understand they happened in real life.

I was in Algebra 2 / Trig, which was the last math class one was required to pass for graduation, so it was mostly seniors. That's how I met Brian. He was a nice, skinny, normal-looking white boy. He actually pursued me. He made me a mixtape with heavy metal ballads, including "Feel Like Makin' Love," which I cannot listen to now without being reminded that everyone in the early eighties was legitimately in a low-budget rom-com that no one ever saw. He was polite, with an outsider's allegiance to libertarian politics and black clothing. I was caught off guard by his interest in me. I allowed his charming, old-fashioned wooing because wasn't that what girls were supposed to do? This would be my first and last attempt at having a school boyfriend. He wanted to meet my parents.

I brought him home. My parents seemed to be equally caught off guard by the sudden presence of normativity. They seemed suspicious of my intentions but tried to act like it was an expected scenario. There was an inexplicable, pleasing element of intentional freak show when I playacted a girl on my own. I think it made my folks a little squeamish, but what could they say? Isn't this what you wanted? Are you going to vomit if I hold his hand? My dad teased Brian, quizzing him about his future plans and wardrobe. My mom made dinner and tried not to squirm every time Brian said something with affected politeness. It was reasonably successful, though notably awkward for all but Brian.

I had an ulterior motive for this relationship. I knew how to act like I cared about his feelings, but I just wanted to lose my virginity. In all my slutting around, I had yet to do the deed. I'd tried a couple times, but it hurt too much and I didn't have the patience to trust any of the older creeps or junior high prey. I knew Brian would take it seriously and feel honored in a Ren Fair kind of way. I made up what I thought girlfriends were supposed to do. I wrote notes and held his hand in math class. But honestly, the cool kids at Huntington High, who were not in any of my nerdy classes, were unacceptably more advanced in this department. I just wanted to get it over with.

I lost my virginity one afternoon on the living room floor. It would've been almost pleasant had my mother not walked through the front door. After Brian and his penis, which got caught in his zipper, made it out of the house, and mom calmed down, she said, "I'm not going to tell your father, but Brian isn't allowed over here again. He was a nice boy, but I'm never going to be able to get the image of his little white ass out of my head."

*Fair enough*, I thought. Brian and I snuck around a couple more times, but I was grateful to have an excuse to get rid of him. He was a nice boy, but I had little use for one of those.

# CHAPTER TEN

# WELCOME TO THE THUNDERDOME

At the end of ninth grade, my dad got promoted again. His new headquarters was located in a place called Barstow, California. I'd heard that town referenced in a Rolling Stones song, so how bad could it be? Dad took us on a car trip to check it out. After three hours east to the San Bernardino foothills, the freeway went up a mountain pass. Once we hit the top of that pass, we came upon the most scraggly, desolate desert hell I could imagine. Don't talk to me about Joshua trees. They're not majestic. Also, I hate U2.

We were not moving to Barstow, thankfully. Even now, Barstow remains possibly the ugliest of the many depressed, midsized shitholes the High Desert in Southern California has to offer. Barstow was the home of America's largest McDonald's. About thirty miles south of Barstow was a smaller shithole called Victorville. It was where Roy Rogers had a museum featuring his dead, stuffed horse, Trigger, and about ten thousand guns. If you turned off the freeway at Victorville and headed into the abyss another fifteen miles, you came to our destination shithole: Apple Valley, California.

"You have got to be kidding me." I said from the back of the car. "Where are the sidewalks? Was that a tumbleweed? I thought they were just in Road Runner cartoons. Jesus, that one's bigger than the car."

"It'll be fun," Mom dismissed.

If you visit these communities today, you will find Super Targets, franchise casual fine-dining restaurants, and home improvement centers everywhere you look. In the mideighties, Apple Valley had two sad little strip malls, a grocery store, a Naugles, and an Olympic Burger. These remote desert towns were created only a few decades prior to this by people who wanted to escape the growing diversity of Los Angeles and have a more welcoming environment for racism, swinger colonies, and religious cults. Any wingnut with some cinder blocks and a propane tank could set up shop in the surrounding foothills.

At this point, I was getting tired. Freshman year was fine, but my ego had suffered under my ongoing outlaw insignificance and normative failures. I slept a lot. I was thirsty and hungry all of the time. I drank milk and juice by the gallon. I tried to hide my consumption by pretending my mother couldn't remember what groceries she'd purchased and putting empty boxes directly into the outside trash can. I was terrified of getting fatter, but I couldn't stop.

We moved into a three-bedroom, ranch-style house on a half-acre of dirt. Mom had sod put in the front and back third of the property abutting the house, with some nice border shrubbery. I was tasked with yard maintenance. I was being trusted with a manly chore, and I was grateful to be contributing to our household in a small way. I became quite adept with a mower, a Weed Whacker, and a desert torture device called a hula-hoe, a tool created for gouging out weeds growing on dirt that's more like concrete. Since two-thirds of our property was weedy dirt, this consumed much of my Saturdays. It was always between 85 and 110 degrees, and the wind gusted at a steady 40–50 miles per hour. My chores helped foster my inner teenage martyr, and I enjoyed the obligation of some accountability for my existence.

I would have rather been an adult by this point. I needed to be an adult with a job that paid enough to impress my parents and possibly repay them for all the groceries. I needed to make up for the fact that I never fit in, no matter how many advantages I received. I needed a way to atone for the fact that I made them work so hard and sacrifice so much. I needed to pay them back for the dog and the bike and the moped because I wasn't normal. I also needed my future livelihood to reflect an adequate amount of notoriety while relying on the strengths I did possess so they would experience some satisfying amount of remorse for underestimating me. Disappointingly, I lacked the focus to address any of these desires, but indulged in endless hours of fruitless fantasy about them nonetheless.

My folks bought me a scooter this time. It went faster and was a little heavier than my moped, so it could withstand the high winds. I drove it into the Martian landscape and found what used to be a river about a million years ago. I started climbing the cliffs down there and wondered if I had the guts to fall off. A few times I hopped a slow-moving freight train that ran next to the river bed, pestering tragedy to play with me. I would always lose my nerve for running away, then hitch a ride back from one of the serial killers that seemed so plentiful around those parts. They were never as menacing as I needed them to be. I either needed the world to pick me off or the next three years to be fast-forwarded.

I clung to the lingering mystic-athlete-tough-girl. Surely, I would distinguish myself in one or all of these areas. My future as the curator of ancient esoterica as well as explosives expert depended on my academic performance. I toyed around with joining the military. I liked the snappy fashion and the allure of hero training, but I was terrible at authority. My nerdy devotions were my best chance at some place I couldn't see yet, where I could make more money than my dad, and wear whatever I want, and be a spy who could read ancient papyrus fragments in a staggering variety of languages.

My tough girl was a reasonably successful ongoing project. I was getting better at faking it. I flung myself into any unusual circumstance that presented itself. I never really mastered any one fringe. I collected street points like Girl Scout badges. Or I just pretended I already had that badge, but my sash was too full to wear it that day. Maybe I would become an effective and practical leader in an all-female math genius terrorist cell, or an assassin, paid to take out wealthy men who are mean to people.

The elite athlete would get distracted by the other two superheroes in my brain. Athletic training requires discipline, which I've never steadfastly possessed. I had to be angry to affect discipline. I had anger. Also, athletics held little promise for a future independent existence for a teenage girl in the eighties. The proximity of "fitness" to "thin" caused internal friction as well. "You can never be too rich or too thin" was the motto of the eighties. I wanted to be thinner, but like a ninja or Navy SEAL, not so I could be more popular. Every time my mother reminded me I didn't have to clean my plate, it made me angry enough for a new workout regimen for a couple weeks, but so I could be the first woman to play professional baseball, not successfully look good in a sack dress. I couldn't shop with my mother without the two of us creating a public disturbance. I wanted 501s, not girl jeans. I didn't possess the requisite boy ass, however. I was caught between my longing for a certain physicality and not wanting to do anything my mom wanted me to do.

Looking at pictures of me from that time, you might not

even describe me as fat. One might say, Rubenesque. Except Ruben had a thing for those pear-shaped pale broads with weak, sloping shoulders, thin flappy arms, and a teardrop flat ass with wide hips. I had the body of a hearty peasant with short, muscular legs that would come in handy if the cow died and I needed to pull the plow. I had the wide hips and a big ass that wasn't flat and a long torso that widened into broad shoulders and short muscular arms. I was shaped like a bulldog who was shaped like a fifties pinup.

Training montages in underdog sports movies would inspire me for a few weeks at a time. They are another spirituality that preaches "fuck you, you don't know me, I'll show you." Underdogs and outlaws are actually closely related archetypes, deified by American mythology. Both provide imaginable futures for misfits, but you have to win. You have to beat the odds. In contrast, America also deifies merciless dominance and nationalistic conformity. These were not the paths for my body. I wanted to be a jock only if it would later help me become the first female heavyweight boxing champion. Rocky told me that if I could go the distance, then they would know that I weren't just some bum.

Sometimes I would get up before school, swallow some raw eggs, and run several miles before the sun came up, listening to *Pyromania* by Def Leppard on my Walkman. Or I would work on my bat speed by demolishing a remotely located chain-link fence. I bought *Weight Training for Beginners* with a forword by Lou Ferrigno (the Incredible Hulk) because I wanted to look like him. I continued to work out because it made me more indignant, which was good, because it didn't make me any thinner. I was cultivating a presence. I earned one aspect of the composite identity I'd long been refining. I fostered the faith that, eventually, no one would be able to fuck with me and I would be a famous champion of something.

# CHAPTER ELEVEN

# REDNECK JAMBOREE

There was only one high school in town, so it had about three thousand kids. Almost all of them were white. They weren't quite as wholesome as the kids in Arizona, but they definitely lacked the disinterested sophistication of those in Huntington Beach. They were middle-of-nowhere kids. Their disposition was harsh to match their surroundings. Many of their parents were just the sort that found the uninhabited vastness of the desert conducive to more extreme and controversial political positions.

I started taking Spanish, which would come in handy when I ran away to Mexico. I made the varsity basketball team. I butted heads with our coach right away. When I wasn't running sets of lines as punishment, I spent some time on the bench. I made my first friends there. Sherri, Nykelle, and Mel. Sherri was a sophomore like me. She was short and sporty and Irish Catholic. Nykelle was a junior. She was a pretty, light-skinned Black girl who was hilarious. She was six feet tall, and her torso was roughly the diameter of my thigh. Mel was a senior and probably a little too hot and put together for all of us.

Mel had a car and a boyfriend in his twenties who lived over in Victorville. Sometimes, after practice, she would take us all to his place. Her boyfriend was also a little too put together for his group of friends, who were always over. Rodney, Jeff, and Reggie. None of them were particularly handsome, but they always welcomed our band of teenage girls. We'd sit around the kitchen table playing quarters with endless forties of Old English 800. I wasn't a drinker yet, so this was an opportunity to earn another demerit badge. I was also finally hanging out with Black people.

Lacking self-esteem and any inhibitions surrounding age or virginity a normal teenage girl might have, it never occurred to me that I should play hard to get. These guys seemed to like that I was curvy and athletic. They liked my jokes. They didn't talk to me like white guys, who were either dismissive, competitive, or controlling. They were just nice. It was a fun place to hang out. There was never any pressure to hook up with any of them. They enjoyed the company, and we got to drink and laugh and dance sometimes.

Rodney was the biggest. He was built like a professional linebacker. He was the sweetest of his crew. He took a shine to me. We never saw each other outside these roundtable gatherings, but I noticed the other guys stopped flirting with me, and he always sat next to me. He was an aspiring DJ. He made me a few of the most amazing mixtapes of the best eighties R&B and house music I'd never heard. Nothing happened that season with those guys except a lasting, friendly acquaintance.

Sherri and I got tight outside of our after-practice transgressions. We were physically similar, both compact and a little thick, but she wore mascara and blue eye shadow. She had red, curly bangs she would Aqua Net high above her forehead, a common practice in the mideighties. She occasionally tried to put makeup on me and do my hair. Maybe she was projecting. She looked like a softball dyke, same as me. She had those little, muscly dyke hands. When basketball season was over, we were the only two of the group that went out for softball.

Sherri had played the year before and was good friends with the assistant softball coach. We were both catchers. Sherri made varsity as the backup catcher, and I went to JV. We would still see each other on the bus to away games and after practice, but I started spending more time with the JV center fielder, Alex.

Alex and I were instantly best friends. She was a little shy, with a protective streak of aloof intimidation, which I admired. She was pretty in a quirky way. Her face was covered in charming freckles, and she had the most amazingly thick dark-brown hair, which looked auburn in the sun. She had braces, and she liked to draw. She wasn't one of the pretty girls. Her outsider station was fixed in that redneck dust-bowl because she was Mexican. Her mighty wall of perfectly cemented dark bangs and highly arched plucked eyebrows kept the unworthy at a distance.

We started spending a lot of time together. She invited me to her house. Her parents were the loving, protective Catholic types I knew from my friendship with Sophia. They seemed happy their daughter made a nice friend and often had me stay for dinner.

Alex had another friend, GeeGee, who lived nearby and went to our high school. Gee and I hit it off right away. She was a year older than us. She was a Black girl whose parents moved her from Los Angeles to prevent her from getting into any more trouble. She told me she had accidentally shot some guy in the leg at a public pool. She started quizzing me right away, taking stock of my experiences. I sensed she'd be impressed with my sluttiness and indifference toward boys. We quickly got good at making each other laugh. Alex, Gee, and I started hanging out almost every day.

GeeGee introduced us to LL Cool J, who debuted in 1985 with *Radio*. Alex and I brought a boombox on the bus to away games and blasted that album on a loop to annoy the other girls. There was something delightful about making those ponytailed jocks with boobs squirm. Hip-hop wasn't cool with white people yet. The Beastie Boys were a couple years away. I knew I was white, but I abandoned myself to cultural appropriation. I wouldn't encounter that term for another twenty years or so, but my own culture had been trying to expel me for some time. In the absence of a political consciousness that might've dissuaded me from reciting early rap lyrics, I became enamored with people who seemed smarter and more intuitive than all the people who'd been boring me for years. It was so much more fun to be around people who were also arbitrarily excluded from dominant culture. This isn't a sympathetic behavior. Our disenfranchisements weren't comparable. My own marginalization was somewhat self-imposed, just like my mother had always maintained. Guilt was readily accessible for me. But optimistically, one born into some amount of privilege may actually develop a richer empathy with a broader world if one's implicit social power is kept uncomfortably lodged up one's ass while learning new things. The dominant paradigm is mean to all of us and produces shitty music.

# CHAPTER TWELVE

# JIZZ PRIESTESS

Everything happened so fast that summer. Alex, Gee, and I hung out at each other's houses almost every day. Alex's parents were overprotective, so most of the time she couldn't come out with me and GeeGee at night. I'd gotten my driver's license as soon as they would let me, and I had access to my mom's Mazda. I took Gee to Rodney's apartment over in Victorville, and she took me to George Air Force Base.

Rodney had an apartment with Jeff. They had a couch and a kitchen table they probably found in an alley. The focus in the living room was the two turntables in the corner, mounted on two four-foot-high speakers. Gee and I would show up. Reggie was usually there too. They had this other friend, Freddie, who sometimes brought speed. I tried it and liked it too much, so I was afraid to do it again. We laughed and drank, but mostly we danced while Rod deejayed. I learned the cha-cha, the Running Man, the RoboCop, and the Electric Slide. Gee would help me while making fun of me. I wasn't bad. I eventually had sex with all those guys, but mostly Rod. I think Gee only fucked Rod and Jeff. Somehow, this wasn't weird. I have no idea what those guys thought of us, but they were always nice.

When we would go out to the air force base, we would go to the NCO (noncommissioned officers) Club. Most of the low-ranking officers there were Black, so it was this sort of private, military R&B club that never checked our IDs. The guys at the checkpoint got to know the Mazda and would raise the gate when they saw us coming. Gee and I never paid for drinks. The men would assemble in a feeding frenzy around us. This was my drug of choice. I have no idea how many guys I went through on that base. Numbers only matter for girls who are planning on a life. Fuck those girls.

It is impossible to explain self-destructive behavior to anyone who doesn't already understand its sinister bliss. I always took dares. My answer was always "fuck yes" or "fuck you." What are the limits of what you can be within the world into which you were born? What happens when you cannot envision a life within those boundaries? You dream of transcendence while simultaneously eliminating yourself from the gene pool. Evolution rewards assimilation. I had no tether to normal human interpersonal emotion or judgment. My still nascent and underappreciated masculinity had no intelligible potential. My femininity was ill-suited to propriety. A persona manifested to handle the available circumstances. I would later think of her as a drag queen, my cruel savior. She did not want romance. She did not want to know your name. There was a power to her compulsion that was all mine. I wouldn't want to twelve-step it away. I wasn't a sex addict. What a lazy, good-for-nothing slob of a diagnosis. I was a shame addict. While fucking a stranger, there would often be a moment of profound emasculation and utter somatic annihilation—usually when they came, no matter where the cum went, or when I'd suddenly notice (from afar) my own body, bouncing rhythmically against a car or a bathtub—that was so far down into the hole, it became beautiful. I think of it as a Negative Nirvana. I go out through the rock bottom. My body is left there. All the darkness washes me warmly and there is nothing left. For a moment.

The comedown from crazy town always sucks. I always

felt like a whore and dirty and all the shame girls are sup-posed to feel. Whatever. Shame is a delicious cookie that you chew and swallow. I was obliterating my body. I did not know what else to do with it. But that was just the first half of my summer.

# CHAPTER THIRTEEN

# ALMOST PARADISE

I don't know what would've happened if Alex hadn't gotten mad at me. I didn't understand at first. She started to say mean things whenever she knew I was going out. I was confused. I'd only ever gotten friends by impressing them with my willingness to not give a shit.

Then, one day, we were in her room alone, wrestling. She kept saying, "I bet I could phase you." This wasn't the first time she'd threatened me with that particular dare. I was on her bed and she pounced on top of me, pinning my arms with her hands. I'm sure I could've pushed her off, because of my muscles, but I laid still as she stared into me.

"I bet I could phase you," she said. She lowered her head near mine, and let her tongue trace the outline of my lips.

Fighting the initial impulse to vomit all over myself because she had indeed "phased" me, I opened my lips against hers and we started kissing like we were in love. We kept on kissing and groping and grinding like we had found what we were looking for. I stopped going to the air force base.

Romeo and Juliet were teenagers and tragic and dumb, and that is still pretty much exactly how first love is expressed. Our young declarations were clumsy and eternal and angry and profound. They were also forbidden and awkward and completely unrepresented. We didn't know what we were doing. Our only model for sex was with older guys who could care less about our pleasure. We were also both a little intense. It's amazing what "playing house" transforms into in adolescence and what passes as a feasible scene.

While Alex's parents were out of town one night, I stayed with her. We got into a playful disagreement and she went into the kitchen. When I came to look for her, she was naked, on all fours, on the dining room table. I think she was trying to convince me of her demonic associations, because sometimes you do that when you're sixteen. She wouldn't talk to me. She wouldn't look at me. It was relatively convincing. The first time I ate pussy was from behind, in a standing position, as a negotiation tactic. This is actually advanced pussy eating. It shouldn't be attempted by a novice who does not know how to discreetly breathe while performing this task, but it was formative, nonetheless. We eventually moved on to phallic produce and more conventional positions.

For the last half of the summer, we spent all our time together. If our parents decided we should take a break from spending the night with each other, we would sneak out and meet at an unfinished apartment development near her house and pretend we lived together and touch each other's boobs and lament the injustice of our forbidden love. I was definitely the boy. I brought her presents and became inconsolably jealous if she talked about a real boy. Maybe, if we could be together forever, we could be like everybody else, just a little different.

We eventually had to come out to GeeGee, who knew something was up. Without a stutter, she transitioned into our friend who was happy for us.

Then school started again. I think Sherri was a little pouty because I didn't hang out with her all summer. She had heard from Mel, who had heard from her boyfriend, who had heard from Rod and Jeff, that Alex and I were girlfriends. She'd also heard what a slut I had been. Dyke Slut. Double fun. She told everybody.

It took two class periods for word to spread and come back to Alex and me. Alex played the femme card, just as I would've wanted her to.

She said, "What are you going to do about that bitch?"

I'd been thinking I would just avoid her, but "I'll take care of it," is what I said. I cornered Sherri in the girls' locker room and asked her if I could talk to her in the nonconfrontational Midwestern way I had been taught, but she ignored me, then she ignored me again. As she waddled away, condescendingly, my anger finally caught up to the situation and I planted my foot halfway up her ass. She spun around and started swinging, but I was bigger. I took her down and got in a couple good shots, but our softball coach, Christine, pulled me off. I was suspended for a week.

When my mom asked me about it, I just shrugged. "What's wrong with you?" she asked. She had recently taken me to a doctor to figure out what *was* wrong with me. I was tired all the time and I ate way too much. The doctor who was unproductively treating my minor allergies sent me to an endocrinologist after noticing a bit of a goiter in my neck. The endocrinologist had to run the thyroid test twice. I was pumping out about four hundred times the thyroid hormone that I was supposed to. The thyroid controls your growth, metabolism, and menstruation. If you're producing excess amounts at these levels, your body will actually start to metabolize itself after you mature at a rapid rate. It's why I ate so much, trying to keep up. It's an autoimmune disease where your body eventually starts to eat itself, so you die. The pitfalls of peculiarity. Many endocrinologists still resist the possibility of an emotional component to this disorder. I'll bet they're all dudes.

I wasn't allowed to see Alex while I was suspended. After

the week was over, we were just getting used to the drama at school when Alex's little sister caught us making out in a closet (literally). She innocently told Alex's mom about it. I got a midnight call from Alex telling me her mom had beaten her. I stole my scooter out of the garage and went to get her. We were running away. She snuck out and got on the back of my Honda Spree and we set off for Victorville, a long ride on a Honda Spree. I called Rodney, the only person I could think of that might house us for the night. When we finally got into Victorville, we had to pee. We stopped to piss behind a tree in a small, public park. The cops showed up and shone their lights on us. Alex ran. I froze. She disappeared while I was hauled back to my parents' house. My mother was visibly shaken by the novel brand of trouble I had gotten in, but she practically put me back in bed.

In the morning, mom took me to school herself, determined to follow a new protocol of supervision. She didn't realize that I'd called a taxi to meet me at school that morning, which I promptly got into as soon as she drove out of sight. In an age before cell phones, when you lose the love of your short life into the night and you don't know if they're okay or where they are, you break open your piggy bank for a cab. I went directly to Rodney's apartment, where Alex was waiting for me. Jeff and Rod had gone to work. We tried to make a plan.

At some point in our exposure to popular culture, we had gleaned, through homophobic innuendo, that gay people lived in San Francisco. That night, Rodney slept on the couch and gave us his bed. The next morning, we went to work with Rod and Jeff. They drove a delivery truck. We hid in the back as they went on their route through Los Angeles. They dropped us off at the Greyhound station and told us to take care. We pawned some jewelry we had gathered from home and bought two tickets to San Francisco. I was terrified, but this was the moment I had been training for. I was called to save a girl in real life. Nothing was more important. I did bring my calculus book just in case my mathematical acumen would provide for us. We arrived in Downtown San Francisco in the middle of the night. We stayed in the women's restroom until dawn.

We spent the next day wandering around South of Market and the Tenderloin looking for these fabled gays and a way to start a new life. We didn't find either. We spent the next night under a tarp in the back of a truck. I remembered Tammy from Huntington Beach had moved to the Bay Area. She lived in the East Bay. We took the train to meet her. She said we couldn't stay with her, but she got us a really sleazy hotel room. Alex and I got to play house for one night. In the morning, we had a dollar left between us. We bought Fig Newtons from a corner store and did cartwheels in a park from the sugar rush because we hadn't eaten in a couple of days. We went back to the city. We went back to the toilet in the bus station. At some point, an old man propositioned me. It took me a minute to even figure out that he was asking to have sex with me for money. I probably should have done it. What difference would it have made? Alex and I got into a huge fight over the fact that I didn't want us doing this for money. She brought up that I had enough experience and that I wasn't taking very good care of her. That was harsh. And it was true.

I soon had to admit that I had no skills when it came to being a runaway. This was a crushing blow to my daydream identity. I wasn't a tough girl. My girlfriend, the one who made me feel right for the first time, told me that I wasn't living up to her expectations. This destroyed any hope I had dared for a future. I even had to throw away my calculus book because it was too heavy to carry around. After about a week and a half in San Francisco, finding none of the gays, I called my parents on a pay phone. They'd purchased their first answering machine just for this occasion. They left a message just for me, calling me Bozy and asking me to come home. What could I do? We had to go home. I wasn't the knight she was hoping for. When I finally talked to my dad, he asked if I was in San Francisco. His magic still astounds me. They bought us tickets, and we got back on the bus.

Both sets of parents were waiting for us at the station when we got back. They were not talking to each other. Alex's parents dragged her away before I could say good-bye. She was still mad at me anyway. My parents wanted to know which of us was pregnant. I didn't tell them anything except that I wasn't pregnant. They took me back to school immediately. Alex never showed up back to school. When I finally called her house, her mother told me she wasn't allowed to talk to me anymore and they were moving her away.

# CHAPTER FOURTEEN

# ROMEO VISITS THE APOTHECARY

I didn't know where they were moving her. GeeGee tried to console me. She took my side, if there was one, and counseled me to move on. But I wasn't prepared to give up on Alex. What else did I have? The worst high school reputation possible?

I went to the school secretary and pretended that my friend who had moved away was having a birthday and I wanted to send flowers to her new school. The secretary gave me the address of Alex's new high school in Banning, California.

Banning was a little over an hour away by car. I don't know why my parents allowed me access to a car after what I pulled. I think they hoped I would go back to my normal level of sullenness and finish high school, then go away. Instead, I ditched school and drove to Banning. I went to the high school and parked and waited and stalked. Alex finally appeared and came over to the car. After some fighting because she thought I'd abandoned her, she got in. We cried and held each other and wondered what we were going to do.

I had to leave her there and come home. I went directly to a tattoo parlor I had noticed above a bar near the high school. A giant, sweaty man told me to sit still and tattooed the name *Alexandra* on my right hip for ten dollars. I vowed to come visit her whenever I could get away and we would figure it out.

For a couple of weeks, things were fine. I would come down, we would make out in the car. I would drop her off at her aunt's house. We told each other we loved each other, and that we would wait it out.

Her mother called her aunt to see how Alex was getting along in her new school. Her aunt was excited to report that Alex had already made a nice friend who dropped her off at home some days. When Alex's mom asked about the friend, her aunt must've given a very detailed description of me and my car. Alex disappeared again. Her mom came and got her that day, dragged her home, and locked her in her room.

I can't remember how I found out what happened. I couldn't tell my parents, who didn't know I'd found her, or that I was stealing the car and ditching school to go see her. I couldn't tell GeeGee because I did realize that I was obsessed, and crazy people, in general, know that you have to hide your crazy sometimes.

The mission grabbed me that night. I pulled the twelve-gauge from under my parents' bed and left the house, telling my folks I was going to Gee's. I had no real plan for the shotgun. I didn't know how to storm castles.

I went to a pay phone and called Alex's house. Her mother answered. I didn't say a word.

She said, "I know it's you, Tara. Alex doesn't want to talk to you. Your parents don't know what to do with you. You've destroyed our family. Why don't you do us all a favor and get rid of yourself?"

What could I say? She had a point. I couldn't think of one reason to not get rid of myself. I went to the local drug store, and for the first time in my life, I stole. They didn't have sleeping pills in bottles, so I stuck two packs of blister capsules into my pants and paid for my orange juice.

In the small desert town where we lived, backyards were

CHEMICALLY ENHANCED BUTCH | 69

mostly open desert. I drove the Mazda into Alex's backyard. I was close enough so that I knew everyone in the house could see me. For a second, I saw Alex's face in her bedroom window, then it was just her mother's at the back door. I started taking the sleeping pills, which was more tedious than I'd expected with the packaging. By the time I got halfway through the second package, I started to feel the effects. It was relatively pleasant for a short time, until Alex's parents came out to confront me.

Alex's mom was definitely the alpha of this relationship. She handed the gun to Alex's dad and started to yell at me. "Blaaahh, blaah, whaah?!" was what she said. I was beginning to nod off in between silly words. At a certain point, they must've realized I was going to die and drove me home. My dad confronted Alex's dad as I strolled into the house. I told my mom I was tired and going to bed. The next thing I remember is my father running into the house yelling to my mom that I had taken something. My folks brought me to the emergency room.

Getting your stomach pumped is unpleasant. The nurse gave me a beverage that she told me was Kool-Aid, which was really ipecac. I puked all over myself, then the doctor came in and handed me a glass of water while holding a plastic tube in front of my face. "When I stick this up your nose, drink this glass of water." I can't imagine anyone in need of stomach-pumping being in an optimal psychological state to perform this task. That's what happens though. I had a tube going in, a tube going out, and liquid charcoal spewing down my chin and hospital gown. My parents were sitting on either side of me. My mother said, "You know, I've been meaning to have Christmas pictures taken."

I stayed in the heart ward for the rest of the night to monitor my vitals, until I could successfully poop charcoal. In the morning, my folks came to get me. They told me that it was normal, under these circumstances, that I speak to a therapist. I was embarrassed that I had caused so much trouble and agreed to whatever they wanted me to do. We drove down the hill to San Bernardino and pulled into a hospital parking lot. I knew something was amiss when they pulled a suitcase out of the trunk.

# CHAPTER FIFTEEN

# CLOCKWORK ORANGE FOR GIRLS

I spent the next two and a half months in a locked inpatient psychiatric ward for troubled teens. Locking a damaged teenager in a facility with a couple dozen other damaged teenagers is an interesting strategy for adults to take when they wish to promote social functionality. I also understood that my folks didn't know what else to do. I had breached the boundaries of control, mine and theirs. We all needed a time-out.

The rules were explained to me. We were all assigned levels, 1 through 6. Level 1 denoted that you were considered a threat to yourself and others. To get to Level 6, there were lists of individual and interpersonal psychological and behavioral hoops through which we jumped. At Level 6, you could take a walk, by yourself, around the hospital, wearing shoes.

I'm grateful that the gleeful obsession with drugging sad teens was not yet a trend. I knew how to check boxes and pass tests, as did most of my fellow detainees. Teenagers suffering from acute existential conflicts are usually adept at manipulation. We didn't really know what was wrong with us. We were hardwired to survive at that age, and our coping mechanisms had simply become conspicuous. We were decades away from earnest reflection and just trying to keep the staff from noticing the smoke occasionally emitted from our smoldering brains. Conveniently, the professionals were rarely much smarter than we were. Especially me.

The psychiatrist, the guy with the Jag whom we met with once a week for twelve minutes, told my parents my relationship with Alex, my homosexuality, was a phase. He made me take that long test that asks you about your bowel movements and whether you think Satan is following you. I don't recall his diagnosis, but I knew that I was never going to see Alex again. Neither of our parents would've allowed that. I thought she hated me anyway. I couldn't talk about our relationship to the staff as if it were real. I processed the demise of my first love by myself. I still have the tattoo.

A couple of the day counselors were nice. I entertained them with stories. We made Christmas ornaments during craft time. Mom still has those. She brought my homework every week. She would play cards with me until the nurse put a stop to it because we were too competitive and disruptive. They didn't understand that my family conveys warmth loudly. There were tutors, supposedly there to help us. I asked them about a stubborn calculus problem once. The look on their faces let me know that they would not be helping me any time soon.

I advanced quickly through the levels while I was doing sit-ups with the bulimic girl in my room and having sex with the boy with anger issues in an empty shower stall. I knew it was just about getting to the place where I could fake it through the rest of high school. They weren't going to let me out until my hustle was convincing.

The mediation process with my parents was the hardest. I felt so ashamed. I cost them money and heartache. I wanted them to know that it wasn't their fault and that I would do better and try harder. Disappointing my mother was still the most gut-wrenching experience I understood. My dad wrote me a card that I still have, signing it "Your chief admirer." That guy. I still cry whenever I come across it.

I got out in time for Christmas break of my junior year. My AP physiology teacher generously sent me a dead pregnant cat to dissect at home. My paternal grandparents were visiting. Gramma didn't like the kitten fetuses, stored in Ziploc bags in the freezer, next to the fruitcake. My parents got me a 1979 Triumph Spitfire convertible for Christmas, and to say, "Good job in the loony bin." It was a piece of shit, but it sure was pretty.

Just when I thought it couldn't get any weirder, I had to go back to school. Not only was everyone still aware of my peccadillos from the previous summer, but they also knew where I'd been for the previous two months. Thankfully, it was the same hospital the head cheerleader was sent to the year before after she tried to hang herself, so it had a bit of star mystique.

GeeGee stepped up and devoted herself to my protection through sustained intimidation at school. Gee was not only one of the five Black students at Apple Valley High, but she was also from LA. Everyone was terrified of her if she wanted them to be. She walked me to all my classes. She was my protector and my friend. She taught me that I was going to have to be a lot tougher if I was going to make it as a real outsider.

Isn't that a trope? The sensitive, troubled, privileged, confused white person being protected and enlightened by the caring, wise, and enigmatic Black friend? I have not always been a sympathetic protagonist. My own pain, which I was still unable to name, felt indulgent to me, so I kept it to myself. It was formless. I had to keep it in the lines for the rest of high school. I'd be famous later.

I wasn't prepared for the fact that Alex had returned to school in the safety of my absence. I had fucked up her life, I had fucked up my life. I took her best friend and destroyed her relationship with her parents. I had spent the last three months trying to convince myself that my eternal love for her had been unhealthy. That's what I had been told. Our relationship became impossible. The first time I saw her at school, I was undone. Had it not been for Gee grabbing my hand and staring Alex down, I would have disintegrated in the hallway. A few weeks later, she left Apple Valley High and finished at an alternative high school. I never saw her again.

I still ditched school frequently. Nykelle was a fucking genius at forging mom signatures and sounding like an adult on the phone. I'd rigged the Triumph with a tape deck and two huge stereo speakers in the back seat. We'd peel out of the parking lot with the top down singing to Klymaxx, Jody Watley, Pebbles, or JJ Fad. We smoked Virginia Slim 120 Menthol Lights and felt like divas. GeeGee and Nykelle taught me how to be cocky, or pretend to be cocky, which was just as useful. Haters gonna hate.

# CHAPTER SIXTEEN

# It's About Fucking Time, Lesbians

That spring I ran into an acquaintance I remembered from the year before. Steph had dropped out and gotten her GED. She had a job and an apartment and told me she got kicked out of her house because she was a lesbian. *Wait, what? I know a lesbian?* We weren't destined to become best friends, but she did tell me about the gay bars. *Gays have their own bars? Where?*

The nearest one she told me about was only a thirty-minute drive. I couldn't wait until Friday rolled around. I was working at the movie theater in Victorville and borrowed my boss's ID for the occasion. It was the most time I'd ever spent planning my outfit. I told Mom I was going out with Gee and got in the car by myself.

It took me a while to find it. Dark, no sign, no windows, entrance in the back. The bouncer had a considerable paunch and a greasy, salt-and-pepper ponytail drooping from the back of a backwards black flat cap. Sitting on a stool, under a dim backdoor lamp, he barely looked at Rhodie Mae's old military ID and knew I was lying to him. After fondling my tits and pocketing ten bucks, he opened the door.

Anticipation gave way to panic as I took in the situation. Is this what lesbians look like? Grand Central will always remain in my distant memory, the hardest, seediest, stickiest gay bar

I have ever encountered. Located in Riverside, California, forever in 1987, it was within fifteen miles of three military bases. The women inside weren't just butch, they were bulldaggers. I'd never even seen other butches, let alone this rare tribe of government-trained militia mullets. Not a femme in sight. I had walked into a prison porn, and I was the bad little school girl.

Until that moment, I was very proud of what I considered my natural ability to look like I knew what I was doing. At least, I thought I appeared undaunted. I must've looked ridiculous. I had dressed like I was going to one of the clubs I had already been to. So I looked like I was going to an R&B nightclub circa Janet Jackson's "Nasty." I was hella fly.

I took a seat at the bar, facing the dance floor. I scanned the room, trying to find someone, anyone I could ask to dance. It was mostly boys dancing. The women were playing pool. I don't remember how long I sat there. I couldn't just leave without talking to someone. And then she came in. She was tall and beautiful . . . and feminine. I watched her for a while as she danced and talked to people. I was gathering the courage to ask her to dance. I finished another Rolling Rock and finally pushed my stool out to get up. I felt a firm, meaty hand grip my left shoulder, keeping me in my place. The voice behind me said, "Sit down, son. That's a man."

The butch's name was Yoli. She laughed warmly and put her arm around me. She took me into the bathroom and gave me a line, then spent the rest of the night playing pool with me. That was my first time in a gay bar. It was less than a week since I'd found out they existed, that there were other gay people and they had their own bars.

When you spend your life knowing that you do not belong in the only world you've ever known and you are given a glimpse of another, tangible universe that might hold promise for a future existence, the first thing you do is lower your expectations. Your heart is filled with gratitude for just the possibility. I felt eager for any vetting process this new world required if they would just let me in. This meant I made out with anybody who came on to me. This might seem similar to my behavior thus far, but it was the difference between destruction and hope.

After a few times at Grand Central, I learned about Robbie's in Pomona, an honest-to-Minerva dyke bar. At Robbie's, for the first time in my life, I was cute, not in spite of what I was but because of what I was. I learned there was a name for people like me: butch. In a dyke bar, butches are hot. And a cute, smart butch who could dance was really hot.

It was the eighties, the last full decade of the glory days of dyke bars. I was still very young and naïve, but I'd finally found the portal at the back of the closet, and I was setting off from the Shire. There was a whole other world no one told me about, and I might be king someday.

I started dating the first feminine woman who wanted to date me, which is what all young butches do. No one had ever taught me anything practical about what it might be like to be attractive. Nobody thought it would come up.

Tiffany was in her midtwenties and worked at a furniture store and had a condo. She wasn't destined to be an appropriate lifemate for me, but she was a good practice lesbian relationship. We went camping once. I made a bunch of grand promises I would never keep. That's another thing young butches do. A lifetime of low self-esteem and a lack of normal opportunities for flirting practice where you're the "guy" sets us up for at least a decade of devoting ourselves forever and often to a series of inappropriate girlfriends. We ignore all intuitive misgivings about the relationship, because we can't imagine anything better. We never want to hurt someone else's feelings. We still secretly think we're knights from Middle-earth.

Another unfortunate thing happened in this tiny span of time. I was hanging out at Robbie's when the varsity softball coach from my high school walked in. I was hoping to play varsity that year. I knew it was a bad idea to let her see me. I tried to duck out. She saw me. *Shit.* I didn't know how to play it, so I pretended like she didn't see me. I didn't talk to her. Three days later, I was called into the vice principal's office and told that numerous mothers had called the school, expressing concern that I might be sharing a locker room with their daughters. The school would appreciate it if I didn't play sports anymore.

I was kicked out of high school sports for being a lesbian. Thirty years later, the irony of that punch line makes this story a hit at parties. In 1987, I was just pissed. That bitch. That spineless bitch. Nobody's fucking mother called the school. This is the way you save your own ass? By throwing me under the bus?

The thing about 1987, though, is that it was still in the eighties. I lived in a small, conservative town in Southern California. Reagan was president. This was the height of the golden age for televangelists. AIDS was still relatively new and scandalous and had made all gay people a public health hazard. Teachers were losing their jobs just for being gay. As excited as I was about my new identity, I also knew it meant there was something wrong with me that I should hide. That coach was hiding too.

We never talked about it. I never put up a fight. I stormed home and announced to my parents that I didn't want to play sports anymore. "That's fine, you can get another job," they said. I didn't tell them. I'd already put them through too much.

I came out to my mother during one of our frequent

conflicts over just what the hell was wrong with me. "I'm gay," I shouted. I hadn't been expecting to tell her. It actually calmed her. Mom is a problem solver. Confronted with an actual problem, she springs into action.

Chastity Bono had just come out to Cher and the world, and also had a mullet, so Mom had a cultural reference that drew aspirational parallels between her life and Cher's. She called Barb, the lesbian from the seventies, so I had someone to talk to. She bought me a copy of *Rubyfruit Jungle*. She was grateful that I had an identifiable disadvantage; something *was* wrong with me. I was grateful for this as well. Now we both had something else to blame, instead of each other or ourselves. My mother has hated most of the lifestyle and wardrobe choices in my life, but she has always been supportive in her own solution-oriented way. This wasn't going to hold me back.

When she told my father, they both admitted that they had individually suspected this since I was eight. *Might have been nice to have a family meeting.* Since neither had a moral conflict concerning the revelation, they both set about imagining how a successful lesbian might look. They got me golf lessons at their country club. Even then, I wouldn't wear golf shirts, and I might have scared the club pro a little. But it was a good way for all of us to negotiate our new circumstances.

When I brought my new girlfriend Tiffany home, they were unimpressed. *It's one thing to be gay, but don't be gay with her.* But because of all the recent drama, they tried to be supportive of this new direction, even though she was an adult I'd met at a bar and I was still seventeen. The relationship was just boring enough to be a welcome departure from everything else that had occurred. They were willing to bargain for boring. *Just get through school. Don't get weird again.* They'd also lowered their expectations.

It was a fragile yet workable ceasefire. When I came home and told my mom a boy in my math class had asked me to the senior prom, she simply set aside her exhausted confusion and let herself get a little excited about getting me a dress.

Barth Monk was in my calculus class. If ever there was a Platonic Form of "Nerd," somebody would make a glorious statue of Barth. He had the extra-thick glasses that made his eyes look bigger and thick, wavy hair he parted on the side. He had acne under his movie theater–manager mustache. He wore Izod shirts tucked into his pleated Dockers and penny loafers with real pennies in them. He was the only person at school unaware of my reputation because nobody talked to him, so he was nice to me. Of course I agreed to go to the prom with Barth.

Mom and I started off at one of those stores in small towns that specialize in prom dresses and evening wear for Rotary Club soirees. 1987 was the year everybody went around looking ready for their glamour shot at the mall. It was an epic year for colors of taffeta and poofy sleeves. I refused to even try them on. But after some lengthy and contentious debates with my mother in front of the clerks, centered on "what everyone else would be wearing to prom," I said, "Fine. You asked for it."

When I emerged from the dressing room looking like a homemade tissue box cozy, even my mother couldn't contain her laughter. "You like it?" I said. "How about in coral? Perhaps the sleeves could be a little bigger?"

She relented, "Okay, let's go to Nordstrom's."

We drove to an actual department store. They had prom dresses too, but we now both understood that I could not wear what the other girls would be wearing. Neither of us knew why, but we agreed I could not pull it off. We found what we were looking for on the sales rack in the cocktail dresses section. The dress was black and backless, with long sleeves and a collared neck. It had a large, sequined sash in front and was slit up the back of the skirt. It accentuated and flattered my adult curves. It was Alexis Carrington from *Dynasty*, rather than Mallory from *Family Ties*. In retrospect, I was wearing drag. It's the only way I could pull off female. And the only drag that suited me was slutty bitch. It was the perfect dress for that. My mother was thrilled and thought I looked classy.

Poor Barth. I didn't spend much time with him at prom. I danced on the tables with Nykelle and GeeGee. Sherri came wearing one of those poofy taffeta things looking like a grumpy pug. We just laughed at her. We'd been training for this event by listening to "Meeting in the Ladies Room" on a loop for weeks. The three of us dared anyone to say anything to any of us. Even the teachers looked indignant. The two Black girls and the dyke made it their show. Hillbilly High was almost over for them, and I'd nearly made it to the end of the worst year of my life.

Mom got called into the school counselor's office near the end of my junior year. She was a tightly wound woman who informed my mother that she thought that high school wasn't a good environment for me and that my presence was disruptive for the other students. She thought it would be best if I got my GED and left.

There have only been a few instances in my life when my mother has publicly used her magic in my defense. Most of the time, I was in trouble and it was my fault, and she spent a good deal of time apologizing for me and assuring authorities she had things well in hand. This was one of those rare moments where she decided I was being unjustly persecuted.

Mom had just had a fairly shitty year with me and was not in the mood just then for unsolicited judgement. She stood up, flexing super-intensity, and told the counselor that if she spent a little more time putting herself together in the morning, she might have a better chance of getting laid, and then maybe she wouldn't be such an uptight bitch. She said that I was the smartest and most capable student in that shitty school, and they should be grateful to have me. She informed the counselor that I would indeed be graduating from Apple Valley High School, and if she heard that the counselor or anyone else was being at all unhelpful toward that end, she would return with my father and their attorney. "Are we done here?" Smiley face.

When we returned to the parking lot, she turned to me and said, "You will be graduating from this high school. Your grade point average is in the toilet after this year, but you managed to get a high score on your SATs. If you don't get straight As your senior year, understand that you will be going to the local community college with all the people you just went to high school with instead of going off to college." That was logic I understood. My mother doesn't accept punking out, even from hell.

I spent most of that summer working and going to Robbie's, or hanging out with GeeGee. I would sometimes spend the weekend at Tiffany's house. My parents relaxed restrictions they knew I would disobey. It was an unremarkable summer, except for one event.

Tiffany took me to my first gay Pride celebration. It was in Long Beach. The only moment I remember of that entire summer is standing on a small hill, looking out on the sea of freaks who had assembled in the sun. It was a moment of stillness. No obsession, no destruction, no rage, no disappointment, just belonging. That was long before large corporations and cynicism were official Pride sponsors. I cried and cried.

Gee and Nykelle graduated. When I started school again,

I was on my own. My cocky, fuck-you face was in peak performance shape. I had shorter days because they wouldn't let
me take PE anymore and I was taking math at the community
college. I had to get As. I had to escape. I don't remember my
senior year. My only friend was LaDonna the security guard.
I spent my lunches in the parking lot with her, smoking cigarettes. I attended school and got As. When I graduated, I
walked around flipping off some teachers and students who'd
been mean, but it was a day of liberation.

CHAPTER SEVENTEEN

# THE RAINBOW AGE

My relationship with public education was finally at an end. My sentence in the world in which I did not belong had been served. As much as I wanted to light the school on fire with my mind, I was just grateful it was over. My time in the halfway house was about to begin: college.

I got my ticket to somewhere else in the mail when I got accepted to Cal Poly Pomona. Pomona, California, is neither exotic nor prestigious, nor very far from Apple Valley, but it was out. It was a math and sciences and agricultural school. Math had finally come through for me. I registered as a finance major.

My mother was as excited as I was that I was going to college. She'd had to drop out when she got pregnant with me. She was proud of me. She wanted me to make a life for myself that would be happy and have enough social legitimacy to reflect positively on her. I didn't want to let her down. I lay on my dorm room bed and luxuriated in the possibilities.

It's thrilling when you first start to feel like a grown-up. New expectations of responsibility feel novel and important. I loved choosing my classes and buying books and making beefaroni on a hot plate. And I loved being gay. Gay, gay, gay. I wasn't about to be in the closet here or take any shit. I had new expectations of the wider world.

Young queers are often years behind their normative peers in having a strategy for our real-life future. The age is growing dangerously near when we may have to give up on finding that fairy godmother that hands us success and punishes everyone that was mean to us. We've expended so much time and energy on survival that when we finally get the opportunity to make a few life choices for ourselves, all we can think to do is be gay. It's the most exciting thing we've discovered about ourselves, and we want to learn everything we can about our people. We may call it the rainbow age. I wanted to be successful for my parents, but I had a new allegiance to a world of misfits who had grown up angry and confused and fucked up, just like me.

Southern California in the late eighties was absurdly conservative. It's the birthplace of the modern religious right. It was shocking how openly people hated the gays. People on campus weren't just targeting me with whispers like high school. The Campus Crusade for Christ was organized around how immoral and disgusting homosexuality was. We were the big threat at that time. I was finally marginalized legitimately. My pain had a name. I finally had a purpose. I had a fight. I could be a superhero.

I divided my time between my studies and being gay. I got good grades. I loved grown-up school. I started to discover new gay bars in LA, which was only an hour's drive away. I was still dating Tiffany, but that wouldn't withstand my new freedom for long. Our relationship was the beginning of a long period of self-discovery through serial monogamy. I was about to suck that stereotype dry, but not before a brief interlude with another butch dyke cliché. She came along that Halloween. Marianne.

Marianne was a pretty straight girl, but not in the junior high kind of way. She was something brand new in the college kind of way. She lived across the street from my dorm in a little cabin that was next to the school's extensive greenhouses.

She was one of the caretakers. She had short dark auburn hair and dark brown eyes. She didn't wear makeup and she constantly picked at or rubbed everything with her fingers in the most charming way possible. She had a clever, crooked smile she hid with those same hands when she was nervous. She knew what she was doing. She talked to me like she knew all about me. She smelled amazing.

A few people from the dorm were going to *The Rocky Horror Picture Show* on Halloween. Marianne came along. She made sure she sat next to me in the back of the car. On the way home, she held my hand in the dark. We made out behind her little cabin that night for hours under eucalyptus trees. I finally got to kiss the pretty straight girl, and it was amazing. I felt that giddy intensity that is the best part of life, when you cannot get enough of that smell. I didn't get back to my dorm room until early the next morning.

My roommate at the time looked like the guy I went to prom with but was twice his size. We called her Moose. She was an acutely closeted lesbian. She wore a wedding band to symbolize her intentions of marrying Jesus and becoming a nun after school. When Tiffany called that night looking for me (we all shared a pay phone at the end of the hall), Moose tattled on me, and she didn't tell me she had until it was too late.

When Tiffany came to pick me up for a date the next day, I was intending to break up with her. I was filled with guilt but feeling brave because I was totally in love with Marianne. Tiffany played it off until we got to her condo and up to her bedroom. She shut the door, turned around, and punched me in the face. I panicked and tried to jump out her second-story window, but she pulled me back in. She started yelling at me, then insisting that we try to make it work, then yelling at me again. It was an extraordinarily uncomfortable evening and a good lesson for me that I didn't learn from. When she brought me home the next day with a shiner, I was ready to start my new life with Marianne, who thought the black eye was funny, which it was.

Marianne and I dated for a glorious week and a half before she left me for a sensitive, smelly, hairy, vegan, Hare Krishna skateboarder guy who lived in my dorm, because that's usually what happens when pretty straight girls take a walk on the wild side. Another valuable lesson wasted on me. It took me another five years to get over Marianne. I like to think she still thinks about me.

Finance majors were not my people. I switched to pure math. Maybe I'd be a teacher. I couldn't quite see what I was going to look like as an adult with a career. The giant cloud of gay obscured my view. Cal Poly had an amazing integrated general education program for all your humanities requirements. I was introduced to philosophy, Buddhism, and archetypes in fairy tales. My lifelong interest in mysticism was reignited. It's common for misfits to have an interest in "higher truths." We all want to be wizards and feel superior to the norms.

I switched my major to philosophy. I was fascinated by mystic sects within the Judeo-Christian tradition. Cal Poly had a Campus Crusade for Christ chapter with several thousand members. Their Gay Club was me and five fags. I wanted to argue with conservative Christians, but I knew nothing about the Bible. I was certain I could discover some new hidden secrets of Christianity to use against the mean Christians. Their views seemed very unloving. While studying the Bible, I started going to the gay bars in LA three or four nights a week. I didn't drink, but gas and cover charges were expensive. I needed a job. I answered an ad in the paper looking for delivery drivers for a nearby produce company.

The route started at 5:00 a.m., three days a week. I could

be done in time for afternoon classes. I was an eighteen-year-old girl. I told the guy my dad was a truck driver and had taught me at an early age. Unbelievably, he hired me. It was a steep learning curve, but I became a truck driver. I felt like the fucking king of the butches. I got muscles and calluses and dirty, and I was a little terrible at my job. It took me several weeks to even realize there was a ramp at the back of the truck and another few weeks to develop the strength to load a whole stack of watermelon up that ramp. I persisted like the underdog sports hero I knew I was in my heart. I was so proud. My mother was so irritated. Maybe because it was a blue-collar job or a boy job, but it was likely the clothes. But if the baby boomers actually wanted their kids to be better educated and more successful than themselves, they shouldn't have spent so much time calling their Gen X spawn lazy, spoiled babies. I tried to become my grandfathers, the only generation my parents had any respect for.

I was doing it all. Studying mysticism and being a tough guy. I even went out for Cal Poly's softball team. Cal Poly had the rare status of having a AAA softball program. They actually had scholarship money for girls. I had never played with girls who could play like that. I didn't make the team because they said I didn't have enough experience, but they let me be their practice catcher for a season. At least I got a bunch of tough bruises and broke my thumb. I would catch Marianne watching me walk by in my dirty, sporty clothes. She totally missed me. Probably still does.

When *The L Word* came out in the early 2000s, I was most amused by their depiction of LA lesbians all being fashionable and superficial with nice cars. It was funny because it was true. I was living the late-eighties version, where they all had big hair, makeup, and Jeeps. Madonna had just kissed Sandra Bernhard on some awards show. For a moment, it became a thing for famous actresses to go to lesbian bars. I once danced with Kim Bassinger at the Palette, a bar specifically created for lipstick lesbians. I owned Hammer pants, a bolero hat, and numerous bolo ties. And vests, lots of vests. I wasn't quite thin enough to replicate the eighties version of Shane, but I was a snappy dancer and enthusiastic. The LA scene privileged fashionable "soft butches" as they still do today (Ellen). I've never been a dandy, but I was accustomed to wearing clothes that weren't my natural style. I met my next girlfriend at some bar in West Hollywood. Kelly.

Kelly was a light-skinned, peppy, attractive Black woman in her early twenties. She was attending Cal State Northridge to become a health inspector. I wasn't cute enough for Kelly, but I was persistent. I learned that gay Black people are different than gay white people.

First of all, gay Black people in LA in the eighties were T, not gay. I learned about white parties and I learned that there was a whole gay club just for Black people called the Catch One in South Central. It was the most fun I ever had in a gay bar. The music was extraordinary. I learned about line dances. I learned that a whole group of people at a club could enter into a collective, altered consciousness during a line dance. And although I was a good dancer for a white, butch dyke, I would never dare to compete with a Black gay man. Often, as the only white person there, I was given conciliatory encouragement for my efforts, which was affirmation enough.

Kelly had a group of friends who were also too coordinated and stylish for me, but they were always sweet and included me in their outings. They were amused by my efforts to keep up. I added pastels to my wardrobe and tried new things with my hair. I invested in light cotton trench coats with padded shoulders. Kelly and I had an adventurous and satisfying sex life. She moved to Hollywood when she graduated, and we discovered Pussycat Theaters and adult novelty stores. We bought my first strap-on: a deeply unsexy pink plastic novelty appendage with a white elastic waistband.

I also learned that many Black gay people didn't officially come out to their families. Even though being gay was the most important thing in my life, somewhere inside, I understood this wasn't my rule to break.

Still, it really hurt when Kelly started hanging out with this guy she worked with. He was the one she took to family events. She never talked about her family with me. I knew she was having an affair, but she always denied it, even after I walked in on them having sex.

It made me feel crazy, but I couldn't break up with her because she kept denying it and I didn't want to face the truth. She wanted to do gay things with me and everything else with him. Not being in control had a crushing effect on my psyche. I was usually the one in control, but this time, I wasn't cute enough. I wasn't a good enough dancer. I was too fat. I was a dumb white girl who didn't know anything.

I was also kind of a sociopath. I wasn't weepy because Kelly may not have loved me. I didn't like being a chump. It turned out that there was something a boy could do that I couldn't do, and it felt like a betrayal from my new world. My jealousy was obsessive. I couldn't tolerate the possibility that I was not good enough at something.

I conceded defeat eventually, but not before finding someone else to date. This next relationship would be my education into the hippie, intellectual, folk singer lesbian subtype.

I continued to do well in school. At the end of my second year, I quit my truck driving job and started as a canvasser in LA, for the California League of Conservation Voters. Canvassing is a horrible job, and one that all bleeding-heart, liberal dumbasses should be sentenced to perform in their lifetime. Perhaps organizations that rely on individual donations have gotten more sophisticated over the years about targeting their fundraising efforts. But in the neoliberal spirit of completely ignoring socioeconomic nuances, these people made us go everywhere. Being a nineteen-year-old white lesbian fundraising door-to-door for environmental causes all over Los Angeles is a valuable education. You learn all sorts of things about yourself, the people that you're talking to, and the people who sent you out there in the first place.

Rachel was my boss. She was British, with a real English accent. She'd gotten her first in English literature at Oxford, whatever that means. She seemed really smart, because of the accent, and a little snobby, which was totally hot. I set about wooing her with the novelty of my American, tough-guy, truck-driving swagger. She was initially hesitant because of my age and her position, but I was getting good at this. I knew she couldn't resist my charm for long.

Rachel had access to mystical fairy worlds suburban American culture tends to either deny as fictitious or demonize as sissified. Intellectuals, Europeans, artists, folk singers, tea . . . they're real? Please explain.

The most fun game I ever played was winning an argument with Rachel, especially when it involved overturning her pretentious assumptions about me. It made me adore her and want to do it again. I'd never met anyone more privileged than me. I figured she could defend herself. She used big words I didn't know, and there was always that accent. It felt like a real challenge to my intellect. She casually opened an even bigger world for me. She didn't know it was special.

I had Thai food and Indian food. She showed me a sun salutation on the beach in Malibu. She took me to the woods with a bunch of naked Wicca lesbians where we stood around a fire, holding hands, invoking directions, and channeling the goddess. We went to a work retreat in the Redwoods, and I danced in a drumming circle and went to a higher plane of consciousness. I'd done that at clubs, but it was different with trees. We went to plays. I added flannel shirts to my wardrobe. I eventually became a vegetarian after months of deriding the practice as unmasculine. I never did get into folk music. My mother considered it an unforgivable evil in the world, like littering. Also, overly sensitive men often enrage me.

Her dad was a gay director. Her brother was a gay actor. Her mother was a casting agent who sounded like Ursula the Sea Witch. They were all very fancy. Our coworker and friend Richard had a boyfriend who was a slightly famous artist. When he sold a painting, he held fabulous parties with minor celebrities and caviar. I was still, potentially, as intelligent as these people, but I had no practice with this world or its vocabulary. I entertained them with amusing stories about the worlds that I did know. They thought I was funny, like a hamster with a hat on.

My debut as their exotic, suburban/working-class performance artist was successful. I hit it big one night when we were at some arty party in a warehouse in LA. While Rachel was inside playing an actual zither, harmonizing with several other women on some ancient Celtic canticles, I was outside on the roof, being suspended off the side of a third-story ledge, winning a bet with some gay men that I could pee off the side of the building without hitting the wall.

I took Rachel to my world a few times. We went to the Catch one night. Her brother came too. They appreciated the music with that same face that fancy people get when they taste authentic "street food." They say "mmm" and use the word *fantastic* a lot. I learned that British people can't move their hips. They dance moving solely their shoulders.

I also took her home to meet my parents. Mom hated

Rachel. She had liked Kelly, who was cute and thin and stylish and enthusiastic. Rachel was snobby and had that accent. My dad didn't care for her either, but poking holes in her underestimations of us amused him in the same way it did me. Mom especially hated Rachel when I told her that instead of completing my fourth year of college, we were going to India.

The first Gulf War changed our plans when the American government issued a travel warning concerning Muslim countries. Instead, we traveled for two and a half months through Mexico, Belize, and Guatemala. My high school Spanish came in handy. We went to ruins, stayed in huts on the beach, rented a dirt bike in the mountains of Guatemala, and stayed on a tiny island off the coast of Belize. It was only because of our obliviousness to our own entitlement that we were not more of a target for harassment. We made it home with plenty of stories and various lesbian fashion items made from colorful Guatemalan fabric.

By the time we got home, another life was waiting. I'd spun the Mexico trip as educational to my parents, which it was, but there was no way to rationalize my next life choice. Rachel had been promoted to the CLCV's office in San Francisco. I wouldn't be returning to Cal Poly. I was finally moving to San Francisco. I couldn't say yes hard enough to San Francisco. I assured Mom that I would totally finish college up there. I'm sorry, Mom.

# CHAPTER EIGHTEEN

# MAJOR LEAGUE HOMO

I've always hated that game people play with regret by asking others, "Would you go back and do anything differently, knowing what you know now?" You big pussy. Walk it off. Your terrible decisions are the only things that make you at all interesting. My imagination rarely replays things. I can barely remember half the stories I'm telling. I prefer to manipulate the future in my mind, where I still have the chance to be a wise kook that people leave offerings for in my cave temple. But if I had to pick a moment in my life, like if a genie was forcing me, to go back and whisper some hard-won insight to a younger me, I would go back to early 1991, when I drove over that hill by Candlestick Park and saw the San Francisco skyline for the first time. I would tell that twenty-one-year-old dummy, "Pay attention. This is special. You'll never see anything like this again."

This time, San Francisco was exactly how I remembered it from all my previous lives. Somehow, everything seemed normal, even though nothing was. Maybe this is just the way things should be. Maybe my fantasy life had been so present for so long that it wasn't jarring to witness its materiality. Perhaps I'd been suppressing my shock reflex for so long that I no longer had one. Maybe I just knew I was home.

I was ill-prepared to fully appreciate the gift that was San Francisco in the nineties when I first got there. I was called there like the rest of them but knew so little about my own mojo. Everybody else here seemed to know so much. The dominant American cultural model enforced in white suburbs nationwide has a perverse way of obscuring alternative possibilities to its lifestyle and tastes. It takes a while to shed those layers of norms, no matter how miserably you've failed at embodying any of them.

The first time I saw a girl with a shaved head, jeans, a white T-shirt, a thick man belt, big black work boots, and a chain hanging from her wallet, it was like looking into a special issue of *Vogue* created just for me. The first time I saw the guy in the pink thong and heels walking his three pink poodles, and he gave me a flower, I felt like I was Charlie Bucket and Willie Fucking Wonka had just handed me the keys to the Chocolate Factory. The sun felt different here. It was more distant, but in a way that reminded me of my Midwestern childhood, like God was nicer here. I belonged here. I still had no style of my own beyond the performance pieces that emerged when I wanted to make a new girl fall in love with me, but I could not let my new city know what a nerd I really was. Nothing was more important than impressing her.

We moved into the Castro. This time I found the gays. Everything was gay. The hardware store was gay. We had a gorgeous, second-story one-bedroom with a balcony facing downtown and the Bay. There was nothing ugly in San Francisco. Not one thing. The beneficent old whores, those worldly, loving Victorian structures, smashed up against one another, smiling in gaudy colors, eager to provide sanctuary at impossible angles. Layers and layers of paint, indoors and outdoors, provided their own fleshy history and a voluptuous backdrop to new enthusiasm. Constellations of fossilized gum established a new Pantheon of eternal archetypes on each segment of sidewalk. The overcrowded and complex matrix of power lines, delineating the new rules and chaos

of the overhead airspace, also intimated the cosmic bonds
of the indoor consumers. Even the garbage looked like some
modern art installation. It was the early nineties, after all.
And I had come to the right place.

Out of a sense of inescapable guilt, I tried to enroll in
classes right away. Because of the timing of our move, classes
at San Francisco State would not be available to me for an
unforgivable amount of time, so I got a job as a bike mes-
senger. I only made minimum wage, but it gave me a chance
to wear weird clothes and hang out in the financial district,
reading Hegel atop various public statues, while people in
suits stared at me. I was sure they were jealous. My dreams
of becoming eccentric started to look promising.

I went to bartending school and got a job at a "sports" bar
in the Tenderloin. The guy who owned that bar turned out
to be a sleazy aspiring mobster, later indicted on trafficking
charges. He made me wear a T-shirt that was two sizes too
small and required me to solicit patrons for quarters to keep
the jukebox going. It was mostly regulars who drank there all
day and warned me about the owner. I learned to make blow
jobs, Long Islands, and rusty nails. I only lasted three months,
but it made me feel interesting. Everybody in San Francisco
was interesting. I had a lot of work to do.

I started at San Francisco State in the fall. I majored in
philosophy again and took classes in Old Testament folklore
and the origins of Christianity, but I couldn't resist the novelty of women's studies classes. Cal Poly hadn't offered them.
Surely, I should also be an expert on women. *Thelma & Louise*
had recently come out and offered female anger and violence
to the mainstream. The nineties would be turning that into
a vibrant spiritual community in San Francisco, and I was
ready to worship. Alas, was there ever a young butch dyke
taking her first women's studies class who didn't screw up

their concurrent relationship because of the hot babes they met in it? I doubt it.

The difference between LA lesbians and SF dykes was revolutionary. I never knew I was allowed to be that butch or that disdainful of mainstream fashion. The progress toward my own personal style began accelerating back to a similar place as when I was six: jeans and T-shirts. My hair went first. I never wore my club clothes again. Pastels and shoulder pads were permanently purged from my closet, lest someone discover my previous affiliations. My flannels were allowed to stay.

In the face of my new city's undiscovered mysteries, the drive underlying my intellectual pursuits was now largely to fulfill a promise I had made to my parents. They still supported me, though they hated the decisions I was making. I wasn't ready to tell them who I really was because I was still so far away from having anything to say on the subject. They just hoped San Francisco was a phase I would outgrow soon, like the rest of my life. But secretly, the expectation that I would become a respected professional was quickly going the way of my bolo ties. Guilt got me to school most days, but the city was so seductive. College had been my road to redemption, but now it was a burden. My newly formed suspicion that academic pursuits were elitist and ineffectual matched my new proletariat wardrobe. I wasn't ready to tell my mother that either.

And then one day, in late 1991, the queers showed me they were the ones who ruled this city and my allegiance. They pulled me out of class and into the street. I can't imagine how we all found out. No cell phones. No social media. A beacon fire was lit in the Castro. The state assembly had recently passed a minor bill called AB 101. This legislation simply added "sexual orientation" to the language of an existing nondiscrimination law in California. That morning, word reached some queers that Governor Pete Wilson had vetoed that bill, caving to pressure from religious groups. Within a few hours, we'd all heard the call.

You didn't want to fuck with the queers just then. Many had just come through a decade of uninterrupted loss and a president who had watched them all die. We all lived through Reagan and the Moral Majority. By the time I got there in the midafternoon, thousands of queers were assembled in the Castro. I had left in the middle of class like I was in the Queer National Guard. If you Google this day now, you will find estimates anywhere from two thousand to fifty thousand people. I don't know. There were a lot of angry fucking homos. People had bullhorns and signs. There were speeches and rallying cries. Then we started marching down Market Street. We filled blocks and blocks. I was caught up in the Holy Gay Spirit. The eighties had been like being left with your pervy, rich, Bible-thumping uncle as your babysitter. There wasn't a single queer on that street that hadn't been diddled by the eighties. The fury smelled good.

We stopped in front of a state building on Van Ness, just off Market. I was on my own in the crowd, waiting for instructions. Strangers smiled at me and held my hand. Then, we were on the move again to another state office building close by. When we got there, cops in riot gear were lined up in front of the doors. They were behind those temporary police barriers that look like bike racks. I worked my way to the front. I didn't want anyone to think I was scared. Several glorious queens were lined up to my right, facing the police. They were yelling really mean things at the cops. I was entranced. I'd never witnessed such defiance. One of the cops got sick of it and sprayed mace at them. In unison, as if it were rehearsed, at least three of them pulled mace out of their own purses and sprayed back. I stood there awed, thinking that I would kill or die for them in that moment.

The cops were outnumbered by a lot. We started pulling at the barriers. They pulled them back, trying to keep this symbolic boundary in place. We won. The cops retreated into the building through the large glass entrance. A bunch of queers started using the metal barriers as battering rams, smashing the glass. A few more used the poles of their fucking rainbow flags to smash some more glass. (That's what rainbow flags are for, in case you forgot.) People started lighting shit on fire. Someone sent a Molotov cocktail through the window of an office, just to the left of the entrance, lighting the room on fire. There was now nothing but shattered glass between us and the cops. They brought fire hoses from inside the building and started spraying the crowd from the marble steps, just inside the entrance. I got it from the one on the left. I had mainly been a witness because I didn't understand my own agency in this situation, but that fire hose felt like a baptism. It made me a participant in something important and real and bigger than my ridiculous world.

That night has always stayed with me, like a secret magic elixir kept in my pocket that recalls the productive elegance of rage and property destruction whenever I need the scent. I wish I could say that experience altered my course, turned me into some kind of insurgent superhero, that I devoted myself thenceforth to radical activism.

But, of course, girls.

After the excitement of that night, I went back to my daily life, which only hinted at an adult existence. I temped at a customer service call center for a department store and I went to school. Shortly after constructing a life-size papier-mâché tree in our bedroom and ruining Rachel's teak salad bowl, I convinced her to move out of our charming Castro apartment she was perfectly able to afford into a Lower Haight dump at half the price.

It had its charms, though they were too subtle for Rachel to appreciate. It was a large apartment building on Haight and Buchanan. The gay men who owned it took over most of the top floor, turning it into a fifties memorabilia museum of sorts. I took it upon myself to sand and paint the wood floors, pretending I knew what I was doing. It was cold and smelly and dark, and I loved it. There was a shitty old-school coffeehouse around the corner called the Horseshoe. You could still smoke in coffeehouses back then, and I felt very bohemian, reading Kant and chain-smoking, stewing in the stench of coffee, smoke, and shit. I learned the entire catalogues for Miles Davis, the Gypsy Kings, and Tom Waits while I affected the role of a mysterious intellectual who was also almost always the only girl in the joint. Skinny, coffee-addled, sensitive misanthropes made satisfying targets for my fledgling efforts to deconstruct my lifelong training to accommodate male egos whenever they offered me their insight on Kant.

I was just discovering the filmy treasures my new location had to offer when I fell in love with a hot femme in my women's studies class and moved out.

Rachel and I still had good arguments and I was very fond of her, but I couldn't maintain devotion to my hippie phase when the chance to be a knight presented itself.

Ellie was a period piece out of a Brontë novel. She had porcelain skin and a flurry of perfect freckles across her interesting nose and dramatic cheekbones. She had mythical black hair with a small silver blaze above her right temple, despite being in her early twenties. Ellie had trained in ballet her entire life and probably would've been a famous ballerina had the discipline not given her the body of an Olympic gymnast. She also studied classical piano and had gone to a fancy arts high school in Michigan. She lived on gas station brownies and coffee with cream that she refused to stir in. She studied Chaucer.

Her occasional inclinations to inhabit the fey lands of the *The Mists of Avalon* did not startle me, and I happily indulged my lifelong impulse toward gallantry. Ellie was my introduction to high femme. High femmes may look similar to pretty straight girls, but these ladies are queer as fuck and not squeamish about calling your bluff regarding the superhero you always secretly suspected you were. They would like it to be true as well. For butches, this means you finally get to roleplay all the epic identity fantasies you've always had, out loud, with another person. At first, being in a relationship with a high femme feels like the best thing that has ever happened to your self-esteem. It also means you better not fuck up and break character. You belong to her, and so do your imaginary superballs.

Now I was working as an engineering assistant in the student union on campus. Basically, I changed light bulbs and snaked the drain behind the Chinese food kiosk in the food court. I was entrusted with the working-man secrets of the student union and an enormous set of keys on a retractable key ring that hung from a carabiner on my belt loop, just like Schneider from *One Day at a Time*. Double Butch Bonus. I joined the softball team for San Francisco State. It was definitely okay to be a dyke on this team.

Ellie and I weren't quite ready to live together. I moved out of the lower Haight and into a cooperatively run lesbian flat on Valencia in the Mission. It was run by two intellectual, vegetarian lesbians who tried to have house meetings and institute chore wheels but lacked the foresight to rent to women just like them. Instead, they rented to a swarthy, scary, klepto butch with a thing for knives, and me, who had my head too far up Ellie's vagina to be of any use. Maybe they thought we were cute.

Still, the Mission was magical. I discovered Good Vibrations just up the street and got myself my first real strap-on: a leather Texas Two-Strap and big black silicone dick. Now I really was a pirate.

School was farther away from the Mission and Ellie lived near school. I didn't spend much time in my cool new household, which I probably would've enjoyed. Butches could possibly be the most productive, dynamic, well-liked people in the world if we weren't always so busy getting some cute girl a latte and trying to remind her of her father. Ellie and I listened to Kate Bush while we fucked in the bedroom of the house she rented from a guy who reminded her of her father. We took picnics in Golden Gate Park. I went to work and class and softball practice. The first few months of a new relationship are so sparkly. Ellie's quirks charmed me and she fostered my masculinity. It was like archetype happy hour with free pussy snacks.

I made a friend on the team, Ed. Ed called me Bob. I'd never been friends with another butch. Ed was big, like almost six feet tall, with a cute baby face. We'd snort at each other and say piggy things about girls and try to hurt each other on the field. When the team went to a tournament in Bakersfield and stayed at a Motel 6, Ed and I and another butch on the team who was almost forty naturally shared a room. Ed and I shared one of the beds and gave ol' grumpy her own.

It wasn't long before Ed and I started touching each other in the dark. I feel a little sorry for straight guys in these situations. I'm sure this happens to young, straight jocks with more frequency than I'll ever know, but they have a more terrifying level of stigma attached to incidental man-on-man gropings. And while butches do internalize much of the same homophobia and gender regulation straight men do, there's more latitude for us because we're already gay. That doesn't mean we go around telling everybody about it.

As the initial exploratory brushes intensified into more thorough probing, accompanied by heavier breathing and soft slurping noises, the old butch in the next bed finally told us to either cut it out or take it outside. We were too excited to stop, so we took it down to the pool, which was closed. We hopped the fence and fucked in the whirlpool.

Butch-on-butch sex is pretty hot and not nearly as fraught with all the identity anxiety that accompanies homonormative sex, which is also hot for different reasons. You get to fuck a masculine person without the icky things associated with fucking men, including shame. It's a dirty sweet secret that doesn't penetrate your own identity insecurities. It's self-affirming and shouldn't count in a normal cheating way.

We were pretty exhausted the next day for our doubleheader. When we climbed back in the bus for the long ride home, everyone fell asleep and Ed started fingering me under a towel. It was hot, but really it assured me I was part of a different world now. Nobody was going to kick me out because I was a dyke. They were going to shove their fingers in my vagina. I would have to start letting go. That's what your twenties are about, isn't it? Your damage is still just beneath the surface, but you've likely moved your body far enough away from it that you're not sustaining further injury. Your defenses have relaxed just enough to allow moments of reflection during a good hand job.

Part of the character I played with Ellie was husband, and the bit of that archetype that was glaringly absent was the role of provider. That's what my dad was. I needed a real job so I could take care of her. Also, if I worked full time and went to school full time, I would feel like my parents could respect me a little. They subsidized my existence while I went to school. I always worked, but I didn't need a full-time job. At the thought of that, I felt unworthy of my own skin, especially when I still had no idea what I was going to do with my impractical degree. I needed to overcome some real-world adversity to legitimize self-respect. Someone at school told me about Veritable Vegetable.

# CHAPTER NINETEEN

# BUTCH UNIVERSITY

VV was a woman-owned, women-run, all-organic produce distributor in San Francisco. Founded in the seventies, it was the nation's first distributor of organic produce. The early history of the organic food movement in the US can largely be found in its financial records. In the late seventies, it incorporated a feminist vision into its operating mission and started training women to drive trucks and forklifts. Hundreds of dykes across the country owe at least part of their identity to their time spent at VV. I could barely believe that such a place existed. I was destined to work there.

I took my six months of truck driving in LA and my youthful enthusiasm to their warehouse down by the bay. They had a small corner warehouse at the end of a long row. Outside, they had an antique Mayflower semi-trailer set up on its supports with windows and a staircase leading to a door. It was their break room. Could this place be any cooler? I needed them so much more than they needed me.

A crusty, crass older butch named Sue and a scary, hot redhead named Hannah conducted my interview. Sue was charming and funny, but I could tell she didn't like me. I tried to impress the femme, who was the kind of person who was only impressed if she chose to be. They knew they were the gatekeepers for an SF cult that employed butch dykes. They had reservations due to my youth and spotty work history. I looked like a desperate puppy at the pound. Miraculously, I got the job.

I pulled produce orders on the graveyard shift. They gave me an army-green Ben Davis warehouse apron, utility knife, fat black marker, and clipboard. They gave me an old red steel hand truck that no one else liked because it was heavy. It was my new superbutch signature accessory.

I loved being sore and tired at the end of the night. I loved building intricate pallets of different sized boxes of produce. I loved getting my orders right. I loved learning new tricks with my hand truck. I even loved the produce. Being from the preglobalization Midwest, I didn't know anything about fresh produce. I'd never seen fresh herbs. I didn't know kale was a thing. I'd never eaten a mango. Then there was the rest of the night crew, who were quite everything I thought an outlaw chick gang should look like. Hannah usually wore all black and boots with heels and dark red lipstick as the assistant night-crew manager and could belch louder than anyone else. Sue had a flattop and walked with a cane and poked people with it and said funny things. There was Dee, who was over six feet tall and Samoan. She made me feel kinda girly. There was Shea, a thick, muscled Black man, whose presence confused me. It was a couple hours before somebody whispered to me that Shea used to be a woman. I had no context for that. But this was the Emerald City, after all. What did I know? That's neat.

One of the drivers who did the local route was Hart. She was one of those straight girls who manages to be queerer than most lesbians. She was tall and cute and loud and hilarious. She had Bette Davis eyes and a potty mouth. Then there was Joan. She wore a beret like an arty revolutionary. She was the head receiver and the one who primarily drove the forklift. She could also drive semis. She often wore a baby bottle of red wine tied around her neck. She told me she had voted against my hire because it would be disruptive. I didn't understand what she meant.

There's a special camaraderie among people who work the graveyard shift. It only takes a few weeks of working hard through sleep deprivation and bumming your crew cigarettes to earn a little validation. They may still think you're young, cocky, and stupid, but you're a new member of their all-girl vampire chain gang now, so at least that part of you must be okay. Seniority on the night crew controlled the stereo, establishing anthemic playlists for us. Our rotations included the soundtrack for *Saturday Night Fever*, Ween, Nirvana, and Sir Mix-a-Lot. We routinely broke into spontaneous song and dance numbers just like the street scene from *Fame*.

I purposely took classes that started early in the morning so I could go right to school after work, then sleep on the grass in the quad until Ellie was done for the day. It felt exhilarating to be exhausted, like I finally had a right to my own air. I was the smart, hardworking tough guy Ellie had been waiting for.

Ellie and I got a place together. We found a nice one-bedroom in the Duboce Triangle. It had vintage tile on the mantle of the inoperative fireplace and ornate molding around the bay windows.

I needed to get a cat. Cats and strap-ons are everything young lesbians require to set up a new household and comprise the entire list of disputed joint property when your relationship eventually ends in a firestorm of jealousy and identity implosion. A pet of my own would provide a yet unfulfilled segment of my identity. Butch dykes require an animal familiar for full initiation. Unless they're allergic, then they're soft butches.

I went to the Humane Society, which is traumatic for those

of us who disappoint our mothers. Just as my thoughts were tumbling down the morose hole, I rounded another of the endless rows of cages, and a yowling targeted me as if I were late to an appointment. The yowling continued as I sped up to discover the source. When I arrived, I found the cage that contained the first real love of my life. I was face-to-face with the scrawniest, loudest, smartest calico that ever lived. She looked at me as if she had been waiting for me. She had made herself hoarse yelling for me. I had the guards open the cell, and Bell jumped onto my shoulders and stayed there for another fifteen years. This story is incomplete without Bell.

Ellie got a cat too, a fat, long-haired beast named Princess.

We moved into our apartment in fall. My parents decided to pretend like I had a normal life. They were coming for Christmas, for inspections.

Ellie was the fourth girlfriend I made my parents meet, so embarrassment and failure framed my anticipation. But this was going to be in my new apartment, at Christmas. I was working full time and going to school full time. This was a solid moment of productivity for me in my mind. Ellie was pretty and could hold a conversation. Maybe this wouldn't suck.

All young queers must go through this experience. The thought of your parents coming in their first diplomatic capacity is daunting. You cannot fully envision what you're trying to prove to them. After a few years of not living with them, when you're not imagining them judging you, your life seems pretty together. But at the thought of their arrival, you suspect that your life is only slightly more substantial than when Barbie married Captain Caveman and you invited them to the ceremony. You try to ignore your insecurities about the weight of your relationship and the transient nature of your furniture. Surely, they can find some pride in your work ethic and be happy that you've managed to get such a cute girl to love you. And maybe they'll see your awkward lasagna and DIY Christmas decorations as slightly more mature versions of the hand-drawn cards you used to make them and be similarly charmed by your efforts. Perhaps they could stick the whole experience up on the refrigerator of their heart.

Maybe young straight couples go through this rite of passage with some similar discomfort. But for them, Mom and Dad's first official visit provides legitimacy to their adulthood like a UN resolution to recognize a new state. The gender roles and assumptions of responsibilities for straight couples are accompanied by timeless and respected models for honoring the new assertion of adulthood as if it were real. The effort must be validated. The torch must be passed.

My parents had never been participants in my little role-playing experiments. My mother was not about to politely encourage my novice attempt at masculine integrity. I was still her daughter, and in 1992, there were no popular culture models to aid her understanding of my gender craft project. She had largely let go of the fantasy of my undiscovered femininity, but she still wondered just what the hell I was doing.

I hadn't specifically explained to my parents that I was trying to create a lifelike diorama of normativity for their benefit. Holidays pull back the curtain. Away from my mother's gaze for several years, I thought I was replicating an esteemed model of masculinity in the style of post-WWII grit, swagger, and natural aptitude with machinery. We shall call it old-school butch. Without either of them there, I imagined it was going pretty well.

"What are you doing?" was the review I received.

To them, I was a twenty-two-year-old girl with a history of making poor decisions. That was fair.

"How are your grades? What's your plan after graduation?

Your little friend is kinda weird. Why are you working in a warehouse? No, we don't want to go see it. You can't afford this apartment. What does she do to support herself? Does she pay rent? I hate cats. Don't you think you would look nicer if you grew your hair out a little? Do you need new shoes? Why must you always make your life so difficult? The lasagna is fine."

Irritable bowel syndrome and tears. Was I even a real person? What was I doing?

That first visit from my folks put quite a dent in the hull of my mystery ship. I saw flashes of what my life looked like through my parents' eyes. I was playing house, just like when I was seven.

Thank god I had to go back to work. It was becoming the only thing that made me feel okay about myself. I did things right. I was useful. I looked hot in my apron. The crew was starting to warm up to me. We used to go get breakfast together on Friday mornings after work and drink beer and laugh loudly. It was my first taste of something like real life. The satisfying repetition of well-defined productivity in my work world was starting to point out the nebulous fictions that dominated my other worlds.

When I started back to school, it was clear my initial enthusiasm for overcoming exhaustion and conquering the odds had been related to my misguided hope that it would impress my parents. The breeding stamina that accompanies a new relationship was also tapering off. I started skipping classes and making excuses. By the time my physics final rolled around, I could not stop myself from sleeping through it. The woman sitting in front of me had to wake me because my snoring was distracting her. I received the worst grades of my life.

The compelling romanticism of my relationship with Ellie

began to dull next to the vividness of the personalities and culture of my job. I never introduced Ellie to my work family. I just knew the two worlds wouldn't get along. I didn't know how to play blue-collar tough guy and pretend knight in the same room at the same time. My identities were conflicted as they'd always been, and I couldn't blow my own cover. I started to resent the expectations on my relationship self even though I was the one who established them. Butches, you know you love being the martyr until that moment that you don't anymore.

I also didn't want Ellie to meet Hannah.

A bunch of people from work were going to see a show at a bar south of Market. Ellie didn't mind that I went, but she didn't know that I had a crush on my boss.

Hannah was a presence. She was funny and smart and larger than life. She too could be classified as high femme, but more Marlene Dietrich than Helena Bonham Carter. She had red hair that she dyed redder. Deep red lipstick and black heels. She flared her nostrils when she blew smoke through them. She had a scarlet *A* tattooed over her heart. While I could've had a productive friendship with her, bonding over past experiences that I assumed we shared, I played the naïve, cocky boy deferring to her feminine authority.

When I got to the bar, I had a couple beers with other co-workers before strutting over to her corner barstool. I was wearing a sleeveless T-shirt to show off my new work muscles. I asked if she was having a good time. She looked up from her cocktail to stare at me. I tried to make small talk. I tried to make her laugh. She stared, blowing smoke in my face.

Instead of salvaging my shrinking dignity by leaving, I made a game of making her talk to me. After another few minutes, she leaned toward me, sank her teeth into my left shoulder, and didn't release. I made every effort not to react to the pain. She continued to bite down until she broke the skin. Then she turned back to her drink and lit another cigarette.

"Okay then, I'll see you at work," I said. I still have a small scar.

I was hooked after that. She allowed me to give her rides home sometimes. One morning, she invited me in. She brought out one of her dicks. "Fuck me, boy," was what she said.

She was so much better at this than me.

The tension had been there for weeks, but I failed the test. She was rightly put off by the guilt I expressed and the fact that I immediately ran home to Ellie. My superficial moral conflict bored Hannah. What a whiny chump I was.

I tried to figure out how to make her love me again, which led to sustained awkwardness at work for some time. Hannah never encouraged my advances again. Our friendship also ended, which I mourned more deeply than our affair, but my ego wouldn't allow me to tell her that.

Ellie had, indeed, grown suspicious. We fought constantly. The identity I'd lovingly cultivated for her began to disintegrate. I failed all of my classes. School seemed inconsequential in the shadow of my moral failings. Everything started to unravel. My gallantry buckled. My swagger deflated. I had to admit to my parents that I didn't want to go back to school. Everything was a steamy pile of guilt and shame. My parents told me I could support myself until I got my shit together. I was grateful for that. At least I could be a crushing disappointment on my own terms.

It did mean that I couldn't quite afford our rent and food. Ellie and I were still hanging on as a couple. I couldn't face another failure just then. I broke our lease. We didn't get our security deposit back because of the nail holes I put in the oak moldings around the bay windows putting up those stupid Christmas decorations. We moved to a new live/work "artist" loft downtown on Sixth and Market.

It was one room with fifteen-foot ceilings and tall windows. There was a loft for our bed with a tiny staircase. Under the loft, there were a hot plate, a dorm fridge, and a sink. We had to share bathrooms at the end of the hall. You could get up to the roof if you wanted. It was cheap and the neighborhood was unmistakably in the city.

Ellie wasn't happy about it. It was a tight fit for the two of us and two cats. The old apartment and neighborhood had matched Ellie's character. It had been quaint and quiet. The new place was harsh and noisy. I was starting to have an affinity for harshness and noise. Ellie also didn't match the way I felt about myself at work. The romance that had so captivated my ego in the beginning now clashed with loud laughter, sarcasm, and hard work. It was time to be a tough girl surrounded by tough girls.

I had put us on a waiting list for a larger room in the same building to make Ellie happier. But when the new place became available, Ellie moved out with Princess. Our performances had become irreconcilable. Also, she never believed I never slept with Hannah. And I never admitted it.

I suspected that I was a no-good dick. My track record was terrible. I moved into the new room by myself and resolved to take a break. I helped Ellie move her stuff, and I settled into my very own first apartment.

I was lying to myself about the break. Joey had already come along.

CHAPTER TWENTY

# THE MISSION

I didn't know what the hell to do with Joey. She was a new truck driver at Veritable. She didn't need me. She didn't need rescuing. What was I supposed to be for someone who didn't need me to be anything? I didn't even know that she liked me at first. I had no frame of reference for Joey, but I really wanted to be ready for her.

Joey was beautiful, but not exactly feminine. She wasn't butch either. She was a tough girl, an original. She buzzed her black hair. She had big, fierce brown eyes that protected her soul. She was guarded, aloof. Shit, I can't do aloof. How was I supposed to play this?

Our first "date" was a bike ride that turned into a contest of wills. We rode all the way out through Golden Gate Park, the Presidio, then across the Golden Gate Bridge. We turned up the steep, winding road on the other side that leads into a wildlife area. We followed the road until it crested into a scenic overlook. We locked our bikes and walked down a steep path that led to a small, secluded stretch of beach looking onto the Pacific. We sat there in silence for some time. I thought I could sense some sexual tension, but how could I be sure?

On our second "date," she came to my place and we watched a movie, in the dark, on my bed, in silence. Again, after a long period of possible tension, I walked her down to the bus stop. She looked as if she were wondering if I were stupid. An encouraging development.

On our third date, an epic hike through the Redwoods, I lost our staring contest. As I was hiking behind her, trying to keep pace, I began rambling uncontrollably. After nearly an hour of my corny babbling to mask my growing anxiety about the status of our association, she suddenly wheeled around, flung me against a guardrail, and kissed me, hard.

I pushed back, shoving her into the opposite guardrail, and kissed her back. Making out with Joey was like being in a really sexy fight. I hadn't anticipated what was behind those eyes.

We returned to the city, and to her apartment in the Mission. It was sparsely appointed with cool, tough girl stuff. She lit some Mexican saint votives and put on PJ Harvey loud. We tussled and fucked and came until the next morning.

I'd had glimpses of the dusky, dangerous magic of the dyke realm in the Mission, but I didn't understand the scope of its possibilities until I was initiated. I didn't know if I could ever be cool enough to make it there, but it was the enchanted rock-'n'-roll Amazon treehouse compound I had been promised. Saint candles and twinkly lights, produce crate shelves, ironically repurposed and defiled iconography, futons on the floor, and dark coffee, dripping into a mason jar the morning after profoundly hot, but somewhat painful, sex.

I woke to the view from the floor and the smell of paraffin and sweat. The night before was a blur of power exchange. I didn't know who had been the butch or the top. How was I to respond? This was advanced queerness.

Had I been even remotely self-aware, perhaps I could've summoned the adversity and darkness I had actual familiarity with and manifested a viable queerness that might have enjoyed the uncertainty of unregulated passion. My paradigms had not yet been dismantled, sadly.

Joey and I enjoyed many adventures over the next several months, but my anxiety about the lack of definition in our relationship and gender roles accelerated over time.

I agonized over the fact that she would never call me her girlfriend or hold my hand in public or tell me how she felt about me. She was masterfully reserved. And I was a dork. I did not understand the promise and beauty of what was being offered to me. It was the opportunity to be unplugged from the Matrix, but she didn't explain that to me. My insecurities bored her.

I thought this new amorphous identity required more accessories. I needed to be a part of the world she seemed to easily navigate. I had to be like those other scary cool dykes who lived in the Mission and knew about cool dyke stuff. Everybody I wanted to know lived in the Mission.

A new apartment seemed like a good start. One spring day I rode my bike though the side streets all over the Mission and eventually came upon a For Rent sign in a bay window on Lexington Street, which is more of an alley. I knew it was a haunted magic Hobbit hole even before I saw inside. Step One, the perfect pad.

The door was open. The landlord was inside painting. A straight couple was looking at the place—*Where the hell did they come from?* They didn't deserve this apartment. It was a one-bedroom railroad flat. The door opened into the dark living room with a built-in buffet. To the left, a bedroom with a bay window overlooked the street. The kitchen was huge with an old-time Wedgewood stove, the kind with the feet. The bathroom had been painted a streaky royal blue and had a clawfoot tub and light fixtures made from blue glass bottles. I loved this apartment like it was an undiscovered part of my soul.

I started making conversation with the landlord. I wasn't going to leave until he agreed to give me this apartment. Well, I did leave, but only for the ten minutes it took me to go buy a case of High Life, the beer I had seen empty cans of in the room he was painting. After a couple hours of drinking with him and then telling him that I loved the bathroom and he didn't have to paint it, he gave me the apartment. Five hundred and twenty-five dollars a month. I hope the millennials who now occupy that place choke on that.

I moved in the next month. The downtown loft had just been the waiting room to my new identity. Nine Lexington was a shiny new skin. I laid on the living room floor that first night, with no furniture, feeling safe. Bell patrolled, eliminating evil spirits before curling up on my shoulder.

I got an antique sleigh bed at the thrift store at the corner. I also picked up a framed, decaying lithograph of Jesus before Pilate, a triptych of ink-drawn topless hula girls, and a wooden, Malaysian god icon. My first knickknacks. I got my own CD player and PJ Harvey CDs along with a coffee grinder. There were half a dozen Mexican grocery stores within two blocks, each stocking a variety of saint votives. In the built-in buffet drawers, I discovered an old cabaret album titled *Bottoms Up* and piles of forgotten glitter. Magic Gays had lived here. Maybe I could be a San Francisco dyke after all.

Joey liked my new apartment. She may have also been skeptical of the newness of my worn relics. We broke the sleigh bed anyway, twice. And my new affectations immediately felt familiar to me, regardless of their hasty assembly. She especially liked my cat, who actually was a little too cool for me.

My alley fort was the perfect location for everything that was perfect about the Mission in the nineties. It was between Mission and Valencia, and Seventeenth and Eighteenth. The

Elbo Room was fifty feet away, which turned out to be the former location of Amelia's, the last full-time dyke bar in San Francisco (at the time) until it closed in 1989. Providence. They still had the old black-and-white photo booth that made everyone look hot. Leather Tongue Video was around the corner with obscure cult classics and bizarre porn for educational purposes. The best burritos, the best falafel, and the best dive bars were all within blocks.

Dating life for dykes in the Mission was a craft. Every encounter needed to be a montage of urban obscura, irony, and frugality, an edgier incarnation of the date-day scene in *Breakfast at Tiffany's*. In a pinch, all three could be had at Esta Noche, the Latino drag bar two blocks away. Joey took me to the St. Francis Hotel in Union Square to ride the glass elevators on the outside of the building. This experience wasn't just free, but it also scored bonus points for walking through a fancy hotel filled with fancy people in scruffy dyke costumery.

One was also expected to have independent interests so as not to appear needy to a tough girl. I was pretty terrible at this. Spending time alone in my life had been fine when the whole world was against me and I could fantasize about my latent superpowers. But if there was hope that an attractive person was actually attracted to me, all my focus was spent trying to be more attractive, wondering why they wouldn't want to spend all of their time with me. I visualized them watching me do things and thinking I looked cool. Most Sunday mornings, I'd walk up Valencia to the Italian deli on Twenty-second and buy the *New York Times*. I'd have breakfast at Boogaloo and read the paper. I'd finish the crossword on my back stoop with strong coffee and my cool cat in the sun. I was sure Joey could see me.

If Joey was pretending like she didn't know me for a few days, I would accept invitations from people who allegedly wanted to hang out with me. I was a terrible friend. I was never sure why people would want to do stuff with me. My coworker Hart ignored my awkwardness. She took me to bars and showed me how to hang out with another person and enjoy myself. It was like a date, but you didn't have to worry so much. She wasn't a dyke, so she didn't give a shit about my accessories. She made me laugh.

Another coworker, Jules, introduced me to some arty aspects of the Mission. She was the one who first took me to LunaSea, a dedicated amateur performance space for queer women. There was always a friend of an acquaintance doing something there. There was networking time after the performance while everyone smoked, where you could be seen and get credit for your attendance. I logged many hours there watching some disturbing and often terrible queer performance art in that tiny theater. I hadn't yet been exposed to this niche of queer culture, but it seemed important. I tried to moan and snap my fingers at the appropriate intervals. Most performers there were processing their experiences with significant sexual abuse. I'd never shared my own experiences with, say, men capitalizing on my situational vulnerability. All that stuff happened to the other, secret, terrible-at-being-a-girl me. It couldn't have happened to the me I was trying to be in that space. It wasn't butch to talk about how many guys I fucked with in high school, or junior high, or grade school. That just made me sound gay. Besides, I wasn't raped by my stepdad; I just had a secret character flaw that felt uncommon and unsympathetic.

I felt protective of the women who did perform, though. That has always been my job. I felt a precognitive connection to the performers. I was both like them and the one who should protect them. Some of the pieces were good, but no matter how uncomfortably awful or unnecessarily loud a piece was, I could always discern the tiny corona of beauty glowing around the total eclipse of terrible as they publicly externalized their pain. I didn't intellectualize then how essential good and terrible queer performance art is to our history and solidarity as a community. It was but one of the mediums through which our combined discontent and wrath could be vented and transformed. We were a collective din of the damaged. I took it for granted that we were all a part of the same club and I should protect the vulnerability of it with my life.

In our personal lives, we were all horrible at actual intimacy and trust and vulnerability. Joey and I continued to struggle for dominance in that irritating and irresistible way young dykes do when we're trying to protect our squishy parts. I protected myself by demanding small gestures of uncynical affection. She protected herself by not returning my phone calls for a few days, then showing up at my apartment for sex, acting like I was silly.

Some new people came to Veritable. I clearly remember meeting Pally and Rina for the first time near the north bay door in the warehouse. Pally had ass-length dreads and lots of tattoos and facial piercings at a time when those things were just starting to become mandatory. I was sure I'd been at a party with some of the coolest queer girls in San Francisco, but Pally and Rina didn't give a shit about anything I'd seen. They looked like rock stars. Just being near them made me feel like a nerd.

I introduced myself like I was the head of the Welcome Wagon, back in Iowa. I invited them to a Thanksgiving party at my apartment like I was in charge of the prom committee. After they looked at me like I'd interrupted their nap, I scuttled off, trying to minimize the inconvenience I'd caused.

Around the same time, Zoe started on the night crew.

She was from a world I understood. She was polite and bubbly. She didn't have any tattoos or attitude. She was either straight or inexperienced when she got there. And she was really cute. She had sexy green eyes and a softness that pushed that goddamn straight-girl button in my gut the second I saw her. I was still dating Joey. Maybe she actually liked me, and maybe I was cool enough. I obsessed about it every day, so surely I was in love with her. I was the enigmatic tough girl I always wanted to be with Joey. But Zoe seemed so familiar, like an old friend had dropped into my crazy new world and she needed a tour guide.

I offered my sage guidance to help Zoe become more comfortable with the city and the night crew. I was sure I wasn't flirting with her. I already had a girlfriend who scared the shit out of me. I loved Joey's playful challenges to my self-esteem. I wouldn't screw that up by falling into something that seemed so unedgy, I told myself. I invited both of them to Thanksgiving.

I called my mom for recipes from my childhood. She was excited to help me make my first Thanksgiving dinner for my friends. I bought a Crockpot from the thrift store just so I could make my favorite hotdish with Minute Rice, Campbell's cream of mushroom soup, and Cheez Wiz. Thanksgiving was a success. Most of the night crew came. We felt like family. Joey spent the holiday with her family, but Zoe came.

When Christmas rolled around, I promised my mom I would drive home. Joey was going to spend the holiday with her family again. Zoe didn't have anywhere to go for Christmas. I was just being a pal when I asked her to come with me.

That's what I told Joey, and I think that's what I believed. I felt overwhelmed with preemptive guilt explaining the situation to her, and a little stupid because Joey acted as if she didn't care what I did.

We were sitting at Maya Taqueria on Sixteenth and Guerrero. I was trying to get her to admit it would bother her if I slept with Zoe while I was trying to explain that I wasn't going to. I said, "This would be a lot easier if you would just say that you don't want me to sleep with Zoe because you love me, and it would bother you." After twenty minutes of trying to convince her this was a reasonable expectation on our relationship, and after six months of my anxiety about her feelings for me, she finally relented. It would be the first and last time Joey told me she loved me.

I was actually relieved Joey didn't want to go with me to my parents' house for Christmas. I wasn't embarrassed of her. I was embarrassed of me. How could I maintain my tough dyke façade once she saw where I came from? She would have seen me in a sweater. Zoe understood that world implicitly. It wouldn't diminish how she saw me.

Zoe and I barely made it to the Central Valley before I was reaching down her panties while I was driving. It was that surging compulsion I'd always had, to be the big man, the dominant daddy. I don't know where that guy came from, and I never liked him. Zoe didn't deserve that guy either.

I knew Zoe wouldn't stop me because of some moral opposition to my cheating. I couldn't stop me either. My ego drove that big dummy bus. I didn't know what intimacy looked like yet, and I had no reservations about lighting my life on fire. I had figured out how to win. That was the best drug of all.

My mother wondered what the hell I was doing. I'd told her over the phone about Joey, then I showed up to Christmas with Zoe. Mom hadn't met Joey but liked her anyway because I'd told her how aloof and confusing Joey was. I told Mom Zoe didn't have anywhere to go for the holidays, but she knew exactly what was going on. She did not approve. She was also disturbed, upon rifling through my luggage to wash my clothes, to find I now wore boy's underpants. Double judgment.

We muddled through Queer Offspring Home for the Holidays, which is actually a separate, concurrent holiday few understand, like Kwanzaa. I spent about half the time in the toilet with severe stress diarrhea, so that killed some time. I'm sure Zoe thought my mother was gracious, but she wasn't familiar with Minnesota Nice. Only a trained ear could hear the seething disapproval.

My half-assed offerings of normativity have always confused and annoyed my mother. She even hated my sweaters, the grand compromise. I didn't have a clear picture of what my mother thought my life should look like, but it felt something like living in a neatly labeled Tupperware container on my mother's shelf next to the holiday decorations. Everything could be pulled out at the same time. I had no idea how to be what she may have wanted. I also didn't know how to "be myself." That's a kitty poster lie.

I was happy to get back on the road. At least, until I got closer to San Francisco and to facing Joey. I had made her show me a small amount of vulnerability and tell me she loved me. I had promised to respect that a day before I was fingering Zoe on the I5. Why did I do that? I was still in love with Joey. What the hell was I going to tell her and what was I going to do with Zoe? Damnit.

Letting go of normative expectations and fake identities would've been the only way to have had a successful relationship with Joey. But I didn't even know what my favorite color was. That's something you either know all your life or takes you until you're about forty to figure out. Joey represented a life that required self-esteem and originality. The closest I could come to either at that age was using them correctly in a sentence. The simplest way to characterize my behavior toward everyone at that age would be cowardly and inauthentic.

When I first saw Joey, I fell apart. I didn't even try to lie. I told her I fucked Zoe. She tried to play it off like she didn't care. Maybe she didn't. She said she'd been thinking we should take a break anyway. I was devastated, but I couldn't defend myself.

Zoe called. I thought I should at least be nice to her, even though she now looked and sounded like all the disappointment I felt for myself. She came over on New Year's Eve. When Joey surprised me in the morning at my front door, I had to admit that Zoe was upstairs. That was an uncomfortable way to start the new year. We both knew that was the end.

Zoe and I hung out for a few more weeks, but my self-hatred was seeping into my interactions with her. I wasn't very charming. I was trying to push her away. I knew I was an asshole, and I didn't really woo her with the enthusiasm she deserved. Having sex with her was fun and made me feel like a stud. Then I would just feel like a psychopath for enjoying myself. I finally just broke up with her.

I was alone. Work was awkward. Hannah, Joey, and now Zoe. People were starting to figure out that I was a dick. Still, going to work was better than being at home. Most days, I couldn't leave my bed. I'd always had gentle suicidal thoughts, daydreaming about dying. It was like being with an old friend who didn't judge me. This new companion was horrible. With no one around to designate who I was, I just had to sit in the nebulous pile of shit I knew I was.

I just sat around wondering how I got there. How did I waste all of my gifts and privilege? How did my dad get to be such a good man? He didn't treat women like this. I was one of those guys my parents hate, that I hate. Controlling, manipulative, and weak. There was that one time I tried to be a girl and all I could manage was self-hating slut. What was I supposed to be? I didn't drink at the time or do drugs. I didn't have a TV. I just had to sit there sober, waiting for work or sleep. Bell sat on my shoulder and would tell me to go smoke cigarettes and play solitaire sometimes. I played the version my grandma taught me when I was little that I'd only won twice in my entire life. Smoking and losing. I did that for a few weeks. Then I called my mom.

"Well, I was wondering what you were doing. It seems like San Francisco is a little hard for you. Should you come home now? I don't know how to help you when you're like this. Should you go back to school? We could get you an apartment here. What are you going to do?"

"I don't know," I said. "I'm really sad. I don't know what's wrong with me. I was just calling."

"I don't know what to say to you. You make your life so hard. I don't think I can talk to you when you're like this." Mom hung up and didn't talk to me for a couple months.

Mom's a problem solver. What did I expect her to fix? I remembered the Bo story and how my folks didn't care that I denied them as my parents. They thought it was cute and called me by someone else's name. My mom was proud she returned to work ten days after giving birth to me. I decided she'd never really wanted me but had devoted herself to raising me out of a sense of obligation. Now I was just a failure—at being myself, at being whatever it was that would've worked for my mother, at having common human integrity. She would be justified in abandoning this project.

# CHAPTER TWENTY-ONE

# TRAINING MONTAGE

As I lay there in a fetal position, paralyzed by the thought my mother had finally given up on me, GeeGee called.

"What's wrong?" she said. "I've been thinking about you for days. What the fuck happened? I know you're not right." Gee is an actual wizard.

I tried to explain the delicate dynamics of what I had done.

She cackled, "You're the dumbest smart person I've ever known."

I needed to see her, even though I didn't want to. She definitely clashed with my new cultural aspirations, but I needed a break from self-discovery. I bought her a ticket, and she got on a plane.

Gee didn't understand how important all these interpersonal dramas were. She said they were girls and I was a dumb boy. That's all there was to it. She laughed at me. That made me feel better, like maybe I wasn't the worst person who ever lived. She told me to get dressed and take her out. We would split our time between gay stuff and straight stuff. She'd never been to San Francisco.

I didn't know straight San Francisco at all and wondered if it was even a thing. First, we dressed up and went downtown. I took her to the St. Francis to ride on the elevators. We didn't know how afraid of heights she was until we had to walk down thirty flights of stairs after she bit me. She thought the bar in the lobby looked classy and sat down. I'd always tried to avoid the staff at the St. Francis. They happily brought us drinks and were polite.

Gee was admiring the salt and pepper shakers and told me to put them in my pocket.

"I don't steal. You know that," I said.

"Do it," Gee said.

I shoved the set in my pants, then Gee put a wine glass in her blouse. We went to the bar at the top of the Bank of America building and did it again. We got two pint glasses and a small candlestick. We went to another hotel on Market where she immediately pulled me into someone's wedding reception. Even if you're a Black girl and a butch dyke not dressed for a wedding, no one will say anything to you for approximately twelve minutes while you help yourself to rumaki and pineapple skewers. After we collected a napkin holder and some cutlery from another hotel bar, we headed home.

That night, she was determined to go dancing with me. That's what we did together. She heard about a couple of clubs sponsored by local hip-hop radio stations over in Oakland. I was going old school for the night. The first club wouldn't even let me in because they couldn't figure out what I was and cited their dress code as a way to get rid of me. We got into the second club and I found my spot in the corner. This wasn't my world anymore, but I wanted Gee to have a good time. She immediately had several admirers. She brought them back to my table individually, to see if they would be nice to me.

One of them was successful enough at making eye contact with me and persistent enough at complimenting Gee that he was determined to be that night's winner. He wanted to follow us home.

I didn't care. I was confident we could take him if he got

weird. He followed us all the way back to my apartment across the bay.

I changed into sweatpants and a T-shirt. He assumed I would retire to the bedroom, leaving them to get better acquainted, but I sat with them on the couch. Gee and I have always shared a natural ability for making men jump through hoops. I'd forgotten how much I enjoyed it.

After a couple of hours of watching him dangle from the possibility of sex with GeeGee, she yawned and announced, "Well, I'm tired, I'm going to bed. It was nice to meet you. Drive safe. Monkey, you coming?"

He looked offended and sad and confused.

I said to Gee, "Well, if you don't want him, do you mind if I have him?"

Even more confused and maybe a little scared.

"Nah, go ahead. I'll start a movie. Come join me when you're done," she replied.

I led him to the kitchen, pushed him against the sink, and pulled out his cock. It was pretty big and definitely less confused than him. I laid him on the floor and got on top of him. I made myself cum and was polite enough to let him finish. I was the hostess, after all. After my shower, I found him on the couch, staring at me. I walked past him into the bedroom. Gee was watching *Demolition Man,* one of our favorites. I snuggled up next to her and started watching the movie.

The boy stood in the doorway. "So, uh, what now?"

"Oh, I'm done. Gee?" I asked.

"I'm done too. You can go," she said to him, not taking her eyes off the screen.

After a long pause, he muttered, "I feel like a piece of meat."

GeeGee and I erupted into a fit of pronounced giggling. We laughed that laugh of derision and glee that comes from a tiny spontaneous moment of vindication after a lifetime of subconscious resentment toward the implied power structures defining heteronormative sex that only the two of us share. It went on for quite some time.

He left some time in the middle of it. In the morning, I found his fake gold watch in the living room. It was a knick-knack I'd earned.

After Gee left, I felt a little better. Perhaps her presence reminded me I had come through worse, and I used to have superpowers. I was alone again after she went home, but I remembered I'd spent much of my life by myself, and I used to handle it by daydreaming and training to be a famous superhero.

I thought maybe if I lost twenty pounds and got ripped, Joey wouldn't be able to resist me. Also, if I got a motorcycle, that would probably help. She had just gotten one.

There was a gym on Valencia between Eighteenth and Nineteenth that I'd always been too intimidated by to go in. It looked like a gym Rocky would've trained in. Giant windows comprised the entire front of the building. My dream physique required austerity and discipline. I would not be cowed by its façade.

I went in. The whole place smelled like balls. An older sporty-looking dad guy in coach shorts was spotting for a young, muscly grunter doing squats. This place was way too dingy to be gay.

After junior finished his set, Dad looked over and said, "Can I help you?"

"Um, can anybody join this gym?"

"What do you want to do?"

"I want to get in shape and lose some weight, but I also want to learn how to lift."

"Okay, my name's Jim."

Jim was an ex-Olympic power lifter. He'd opened his gym

because it was the only thing he knew and loved. One room was devoted to training young men to compete in power lifting. The room was filled with pictures of boys winning medals and trophies. The rest of the room was mats, huge metal plates, and bars. The other room had a stationary bike pulled out of a Sears dumpster. There were a couple of old treadmill prototypes that didn't run on electricity. There was a collection of jump ropes in a box and some sawed-off broomsticks for stretching.

I loved this gym. I never saw another girl there. The "girls' locker room" was a large restroom with a sink, shower, bank of lockers, and an inch of standing water at all times. I went there almost every day. I had a Discman. Music was essential for training missions. Queen Latifah and TLC. Nobody was watching. I could listen to whatever I wanted.

I started to lose some weight. Depression is a natural appetite suppressant. Jim warmed to me because I never bothered him, and he showed me some proper form on a simple weight-training routine. I would think about Joey and my mother. Both would eventually be impressed by my discipline and menacing physique and love me again.

I found a motorcycle. A 1976 Honda CB550. It was gold. I had ridden a dirt bike a couple times in junior high, and there was that time I had sex with that guy so he'd let me drive his Ninja. I pretended I knew what the guy was talking about when he sold me the bike. I gave him five hundred dollars and rolled it into the street. He showed me where the brake and the throttle and the clutch were. Then, by my will to not embarrass myself, I drove it away. I named her FatGirl.

By the time Pride rolled around, I'd lost twenty pounds and taught myself how to ride my bike. I went to a leather store in the Castro and bought myself a pair of leather pants and a leather daddy hat. I also picked up a see-through Lycra tank top with a stripe of clear plastic down the front. It's hard to imagine how hot I was. It was almost too much pressure.

Jules agreed to ride on the back of my bike for Dykes on Bikes. Hart was going to ride on the back of Joey's. When we arrived at the lineup in the morning, I spotted Joey and Hart and wondered if I should be aloof. Hart started waving at me and Jules said I should go line up by them. Well, if Hart and Jules wanted to ride next to each other, I couldn't do anything about that.

The drama and buildup of that moment disappeared when everyone started their engines. It was like opening a hellmouth. We took up the whole parade route. The sound of the engines bounced off the skyscrapers on Market, and the goddess shook the diaphragms of almost a million spectators. It's hard to maintain anxiety about romantic kerfuffles in that environment. It's one of those rare, lucky moments that provides perspective and relieves human dread and loneliness.

It also puts everybody in a really good mood. By the end of the day, Joey had started talking to me, then kissing me, then we went home together. My ridiculous plan worked, sort of. It was never the same and what little respect and trust Joey had for me before was destroyed, but we both really enjoyed the sex.

During my six-month training montage on my way back to Joey, I'd convinced management at Veritable to allow me to get my commercial driver's license. It was on my tough-girl list. Plus, Joey was a truck driver. I was still on the night crew, but my skill set became more versatile and impressive.

Two weeks after Pride, I got the tip of my left index finger caught in the lift gate of a truck and ripped it off. Well, the flesh ripped off. It's called degloving. They removed the bone later that morning in the emergency room. Besides embarrassing myself, losing the tip of my left index finger ended up being pretty cool. Not only did I have a super butch story to tell for the rest of my life, but I got $1,200 and two weeks off work. Joey and I went to New York for a week. That was about the last week we had fun together.

She didn't expect much of me after Zoe. And if she was sparse in her affection before, she now mostly left me sitting in the corner like a naughty puppy that piddled on the floor. After we came home, she started hanging out with a shorter, less intimidating butch who had started at Veritable that I was insanely jealous of. It was a matter of weeks before she just stopped seeing me. I deserved that.

I went back to the gym. I had a couple of one-night stands. I got a small tattoo on my left shoulder that looked like a chicken's footprint. I'd seen it on some guy's back on the bus. Someone at a coffee shop randomly stopped me a couple weeks later and told me it was a rune that symbolized emotional protection in the form of intuition. I thought that was pretty cool, but it didn't work. I started messing around with this big butch from work who was six feet tall but also kind of theatrical and gay. She could clog. And then I met Ella.

# CHAPTER TWENTY-TWO

# BUTCH EGO, MORE BAD DECISIONS

Ella was a runaway from Minneapolis. She'd been mostly on her own since she was fourteen. She worked at Leather Tongue Video around the corner from my apartment. Since I wasn't dating anyone, I spent a lot of time renting movies. She was pretty and thin, with a natural musculature that few possess. She didn't have to work out to achieve it. She had long blond hair and a semipunk look that seemed natural on her. As attractive as she was, Ella wasn't quite my style, but my ego didn't dissuade her well-developed confidence in flirting with me.

I was in a rare physical state, driven by depression, self-hatred, and compulsive exercise that made my body look uncharacteristically fit. She didn't know I was used to being the pudgy, insecure nerd. I looked just cool enough to talk to, mature enough to confide in. Or maybe I just looked like a chump. She was in the process of a breakup from another older butch. She implied there might be a possibility that she was afraid of her girlfriend, and she didn't know how she was going to retrieve her things from their apartment. I assured her that I would help. I offered my assistance and protection.

I don't remember if she moved into my apartment right away or if it took a couple weeks. It was fast. Our sex life was animated, but fairly performative on both our parts. Over the course of our life experiences, we'd both made our sexuality primary in our identities. It's how we communicated. Neither of us had many interpersonal skills outside that, nor did we have the self-awareness to understand that about ourselves. We participated in an unspoken agreement to ride each other's hustles for our mutual benefit. I fully invested in being her caretaker, and she committed to the role of badass prodigy. She may have been looking for someone to be a Mission dyke power couple with, and she caught me in a deceptively hot phase. She made herself comfortable in my apartment, and I had someone to take care of again.

At work, Pally and I grew closer. I amused her with stories of how badly I screwed up all of my relationships. She thought my girlfriend collection was stupid, but she must've seen something in me. Pally is one of the smartest, most intuitive people I've ever met. She knows people instantly, and also knows if she likes them or not. She is one of those rare people that has always known who she is and has never felt obligated to prove anything to anyone. It's very alluring. One cannot help being drawn to her and loyal to her. I'm a cat person, and Pally is like a cat. She never feels shame, and you feel honored every time she graces you with her attention. She commands respect just by being herself. I had found a mentor.

When she was feeling more affectionate, she would call me Richie Cunningham, implying she was the Fonz, which she was. Pally was the rock-'n'-roll, nineties tough dyke Fonz. I began to see my own artifice through her eyes, but I didn't know how to combat it. I think she liked having a friend who was smart enough to keep up with her intellectually but was nerdy enough to not understand how cool she was to be a groupie. We were butch buddies, even though *butch* was a word she used to make fun of poseurs, sporty dykes, and me.

When I finally saw Pally and Rina's band perform at a

house party for the first time, I was embarrassed I hadn't been even more deferential. They were so good. I was about to get a rock-'n'-roll education from rock stars. I couldn't believe they talked to me.

Meanwhile, at home, I was trying to maintain my role as boyfriend who takes care of everything and doesn't embarrass my girlfriend around town. Young and inexperienced, Ella still managed to land a job at Stormy Leather, SF's premier leather and latex fetish wear manufacturer. She made cock rings all day to start out.

Ella was driven and special. She, too, was always confident in a greater fate for herself. I suspected I was just a stepping-stone for her destiny. I was indulging my caretaker martyr narrative while being introduced to some of the more aristocratic elements of the San Francisco dyke scene. We were refining our pedigree.

Ella always felt she belonged with the cool kids, which she did. She had ambition and style. We would frequently go to the Bearded Lady Coffee Shop, where the creative class congregated. They got to know our faces. These were the dykes who made the zines, the experimental porn, and the well-attended queer performance art. Their style was largely thrift-store dumpster salad topped with the perfect shop-lifted stripper accessory and coke-fueled trysts with Manic Panic and electric hair clippers. I honestly thought they were lovely. I wished I could be as witty and transgressive as they were. They were all nice to me, even while I was intimidated and jealous.

Ella and I attended some women-only play parties. (You still used that restriction in the midnineties.) There was some overlap with the creative class at these functions, but the women who invested in the leather and toys to impress at these parties were an even more rarefied subgenre. Because these functions were aligned with Ella's new profession, they were also networking opportunities with self-identified dyke royalty. I bought a pair of chaps to do my part.

I always found play parties rather boring. They somehow took the sex out of having sex. Rules, performance, and fashion. Well-regulated power negotiations. None of my strengths. I excelled at improvised swagger and dirty talk. The parties were impressive as spectacle; it just wasn't hot. I probably developed this opinion because again I felt out of place and self-conscious. It was basically a sex tournament, and I didn't want the one thing I thought I was good at to be negatively evaluated. The experience was a bit like attending a High Tea, and I just knew I was going to be the guy who didn't know which dick to use and I might fart while flogging.

Pally met Ella once and instantly disliked her. Pally's assessment of Ella as a poseur and me as a chump wasn't inaccurate. I respected her opinion, but I didn't follow sage advice. I wasn't a quitter. I didn't minimize potential catastrophe or save time by listening to my own intuition.

I instead doubled down on my insecurity and extended my loyalty to punitive outcomes by increasing my liability.

Ella wanted a bigger place, and I still had some ridiculous vision of shoving modified suburban expectations into my urban dyke fairyland, like then my mom wouldn't think I was weird anymore. I decided to leave my beloved apartment and rent us a two-bedroom house at twice the price. This wasn't possible in the Mission, so I was also leaving my homeland. We moved out to an area across the freeway from Hunter's Point at the southern end of San Francisco.

I gave Pally and Rina my apartment on Lexington. It felt like less of a loss, keeping it in the family. I also wanted to provide Pally with an offering. She was who I'd intended to be. She ran away when she was sixteen, which is also when she and Rina got together. She took care of them at that age. She formed a rock band at that age. She moved her whole band up to San Francisco from Pomona in her old VW van. They lived in that van and their practice studios for the first year. She represented a level of badass that required offerings. I really wanted her to like me. Her authenticity was a beacon.

So Ella and I set up our house. We sanded and painted the wood floors and remodeled the bathroom and kitchen. We had a backyard with a two-story fennel plant that Bell liked. We did a bondage photo shoot in our attic. I started driving trucks at VV so I wouldn't have to work nights. When her friend from Minneapolis called and asked if she, her husband, her toddler, and their dog could stay with us until they got their own place, I saw no reason not to share our stability.

Dopey and Jeanette were Ella's punk friends from the West Bank in Minneapolis. They had a young son named Ollie and a pitbull named Six Pack. We gave them the smaller bedroom and let Ollie turn our sun porch into a playroom. I liked the kid. He called me Unko Tawa and drew me pictures of my muscles. I might've liked the dog, but he chased Bell. I disliked Dopey instantly. Within three weeks, he lost four jobs.

One afternoon, Dopey and Jeanette were arguing. I ignored them until Dopey called Jeanette a worthless bitch in front of Ollie, who was crying. I came out of the bedroom and told Dopey that he had to go. He told me to mind my own business. I said, "The way I see it, Dopey, I pay all the bills here, so this is *my* wife and *my* son, and this is *my* house, so take your dog and get the fuck out."

I must've bruised his ego, because he could've beaten the shit out of me. After my brief, shining moment of masculine privilege, Jeanette settled into a constant sulk and mostly avoided me. Then Ella came home and told me there was something wrong with her and she couldn't work.

She had a lump on her inner thigh. The doctors were worried it might be a type of lymphoma. I was distraught. Over the next six months, she would undergo a multitude of tests. They determined it wasn't cancer, but they didn't know what it was. I got a second job on the weekends as a limo driver.

I drove a truck Monday through Friday, and a limo from Friday night until early Sunday morning. I'd never been so tired. We never had fun again. Jeanette and Ella entertained themselves by renting movies from Blockbuster and never returning them or calling Minnesota during the day for hours. (Long-distance calls used to cost money, especially during business hours.) Neither of them did the dishes or the laundry or picked up after Ollie, and I didn't give a shit. I was too tired. If I tried to say anything, I was reminded that I was a dick like Dopey and Ella was sick. I found the outer limits of my inner martyr narrative.

During my endless hours driving, listening to Howard Stern and ongoing coverage of the OJ Simpson trial, I would vacillate between nausea and self-indulgent pride. I knew I was the chump, but I knew I'd gotten there on my own. I fantasized about running away. That had been a lifelong salve. I could always build that shack in the woods. I had done it a million times in my mind because that's what butches do when they are ready, but not quite ready, to get out of an unhealthy relationship.

Ella finally got a diagnosis. She had cat scratch fever. I'm sure there's a joke there, but I was too tired to make one. I was just grateful the doctor cleared her for work.

After she went back to work, I quit my limo driving gig and went back to nights at the warehouse. It wasn't long before Ella was making the most of her lonely nights.

She said I wasn't any fun anymore, which was true. I had gained some weight back from sitting on my ass for twelve hours a day, living on Jack in the Box jalapeño poppers. But it felt like a real punch to the gnads when Ella started acting funny. She denied everything, but my face started exploding with severe stress hives every night at work, telling me she was cheating on me.

Part of me felt like I deserved this for being such a shit-head in all my relationships. Pally confirmed this assessment for me, and reminded me that she "told me so." But she doesn't hold bad decisions against people. She happened to be in a fight with Rina at the time, and our friendship deep-ened in this moment of commiseration. She trusted me as a peer. When I called Ella to tell her I was going to breakfast with Pally, she panicked. She knew her hustle couldn't with-stand proximity to Pally. She told me that if I went with Pally, we were done. My allegiance was suddenly clear.

Ella left that day, leaving behind some notable belongings. Chief among them were Jeanette and Ollie, her stupid cat, Slinker, who peed on everything, and a rotting turkey in the fridge. I didn't want to deal with any of them, so I pulled a mattress down the stairs to a small room behind the garage and started living there. That same evening, Pally and Rina showed up with a twelve-pack of Rolling Rock and an eighth of speed.

# CHAPTER TWENTY-THREE

# ARE YOU EXPERIENCED?

The fairies finally came to my aid. They came through the garage back to my little garden room. We all did some lines on an old AC/DC CD case, and they started making me laugh. Pally and Rina made me feel like I had mafia connections who would make everything okay. I had new rock-'n'-roll friends before I understood the ramifications of that world. They made me feel as if I didn't have a complex existential identity conflict, I just had the blues. And they were there to fix that. It would have been an insult to dwell. I wasn't disappointing my mother and failing as a man, shit just got fucked up. Let's do some drugs, listen to music, play some cards, and laugh.

We made plans to switch pads. They were moving into roomier expectations in life, and I wanted my apartment back. The house would give their guitar player, Mike, a place to live, and Pally could get more pets.

I started doing drugs for the first time in my life. I loved speed so much. I was so smart while I was tweaking my ass off. When I was a teenager, Nancy Reagan told me that drugs were bad and the people who did them were derelict street people. Pally and Rina taught me that some people who do drugs are talented and responsible and stable. They certainly had their shit together compared to me. Pally and Rina were even cooler than those dyke artists at the Bearded Lady, and I was their new mascot.

The house switch was complicated by the fact that I still

didn't have Ella's new number and she was decidedly uninterested in my timetable for moving. She ignored all the messages I sent through Jeanette, who also pretended I was bluffing. I called Gee.

I bought Gee a ticket in secret and picked her up a few days before we were supposed to move. We came through the front door and found Jeanette on the phone. She said, "Shit. That girl GeeGee is here." They had met.

Gee said, "Is that Ella? Give me the phone . . . is this Ella? Your friend here is about to tell me where you live."

Ella must've told Gee that she had a gun because Gee started laughing and said, "Bitch, you better know how to use it. You're only going to get one shot. You have two days to come get your shit, including your friend."

Somehow, two days later, Ella was there with her newer, younger, skinnier butch. They cleaned gelatinous turkey goo from the refrigerator and swept the house. I never saw Jeanette and Ollie again. I had a crew of dykes and a truck from Veritable. We were loaded by noon.

When we backed down Lexington to my old apartment, we found Pally and Rina still asleep. Fairies are magical and wise, but they operate on their own rock-'n'-roll timeline. They weren't really packed, and they were annoyed by our punctuality.

Butch dykes organize intuitively with hive-like efficiency when they are moving people. The whole campaign was done by the evening. GeeGee went home a couple days later, and I was single again in my Mission apartment.

I wasn't depressed this time. I started sleeping with another friend from work, Wendy. We were more like siblings than girlfriends. We were comfortable bickering and fucking, but never indulged in much romance. We did crosswords and smoked cigarettes.

I was grateful to have a second chance at my apartment. I also had Pally. I didn't want to fuck up that friendship by whining. I started going to all their shows and being their roadie. I was hanging out with the band. I was the one invited to do lines with them off the back of the bar toilet before their set. There were lots of chicks in rock bands in the nineties, especially in San Francisco. It was another important platform for women to express their anger and tell mainstream America to go fuck themselves. That was the only theme in the nineties I knew about. And rock 'n' roll did it the best.

Their band, P.W., never got as famous as some of the bands they were better than. Part of the reason was because they were loyal to Mike as their lead guitar. He was ridiculously talented, but he was a guy. This prohibited them from being a chick band in a decade of rockin' chick bands.

They used to open for Tribe 8 occasionally. They also shared a practice space with them. P.W. was better than Tribe 8, but Tribe 8 were all women, and Lynn Breedlove did have those fucking dildos and never minded taking her shirt off. But I was loyal to Pally's band above all other SF chick bands, and I still am.

Pally and Rina taught me about a rock 'n' roll I hadn't experienced. I knew about Joan Jett, but I didn't know about L7. Pal taught me about the Lunachicks. Rina taught me about Hole and Courtney Love. Pally thought Courtney was annoying, but Rina somehow knew I would appreciate her. I remember listening to *Pretty on the Inside* for the first time alone in my apartment. Without foreplay, Courtney shoved it right inside me.

*WHEN I WAS A TEENAGE WHORE.*

I couldn't move.

*My mother asked me, she said, "Baby, what for?" I give you plenty, why do you want more? Baby, why are you a teenage whore?"*

My old darkness suddenly had a voice, and it was perfect. Then the voice said to everyone who had ever judged me, *I've seen your repulsion, and it looks, real good on you,* and I found a prophet. My life is dissimilar in so many ways to Courtney Love's, but she knew things I never told anyone. Anyone who has ever talked shit about Courtney Love can just go fuck right off.

Pally was partial to the Lunachicks and L7. They appealed to my tough girl. L7 sang about women getting drunk and high and being violent and fearless. "Fast and Frightening" is a song about a scary, hot butch dyke. *Poppin' wheelies on her motorbike, straight girls wish they were dykes.* They sang about carrying guns and shoving. The Lunachicks were New York clever. They sang about gender deviants, fetishes and sex toys, and attacking men who are assholes. *She is the jerk, the jerk of all trades. She can build, she can fight, she can bust out your light . . . Never ever ever ever underestimate, she will kill you, kill you with her hate.* How do they know about me? Angry chicks had a voice back then. I was such a nerd. I wished the pirates had found me sooner.

My new friends opened my eyes. They were apostles for this gospel. They took me to church. I got to hang out with rock-'n'-roll people at rock shows. They introduced me to more of their friends. Some of these people were part of a loose group of women called the SF HAGS. The *A* in *HAGS* should have a circle around it like the anarchy sign. I didn't know the origins or entire roster for this group, but Pally and Rina were definitely HAGS. Pally's best buddies in this group were Kegger and Quij. To be a HAG, you were either in a rock band or went to all the shows. You were likely on the guest list or invited backstage. You usually didn't pay for drinks.

And for sure, you had crazy hair, did a lot of drugs, and had a wicked laugh. I was not a HAG. Only because of Pally did the other HAGS allow me near them.

One night, at a house party, as I was being assessed as a sidekick, we were all doing lines when everyone started smoking heroin. As Pally's pet nerd, I tried for casual disinterest. Then Quij grabbed my face and pulled it to hers. She put her lips over mine and shotgunned a giant cloud of drugs into my mouth. It was her way of welcoming me. The moment of affection was affirmed by riotous cackling, and I was anointed as an acceptable presence.

This world was darker and animated at night. It was covered in black and skulls and faux animal prints. It put my suburban upbringing into starker relief. I glimpsed a secret pirate realm whose sole détente with the mainstream occurred during family holidays and occasional mall walks to get to Hot Topic. There were people in this world who never had regular housing or employment, but they always figured out some cash and a place to crash. Pally was probably the most conventionally functional HAG. She always had a job and a place to live. A possibility emerged that the world I had come from didn't need to be as uptight as it was. There could be a more radical rejection of it if I could let go.

Things in my head started to break apart. I couldn't let go of my parents. They were the strongest, most admirable people I'd ever known. But my mother was a crucial leader in the assimilation forces. Pally, my new mentor, didn't hate the mainstream, she just didn't need it. Did I? Could I come up with something original? Pally suggested eyeliner.

This sparked a titillating fight with my own masculinity. There are many masculine archetypes acceptable to mainstream America. It's not all bad. I ingested the good bits of dude from the larger man-pig. There were the tough guys my dad and I used to enjoy, like Clint Eastwood's Dirty Harry. He was stoic, old-fashioned, morally unconfused, and violent. There were the crisp, imposing men of professional sports and military movies. Stamina and discipline are sexy. There were the mystics and scholars who always sounded smart and had a plan, like a wizard or an eccentric cat burglar. My dad is an alpha and a leader and a winner. He is my model of a good man. My grandfathers were working-class heroes. They worked quietly their whole lives to provide for their families and were also artisans. Grandpa Buddy had a flattop and was a mechanic and could fix anything. Grandpa Lee was a dapper woodworker and a cook. I wanted to be a combination of all these. Up until this point, my fight had been trying and failing to become any of these men. This had led to years of identity espionage, messy conquests, and dead-end relationships.

Rock 'n' roll didn't solve this problem for me. What it did was destabilize my models just long enough to wonder if it was all horseshit. I had previously relied on rock 'n' roll to help me flip off the world that rejected me, but now I had rock-'n'-roll friends. I respected and admired Pally almost as much as my father. Rock 'n' roll confused gender assumptions. Men could have long hair and makeup and less-than-masculine clothing and still be sexually powerful and intimidating. Women could reject everything I hated about being a girl and still keep their vaginas intact. Neither rock-'n'-roll gender was anything like either of my parents. Could there be a future for me in this world? I didn't know how to play an instrument or sing. What would my life look like as a pirate? Could I completely reject my mother's hopes for me, whatever those were? There was wisdom and strength to the chick rock bands of the nineties that was important. I would worship there as long as I could.

I didn't grow my hair out. I had a short mohawk. I wore

eyeliner around Pally. We would party on the weekends. We'd snort fat lines and play cards at her dining room table. The cast of participants rotated, but I was always on the list. Pally would hold private salons in her bedroom for one of us at a time to read our tarot cards or do our astrological chart.

I'd amused Pally and Rina by bragging of my limited counterculture gestures, like fucking an air force base in high school. So during one of my private sessions with Pally, she quizzed me about my experiences with men. She wanted to know if I liked being fucked. She asked me if I was a fag. She asked me if I liked to suck dick. Then, as our session was about to end and we were by the door, she shoved me up against the wall, turned out the bedroom light, and started kissing me.

I hadn't expected that at all. I had an intense friend crush on Pal, but I would not have risked coming on to her. As she was the mentor in this dynamic, it was an acceptable escalation coming from her, like an Ancient Greek kind of move. We didn't have sex that night, just a kiss. Over the next few weeks, neither of us mentioned it. She teased me by calling me fag daddy, which no one found intriguing. She told me she was planning a trip back to Pomona, to empty a storage locker she had now that she had a bigger place. She asked if I wanted to come along. That sounded like the most fun ever. She joked that I should bring my dick so I could suck it while she drove.

We left a couple weeks later. I packed my dick because I was excited, but I didn't tell her because I didn't know if she was serious. We spent the drive laughing and talking and doing lines when we stopped for gas. When we got to Pomona, we stayed with Rina's brother for the night on his kid's tiny bed with My Little Pony sheets. In the morning, he gave us the two biggest rocks of speed I've ever seen.

That night, we went to Robbie's, the dyke bar, for old time's sake. We both went there in the eighties.

After a couple of hours of making fun of the softball dykes, the jokes turned again to my fagginess. She said something about how much fun it would be to shove her dick in my mouth in the bathroom, so it was a shame I didn't bring mine.

I said, "Oh, I brought it."

She said, "What are we waiting for?"

We found the sleaziest motel in California just a few blocks away. Pal put my dick on and turned out the lights.

For a minute, I tried playing the domme who had always emerged with masculine entities, but Pal got frustrated. "Why don't you just lay on your back and spread your legs?"

Pal is the only person I've ever allowed to top me and it was fucking hot. I trusted her not to make me feel like shit about myself or emasculate me, and she never did. She effortlessly rode that line distinguishing private fetishes from public respect and care. Over the next few months, we went to a lot of shows, did a lot of drugs, and occasionally, she fucked me until I bled. Outside of the bedroom, we got into a couple of fistfights with men, I taught her how to ride a motorcycle, and she taught me more about letting go of the norms that did nothing but make me feel like shit about myself. This tiny span of my life bound me to the nineties and San Francisco and reminds me that I was a part of it.

# CHAPTER TWENTY-FOUR

# CRACK IN THE MIRROR

Numerous cults in history have been built around intentional hedonism. I've directly experienced the conduit between anarchic, ecstatic, sensual pleasure and temporary transcendence. It's a little scary to get that close to the edge, though. There's something potentially sinister lurking on the flip side if you get sloppy or blasphemous. Halloween thins the veil.

Pally and Rina started adding more heroin to their roster. It was resurging in popularity at the time. I couldn't follow them there. I was too scared of heroin. They did heroin with their other friends. I trusted Pally's ability to do drugs successfully. It just wasn't my scene.

Hart wanted to try heroin with Pally at the Halloween party she was throwing. We were all going. The night of the party, another big butch I worked with, Terri, was hanging out at my place. We were doing some lines and getting dressed for the party. Pally and Rina were right next door in another apartment, doing some other drugs and getting ready to go to the party with us. The thing about doing drugs is how distracting they are. That's why pirates are always late.

It was well past midnight when I got the call from Hart's roommate. Hart had started her experiment by herself. She'd OD'd and was taken to the emergency room.

Terri and I flew out of my apartment and started banging on the door next door. After some hysterical screaming and banging, they emerged. Terri and I lay down in the back of Pally's pickup and we raced to the hospital.

Streetlights blurred above us as time slowed down on the way to the hospital. SF General allowed our crazy-looking crew up to Hart's room. They understood that's what family is in San Francisco, since no one is from there. Hart was hooked to a ventilator. We assumed she would be okay.

The nurse informed us it was unlikely she would recover. Nobody at the party had known she'd OD'd and she was gone too long. We stood there, unable to digest her words. The nurse said they were keeping her alive until they could contact her mother about organ donation. That was too much. Terri and I ran to the bathroom to vomit together.

After an hour of sobbing and trying to grasp the situation, we realized we were the only ones who knew. I called Joan because hers was the only work number I had memorized. Then I called Joey, Hart's other best friend. We hadn't spoken since the last time we broke up.

Death is a big fucking deal. There had been nothing in my life to prepare me for watching the death of a friend. And we were all supposed to be at that party.

I handled things poorly. We all had to work the next night. Hart was still on life support. Pally and Rina set up an altar in the warehouse with pictures and candles. They knew exactly what to do. They took a picture of Hart from the trucking office and placed it on the altar with the others. No one was okay. Everyone loved Hart.

Cynthia, another driver, showed up for her shift around 4:00 a.m. When she saw the altar, she took that picture of Hart back to the trucking office. Fresh grief feels like heavy, constant water, breaking against your chest. Until something ignites it, like it was gasoline the whole time.

I never liked Cynthia, and she never liked me. We were

both divisive personalities, now struggling with the discomfort of this sudden, impossible grief. Cynthia tried to segregate the grief, claiming Hart for the trucking crew. When I saw big Terri crumpled up on the floor, sobbing in anger at Cynthia, a black rage took over my body, and a voice came out of me I'd never heard. It told Cynthia I was going to kill her. I don't remember who restrained me.

When I came to, I was formally reprimanded.

We were all back at the hospital again when her mother arrived and signed the papers to have the ventilator removed. Hart's mom told us her eyes were being donated. Those Hart eyes.

Veritable threw a wake for Hart at Cafe Du Nord. Everyone came. I got drunk and blew smoke in Joey's face, like a petty villain in a cheesy action movie that is going to pay for their insolence with satisfying violence at some point. I regretted it instantly.

The downward spiral accelerated for the next few months. At Thanksgiving, my parents flew me home. This had been a period of imposed distance with my parents on both sides. None of us could see much common ground. I was rejecting their expectations, and they were losing faith. When I got to the airport, I called my mother from a pay phone to warn her that I had a mohawk. When she started screaming, I offered to not get on the plane. She didn't want that. She just wanted me to not have a mohawk. We were at an impasse.

I got on the plane drug-addled and sad. I kept my hat on for the entirety of my visit. My mother implied, upon hearing of my friend's death, that bad things happen to people who do bad things.

I left my parents' house feeling sure my new journey as a novice outlaw had a morality superior to my mother's superficial judgement. I continued to party with Pal and Rina even though I had to share them more with heroin. I was sad because I wasn't part of that club. Pally and I weren't really fucking anymore, even though I really wanted to. I was a bit in love with her, but that was a dead end no matter how I looked at it. I just wanted the big, shimmery rock-'n'-roll super ball to never end.

Knowing when the party's over is a life skill that takes sporty dyke math nerds a little longer to achieve. I was excited when my birthday rolled around in January and we all drove to Reno for the weekend. Me, Pal, Rina, Terri, and Will, a sweet pervy bear cub who started at VV. We still had plenty of the never-ending gobstopper speed ball we'd been feeding off for months. It was a three-day party. No sleep. I played nickel poker so long my fingers were black and slightly infected. There was wrestling and laughing and cake. We returned on Sunday with just enough time to shower, do some more lines, and go to work.

I was a big pile of shit for work that night. Halfway through the shift, Pally told me this chick, Huey, was impugning my glorious work ethic. I don't take that criticism lightly, even if it's true. Pally asked me if I was going to put up with that shit. I couldn't allow Huey's vicious slander as well as let Pally think I was a punk.

I took Huey into an office and yelled at her until she cried.

The next day, I lost my job. They made me come in to do it. I was also banned from visiting the warehouse. Just like that, I lost what little sense of family and identity I'd managed to achieve by that point. My world broke apart, and I was overcome with the terror and grief of sudden catastrophe.

Pally came over and quietly held me all night while I sobbed. The next day, Rina introduced me to the world of unemployment benefits, which I've never told my mother about. After wallowing in shame and self-pity for a week, I knew it was time to do something big.

# CHAPTER TWENTY-FIVE

# TIME FOR GLORY

I knew I needed to stop doing speed regularly. It wasn't as fun as it used to be, and I blamed my love of it for the loss of my job. I also wanted to change my feelings for Pally. I was in love with her, and I needed to let that part go.

This would be my second attempt at materializing one of my private visions. The first time was when Alex and I ran away to San Francisco. The reality was nothing like my daydreams, and we failed. It was time for a second foray into my alternative fantasy universe, lovingly cultivated in my superhero brain.

In my long hours of grown-up daydreaming while truck driving or making clay figurines at four in the morning, I'd developed an intricate fantasy of spending a year riding a bicycle across Europe. I even purchased a giant waterproof map and planned a yearlong route that would keep me from freezing to death but take me through every country. If I camped and lived on potatoes and random encounters with magical creatures, I would make it somehow.

I bought a mountain bike, a full set of panniers, and a backpacking tent. I planned to leave in March. I would start in London. My parents bought my plane ticket. Anything to turn my head from San Francisco. Rina said she would collect my unemployment checks. I cashed in my 401k from VV and sublet my beloved apartment again, to my buddy Wendy.

When I have intricate fantasies about grand adventures,

my imagination generally skips the tedium of practicality. When I arrived at Heathrow, I retrieved my bike from baggage and took it outside on the sidewalk. It was in a box in several pieces. I had tools, but I'd never put my bike together. I'd never put the racks on. I'd never taken even one training ride with my panniers on the racks. This is how I manifest visions. If I've ever possessed anything resembling a spirituality, it's my steadfast devotion to an unseen realm of magic forces that will aid my noble quests if I leap from the cliff of everyday life and self-hatred. I've always suspected they've been watching me, waiting for me to stride onto my intended path to glory.

They also have a sense of humor. It took me three hours to assemble my bike. Most of that time was spent retrieving a tiny, important screw from a drainage grate. Then, when I put my panniers on the racks and tried to ride away, I discovered my bike frame was too short to accommodate the rack system due to my freakishly short legs, and my heels ran into the bags as I pedaled.

I finally MacGyvered a way to ride with all of my belongings and headed toward London, a long, awkward ride by bike.

Highlights of this trip include a one-night stand in London with a French woman who still wanted to have sex with me after watching me vomit on the bus. I got blown off the road by a semi on a highway and a witness took me to an ancient inn, where I was given a room and shepherd's pie. I was attacked by swans on the empty shores of Lake Windermere. I met a charming family in Glasgow who were distant cousins of some guy my parents played golf with. Their lovely niece, Siobhan, let me stay on her dorm room floor and taught me 7-Up is called lemonade in Scotland.

I was gone just over a month. I made it as far as Edinburgh before I realized I wasn't going to make it as a drifter. I was too lonely. I had too many hang-ups surrounding property laws to stay on somebody's property without their permission. I wasn't ready for the mountain yet. I couldn't be that alone with myself at that age. I took a train back to London. It was embarrassing to go home, but I'd accomplished my two goals. Upon my return, I found my way back to being Pally's friend, and I never did speed regularly again. It was cheaper than rehab.

I had to go back to real life. I spent a month crashed on Wendy's couch in my old apartment. This was punishment for my hubris. I found a job delivering fresh salsa. It didn't offer the same community or glamor as working at VV, but I got to take home all the salsa I could eat. I found one of the shittiest apartments in SF. I rented it without even looking at it, over the intercom outside the building. It was a mouse-infested craphole overlooking Howard, between Sixth and Seventh.

Bell and I moved with as much stuff as would fit in the tiny room. She took care of the mice, and I built a loft and a table to hold a toaster oven. It did have a fire escape. It felt like the place I was supposed to start over from. Punitive austerity.

I felt I deserved this setback. I needed the humiliation. The truck I was driving for my new job was just a small step van, which was hard on my ego. I was working with a bunch of straight guys. The warehouse was cruelly located two blocks from Veritable, so I had to look at it every time I went to work, knowing that they didn't want to see me anymore. My apartment wasn't in the Mission. My parents were distant from me. I was failing again. I'd disappointed them and lost everything that seemed important to my identity.

I still went to Pally and Rina's shows. They were still on my side. Nobody else from Veritable really talked to me anymore. You lose most people you thought were family when you lose proximity to their daily lives. People don't want to be around failure and grief if they can help it.

One night, I went to an L7 show with Pally and Rina at the Warfield. Terri was there along with a big group of Pally and Rina's friends, including Patricia. I'd known Patricia for five years by this point but had never really hung out with her. She was good friends with the trucking manager at VV and had worked there as a receptionist for the past couple years.

Patricia was pretty and soft-spoken and sweet. She was so quiet Pally nicknamed her Whisper. She had lots of tattoos that somehow amplified her charming femininity. She'd been coming to Pally and Rina's shows for a while. It was obvious she had a crush on Pal. I couldn't begrudge her that. Pally would occasionally call her over and make her show us her boobs, which were substantial. She dressed conservatively at work but would come to shows dressed to impress a rock-'n'-roll audience. When P.W. (Pally and Rina's band) sang "Drug Slut," she would be among those invited on stage to dance, and the honor of fellating Rina's crotch-held beer bottle was always reserved for Patricia.

I was attracted to her in a quiet way. I thought she was too into Pally to notice. Plus, she was among those VV people I thought didn't like me.

At the L7 show, somebody made the mistake of shotgunning pot smoke into my mouth. I still couldn't handle pot, so I spent the duration of the set in the Warfield toilet barfing my face off, praying to stop being high. I was just coming down when the show ended. We all walked to my place a few blocks away to do some drugs before continuing the evening. On the way, Pally mentioned that Rina didn't like Patricia having a crush on her, and that it had become too much to have both me and Patricia in love with her. She suggested we date each other. She'd also told Patricia to date me.

After we were done at my pad, Pally told me to take Whisper home on my bike. We both did as we were instructed. That was the first time I kissed Patricia. We both liked it.

We started dating that week and discovered how much we had in common. Her high voice and flirty deference had masked her intellect. Our first date started at Uncle Burt's on Eighteenth and Castro, where her roommate was a bartender. I'd never been a drinker and had a hard time keeping up with her. I realized she was also a quiet nerd compelled to infiltrate the rock-'n'-roll circus. I was captivated by this woman who had been so close for so long. There was something different about her. She wasn't broken. She wasn't aloof. She didn't need me to save her or become something else.

We took a calculus class together for no reason, and she did it better. She did crosswords in pen. She went to work on time. She paid her bills. We had rough, hot sex and went to shows together. She did speed with us and played cards. She could keep up with me and caretake around me. She might be perfect. Maybe I could grow up with her.

We'd been dating three weeks when I got into a decent motorcycle accident. I was wearing shorts and a helmet I had gotten at a thrift store that was too big for even my Charlie Brown head. A car turned left into my side as I was going through an intersection. I'd been going to see Wendy. Some witness kindly called her from a pay phone, and she met me at the emergency room. This was the first short period of my life I didn't have any health insurance, so they took me to SF General.

Wendy stayed with me until she had to go to work. I had a broken ankle, some cracked ribs, my calf looked like an exploded hotdog, and I'm pretty sure I had a concussion. Every time they tried to get rid of me to make room for the waves of the unwell and underinsured swelling the waiting room,

I would puke and fall down. The only thing that prevented this situation from being worse was that my ex-boss Sue, the crusty old butch, was my emergency room nurse. Her name was Theo now, and she was a he with a low voice and stubble. I thought that was pretty cool. They set my ankle, scheduled a surgery, and finally got me into a cab around midnight.

When the cab dropped me off in front of my shithole, I was nauseous and weak. There were thirty stairs between me and my crappy futon. I started crawling. My upstairs neighbors, a sweet Cuban drag queen and her boyfriend, one of Fidel Castro's body doubles, rescued me and got me into bed.

It was another setback. I was unclear on what the universe intended with this lesson. When I called my mom to tell her, she was on her way to Texas. Her mother, my grandmother, was dying so she couldn't come.

"I'm sure you'll figure it out. Maybe no more motorcycles. I love you, but you do make your life much more difficult than it needs to be," she said.

"I love you, Ma." We were both too broken to fight.

# CHAPTER TWENTY-SIX

# Eighth Time's a Charm

Patricia came over. She brought me chocolate and doted on me. She kissed my boo-boos and indulged me with dirty talk. She helped me apply for disability, another embarrassment I've kept from my mother over the years. She'd visit most days after work to have sex with me and bring me takeout. I'd sit watching Oprah, playing solitaire until it was time for her to get there. When I became more mobile, I hauled a couple pallets up from the paint store next door and made her a shelf so she could keep some stuff in my tiny room.

We were falling in love, but it was different from my past relationships. We were peers. It felt sustainable. I did have insecure freak-outs caused by shame at being unemployed and broken. I would grasp for my masculinity loudly. She had not grown up with yellers. My yelling would make her quiet and hurt her. It was the first time I realized that some people don't yell. I wanted to be a better person for her. I wanted her to stay with me and be mine.

Patricia could easily have remained nonmonogamous and maintained her free spirit, but she gave herself to me anyway. She stopped fooling around with Pally and agreed to be my girlfriend.

After a few months, I was straining to be mended enough to get a job. I wanted a job. I wanted my apartment back. I wanted to start a life with Patricia, maybe grow up a little. The day after I stopped using my cane, I got a job as a flatbed truck driver for a construction company that supplied big contractors who made things with concrete. Mike, the owner of the company, was a really nice guy. He tried to find a way to ask me if I thought I could handle the job, being a girl and all. I told him not to worry and that I was pretty strong for a girl. He laughed and told me to start the next day.

On my first day, I wondered if I was actually strong enough to do this job. The lightest things I handled were fifty-pound boxes of nails. I routinely unloaded entire pallets of bagged cement by hand. We rented long metal poles with feet called braces. They're used to hold poured concrete walls up before the ceiling is attached. They weighed between 100 and 250 pounds apiece, and I had to figure out how to get them on my truck bed by myself. I lived on fast food and vending machines. I gained about sixty pounds in six months. At least half of it was muscle.

I was proud to be a hardworking tough guy again. When the year I was supposed to be biking through Europe was over, Wendy gave me my apartment back. Reprieve number three. I got a small settlement from my accident. Five thousand dollars each to my lawyer, the hospital, and me. Patricia told me she wasn't going to risk her many thousands of dollars in tattoos if I got another motorcycle. I bought the next best thing, a 1966 Chrysler 300. It was nearly twenty feet long and the prettiest, most impractical purchase I've ever made.

Things were looking up. I'd stumbled into a better version of the world I kept trying to create.

Patricia and I still hung out with Pally and Rina on occasion. One night, we even tried heroin. Pally shot us up. We spent the night unable to move from wherever we landed. It was the opposite of my favorite drug. I hated it. I vomited several times and spent the night wishing I wasn't high. In the morning, I vomited again and felt like shit. And then something inside my body told me to do it again. I was terrified and never did.

Shortly after this, Quij died. She'd gotten the flesh-eating bacteria. I visited her in the hospital while she was dying, with Pal. The only strategy doctors have to combat this affliction is to cut out the flesh around the infection, like firefighters setting a perimeter blaze to starve a forest fire of fuel. Another HAG I didn't know died of the same thing. *USA Today* declared Sixteenth and Mission the black tar heroin capital of the world. Pally assured me that she was safe because she always mainlined instead of shooting into her muscle. It was a small comfort. She and Rina quit for a while after Quij died. We brought them ginger ale and did their dishes.

The world was changing at the end of the nineties. Something was dying, and it was too soon to understand what was happening. People were moving away from San Francisco. There were those who didn't make it through the decade. I was exhausted. The city that had been my refuge and my enlightenment seemed equally exhausted by the nineties. Heroin was the pace at which the city was limping into the new century, subduing the exquisite anger that had been its hailing beacon. The light was dissolving. Speed-fueled, dirty girl punk shows morphed into straight-edge, academically informed riot grrrl shows, a subtle but important transition.

For the last P.W. show I went to at the Paradise Lounge, I came early for soundcheck with the band. They were the headliners that night. The opening band was younger and fresher and from Seattle or something. The nineties ended for me that night when Pally and Rina and I were headed to the bathroom to do a couple of lines before the show. The younger band approached us, telling us how excited they were to be opening for a band in San Francisco. They'd also finished soundcheck and said they were going to go hit the gym before the show. A fleeting golden age ended that day. The pirates lost their port city.

Pally and Rina never stopped working. They never stopped rocking, but they were thinking about buying a house in Oakland with Mike. Patricia and I started thinking about a longer-term plan. The first dot-com boom was in full swing in the South Bay, and rents were being driven up around us. We would never be able to afford anything but my beautiful, rent-controlled one-bedroom. I looked for the community I'd taken for granted, all the transgressive, radical queers who were going to change the world, and saw the scene eroding. Also, I'd alienated almost everyone I knew. That's a lifestyle choice for me. It meant it was time to go.

It was time to grow up. I thought I knew what adulthood should look like and that I should finally go there. I'd lucked into a relationship with a woman who seemed to be a perfect match for me. Patricia was one of the smartest people I'd ever met. She was unfailingly caring and supportive. She had lots of rad tattoos and cool fashion, and she seemed to love me in a new, real way.

I had new dreams of owning a house and settling down, whatever that means. We started talking about places to move. I suggested Minneapolis but didn't want to be pushy because it was my home state. We went for a visit and loved it. Patricia read some article about vegetarian restaurants and the theater scene in Minneapolis and she was all in. At the end of the nineties, the end of my twenties, we were moving back to the Midwest, where grown-ups have backyards and play board games.

My mother was thrilled by the decision. It allowed her to share her expertise on the aesthetic requirements of the Midwest. People just didn't dress or look like us there and nobody would understand. We would be unable to get jobs or find an apartment. "Be sure to grow your hair out and stop wearing your truck clothes," she said. I actually did grow my hair out because I suspected she might have a point.

I thought I had time to make good on my potential. I thought my destiny as an adult with a life that impressed my parents but maintained my unique identity could be found in the place I started from, in a cultural milieu I innately understood. That's where my parents started. They had been realizing their social mobility my entire life. I was certain I would figure something out that looked similar to a success they'd been anticipating. I still had no idea what a career might look like for someone like me. But I was moving back to the old country and maybe I should tone it down.

I'm sure Patricia would've happily stayed in San Francisco. She's one of those people who everyone likes, and she can stay at the same job for years and years. Nevertheless, at the end of 1999, we packed our stuff onto a moving truck, put our two cats and some clothes into my Chrysler, and left San Francisco in the middle of a warm night, at the end of August. We had a difficult time finding a hotel that night because of a Beanie Baby convention in Sacramento.

We had no jobs, we had no place to stay, and we knew no one in Minneapolis. Minneapolis had no idea that we were on our way.

# CHAPTER TWENTY-SEVEN

# THERE'S NO PLACE LIKE HOME

I wanted to buy a house and have a grown-up job. More accurately, I "envisioned" those things rather than wanting them. It was what my new life looked like in my head. I usually have no idea what I want, or even what that word means. But it's important to note that my visions usually come true in some iteration, and there's often unforeseen collateral damage. Yes, I am magic. No, I do not completely understand my powers, but four days after arriving in Minneapolis, we had an apartment and jobs.

We both got jobs working for the Wedge Co-op in their new produce distribution warehouse, Co-op Partners. Patricia still has that job, doing their books. I split my time working in the warehouse, driving a truck for them, and working in the produce department at the Wedge. We'd both worked for VV in San Francisco, so our expertise had hippie-famous liberal credentials. We had a common queer urban confluence of affinities. We were good-tipping, transgressive politics–oriented vegetarians with tattoos who liked to drink and smoke. We were the new butch/femme power couple in town. Minneapolis didn't need to know I was actually a nerd by SF standards.

With our exotic San Francisco mystique and our charming demeanor, we made friends easily. Lesbians in Minneapolis are starved for time with any lesbians they don't already know.

There was a one-woman lesbian welcome wagon named Christina at the Wedge who organized a night on the town for us shortly after our arrival. Minneapolis is a lovely combination of progressive hipster and small town, reserved but warm, inclusive cultural expectations. We joined a euchre club and learned what a snow emergency route is. I then wasted no time in implementing the next phase of our cross-country action plan.

In March of 2000, we closed on our house. It was a boarded-up, abandoned, hundred-year-old mess in a South Minneapolis neighborhood our new liberal friends cautioned us not to buy in. The same one that is, fifteen years later, the home of a new co-op and condo developments, which is likely our fault. It was in a neighborhood with Black people in Minneapolis, which still causes anxiety for white people in the Midwest. So we were those gays who move into a depressed neighborhood and catalyze gentrification, but that wasn't our intention. It was my house the moment I saw it.

To be fair, neither Patricia nor our realtor wanted us to buy this house, mostly because of its condition, and maybe the smell. But my visions will not be denied. It was a big duplex that was cheap enough to use as a single-family house. It had maple floors and a creepy basement. It had Darlene, our next-door neighbor, who was among the first Black families to buy a house in Minneapolis in the sixties. We loved each other instantly.

Patricia made the best of it as she always did, while I set about acquiring new butch skills and buying tools, pretending I knew how to fix up our house. This house was a psychic projection of my soul. It represented the stability of a home of my own I'd always longed for as well as a blank slate to figure out what I actually liked. Another fresh start.

I sanded the floors and erected a fence around our backyard.

I built a deck and fashioned screen windows for our front porch. I added four feet onto our decaying garage so that the Chrysler would fit. We painted the rooms in bold colors, and I made blue-glass bottle light fixtures for the downstairs bathroom as a homage to San Francisco. I didn't understand how to decorate a house like a grown-up. Our whole house started to take on the hue of nineties San Francisco. It was a composite, trial-and-error, never-ending identity puzzle. I tried to synthesize different worlds. I thought I could maintain my disdain for mainstream aesthetics while manifesting an adult reality. It was a compromise. I wanted to create a life my parents could approve of while crafting some sort of individualism.

I started to notice conflicts between Midwestern queerness and the kaleidoscopic upheaval that had been my experience for the past decade. Our Midwestern lesbian friends critiqued the handmade, handset tile floor in my kitchen for the irregularities in the pattern I'd created. Dykes in San Francisco made fun of you if you had matching curtains. There were fewer tattoos here, and no one I knew made porn. Lesbians here didn't share stories of drug use and sexual abuse as a party game. I started to clamp down on my own intensity which had been permitted too much free time in my twenties.

While I'd tried to rid myself of my nerdiness to fit into San Francisco, I now willed myself to tone down the affectations I'd acquired there. The queerness in Minneapolis is both very charming and a bit judgmental. It's a delicate balance of broader cultural norms, kitsch, and carefully placed resistance. It is centered on loyalty and expectations of care. The abiding magic in this town is its people. If you find your family here, you'll never be able to leave.

I met Benny Benson within a few months of arriving in Minneapolis. I was pulling a pallet through the Wedge at 6:00 a.m. As I passed aisle 4, I saw a new person stocking shelves. I thought, *Shit, that's cute. Look at that new baby butch who works here.* I introduced myself and asked if I could buy her a coffee. She said no and looked at me like I might punch her in the face. I didn't know how to interpret that, so I withdrew, wondering if I'd overstepped another unfamiliar, Midwestern boundary.

Over the next few weeks, I saw Sporty Spice roll into the Wedge with a superhot femme girl a few times, which delighted me. I didn't understand my draw toward this young butch, but I knew we needed to know one another. We chatted occasionally at work, but there seemed to be an odd barrier to our friendship. Then one night, I was playing in a euchre tournament at Bar Abilene in Uptown. I saw Benny there with that same pretty girl, but she seemed to be on a date with some bio-boy, and Benny was wearing blue eyeshadow, looking like a wingman. I was completely confused.

The next day I approached Benny at work and asked, perhaps too aggressively, "Are you a dyke or what?"

Benny started to choke up and finally said, "I don't know."

I saw the look on her face and instantly felt all her pain flood my own chest and knew it. I knew her.

In my lifelong quest to find my place in the sun, I've been graciously introduced to a shamanic guide of sorts once a decade. As a child, I spent some time with a fairy godmother. In my teens, I was sent a protector. In my twenties, I found a mentor. In my thirties, I was given a brother. I took her to Cafe Wyrd, a local lesbian café, and we talked about butch stuff and that pretty femme girl she'd had a crush on for years but never kissed. Benny didn't know there were other butches who felt like she did and did the same dumb stuff, just like I hadn't known. I got her laid by sending an older woman after her. Then Benny started going to gay bars by herself and getting herself laid. She played softball with the lesbians who shave their legs and live in the suburbs. We didn't actually hang out that much. I was the big brother. Benny needed to figure out stuff for herself without my shoving. The responsibility I felt for her was my first experience of my potential as a leader since I was a kid.

My intentions of becoming a grown-up were fleshing themselves out. Our house was becoming functional, though still exotic by Minneapolis standards. We had people over for dinner parties. We dined out frequently. I got promoted to warehouse manager at Co-op Partners. This might qualify as a grown-up job, except that natural and organic food still occupied the mental space of youthful idealism in the mainstream psyche, so my parents thought of it more like a really big lemonade stand. But our friends admired the stability of our relationship. We got a dog. Ingrid.

Patricia and I were always sweet to one another. We never fought. We had lesbian couple friends to travel with. We got a big red pickup truck and went to the dog park. I rototilled the front yard and planted native perennials. When my folks came for a visit, they were critical of my job selection and landscaping. They cited my neighbor's less ambitious but fastidious yards and claimed I was being disrespectful and lowering property values. I kept thinking I was creating something that would please them, but it didn't crush me completely anymore when I failed. I just cried for a couple of days then let it go. I became slightly more protective of my life because I had created something more substantial than a by-product of my mistakes.

It's hard to say whether I could've sustained that life, had my brain allowed me to enjoy it. Lots of people fashion lives by assembling psychologically pleasing bits and baubles of expectations and accessorizing with personal cultural affiliations. Bargains on identities can be found at your local Home Depot, thrift stores, and antique architectural doodad establishments. I assume many are content with the identity that occupies their space, how it looks, how it is reflected by their community, their family. Some may even be happy. Some experience ennui. After the briefest introduction to stability, I felt like my brain was on fire and my face was melting.

Don't get me wrong, I truly loved Patricia. I loved our house and our pets and our friends. I wish I trusted psychology more to enlighten me on the demon jamboree that's been banging out maniacal banjo duels in my head for as long as I can remember. Something about my assimilation project started to chafe. I think the destruction began in 2003.

Something was wrong, and Patricia and I both knew it. We weren't bored, but I think we started to wonder if this was all there was going to be. One Saturday night, we were simultaneously assaulted by the fact that we were at home, watching *Touched by an Angel* on a TV with poor reception because we didn't have cable. We'd gone too far. The stability was uncomfortable. And it still didn't impress my parents, so what was the point?

Also, I was fat. That has always been a thing, but I hadn't ever been this big. Since I stopped doing speed in 1998 and started drinking nice beer, I'd steadily packed it on. My job was less than satisfying. My boss was the most repugnant, vile person I'd ever met, as well as aggressive, stupid, and inappropriate. Working for him gave me irritable bowel syndrome and chest palpitations. I had too many sweaters.

I hated being a grown-up. Patricia hated it too, but she tried to be supportive. One morning, we were having breakfast at the French Meadow. I'd ordered a dish that normally came with poached eggs. I don't like poached eggs, so I asked that they come scrambled or something. They gave me poached eggs. I spent the next three hours outside, sobbing uncontrollably in my truck. I think I quit my job the next day.

CHAPTER TWENTY-EIGHT

# TRAINING MONTAGE #2: HIGHWAY TO HELL EDITION

It was time to come up with another new plan. I was never going to become a superhero like this. Didn't I remember that I had been bound for greatness at some point? I didn't know how I was going to become grand, but I thought maybe I should at least finish college. I applied to the University of Minnesota. My parents were thrilled.

Because of my many Fs, they wouldn't let me in the normal way. I was admitted to the College of Continuing Education, into their formerly rebellious dumbass program. The main benefit of this route was that I could take whatever classes I wanted. I could follow up on those dreams of becoming the renowned ancient Sumerian scholar, whose fresh translations of ancient cuneiform finally reveal undisputed proof of alien meddling in human civilization. I took ancient Greek instead. I was spellbound by the beauty and difficulty of it. Translating classical Greek combined the harmony of math with creativity. The uncommon and difficult nature of the activity renewed hopes for my eccentricity. I was also good at it. In fact, I found that if you go to class and do your homework, college is enjoyable and easy. I don't know how anyone completes college in their twenties. As were effortless once again. Compared to my youthful cohort, my insights and dedication were refreshing to my professors. They spoke to me like peers and wanted to hear my stories. I loved school.

I wanted to improve my health and body. I rode my bike everywhere, even through the winter. That's something people do in Minneapolis. I started going to the gym on campus. I started taking yoga, which I had previously deemed too pretentious. I started feeling ahead of people again, which was my comfort zone as a child.

Patricia and I started going to shows again. We started hanging out with the hipster dykes in the Powderhorn gayborhood. We started throwing more fabulous parties. We were popular. People looked up to us.

Patricia was a holy object of devotion for me. We had been together for about seven years and I'd never even thought about another woman. The idea of being away from her terrified me, but when I am not surrounded by soothing chaos, my need for control becomes more aggressive. She enjoyed taking classes, but she didn't need college in the same way I did. She came to the gym with me, but she never needed radical transformation like I did. She never needed to become anything other than what she'd always been. I made her come with me, and then I started wanting time away from her.

I think the exercise might've dislodged some fat that went to my brain. It was both exhilarating and nauseating to do things away from Patricia. I was overcome with guilt over doing things for myself. I wasn't making as much money, and she was paying most of the bills. It was too much pressure that I might not live up to expectations again.

And then the crazies showed up.

I started avoiding sex with her. For old-school butches, there are several ways this happens with regularity. There's Stone Butch tendencies, where you eagerly and arrogantly do sexy things to other people, but you don't want them to touch you. You might even be happy to keep your clothes on most of the time. This is a physical manifestation of the conflict between the body you have, the one that has been disrespected and neglected by yourself and others, and the illusion of the body that makes you a stud. Our illusions are potent for ourselves as well as others. Do not be confused. We are huge studs. Our actual bodies just sometimes aren't a big part of our shtick. Eventually, all illusions lose their novelty.

There's Lesbian Bed Death, which is usually the result of trying too hard to be someone you're not for a person you know too little about, becoming exhausted by the prep work, but finding that you moved in together anyway and now you're just waiting for the other person to break up with you or a bus to run you over.

Then there's deep, existential abjection. You don't know if you'll ever figure out the skin that would make you happy, so you must disappear somehow. There's a private disgust and prostrate fatigue that comes from living in your flesh that makes intimacy terrifying. Every touch reminds you that you're still there. Love starts becoming painful, even more so if it is generous and warm. Without acknowledging or understanding what's going on, you begin chipping away at the first identity that has brought you a taste of genuine stability and comfort. You begin to take baby steps away from the first person who introduced you to the potential of real human intimacy, and you don't know why. And you don't know how to stop it.

That. I had that. I tried to control it by withdrawing into the lifelong sanctuary of my fantasy world, as if disassociation breaks would preserve my commitment. Like if I could just fantasize vividly enough about living in the woods or getting into a fatal car crash, maybe I could keep it together to stay in my actual life. If I could just wreck it over and over again in my brain, maybe I could keep it. But the dark fairies in my head would not be denied. They would find a way to precipitate my downfall. My brain found its way back to an especially useless and self-destructive compulsion I thought I had outgrown.

Straight girls. Goddamnit. What the fuck is that about? The last time I'd dealt with that particular obsession, it was the midnineties and my favorite alone-time activity was creating intricate, time-killing worlds where Gillian Anderson from *The X-Files* or Jennifer Tilly from *Bound* found me irresistibly compelling. Now I was in my midthirties and they were surrounding me again. Unfortunately, this time, they were real people in my real life.

First, I became infatuated with my African History professor, which led me to fail my final. Then, I became so obsessed with my yoga instructor I finally left her a note one day and never returned to the gym at school again. Sigh.

But even while I was losing it, I kept going to school and exercising every day. Patricia and I kept having parties and eating fabulous food. She didn't need to know the seriousness of these crushes. She didn't need to know I was falling apart. Maybe this phase might not continue or become any more destructive. Maybe I might get mugged and shot or run over by a truck before I did any lasting damage.

Patricia stopped taking classes, but we both still went to yoga at the Y. We both lost weight and improved our fashion. We acquired some important friends through breakups. Our neighbor broke up with her boyfriend, and we stopped by to ask her to dinner. Christa was a vet and a Capricorn like both of us. She is dark-hearted smart. She started out needing us, but I had no idea how much I would soon need her. She was one of our few straight friends. They are essential when lesbian drama gets out of hand.

I didn't have to wait long for the drama when one of our

lesbian couple friends broke up. Virginia's girlfriend left her for Virginia's best friend. Not an entirely uncommon hazard for the queers. We sided with Virginia by taking her to some douchey Uptown bar to get really drunk. Coming out of the toilet, I walked into Virginia, both of us ready for our cheesy movie moment. There was a pause while we stared into each other's eyes. Then we threw our arms around one another and kissed like the whole night had been leading to that.

I was filled with guilt and terror.

I'd never cheated on Patricia. I cheated on everybody. There were the obsessive crushes, but I hadn't fucked up in real life yet. Virginia went into the bathroom, and I went out to rejoin Patricia. I didn't say a word.

For two weeks, I had nightmares about Patricia leaving me. Virginia and I didn't talk about it. The guilt was all-consuming. My devotion to Patricia was sacred. This minor transgression had introduced vulnerability in our relationship. It was more than I could bear. I finally stopped us in the middle of a bike ride one day, to confess my sins.

"I kissed Virginia." I was crying.

"Oh. Is that what's wrong? That's okay. She's hot. Should we go now?" Patricia replied.

The next time we hung out with Virginia, all three of us ended up in bed together. Virginia would become our girl-friend for the next nine months. She spent most of her nights in our bed. We even went out as a unit to a few queer func-tions, which made some people uncomfortable. It reminded Patricia and me we could still be edgy. Patricia has an amazing capacity to love. She enjoyed having a pretty girl to dote on. She had next to zero jealous tendencies. Even though she sus-pected that Virginia wanted me for herself, Patricia was con-fident I wouldn't leave. And when Patricia finally had enough and wanted our relationship back to herself, I didn't. I broke it off with Virginia. This was an easy decision for several reasons. First, I really did love Patricia, and the thought of breaking up with her seemed impossible. We were each other's people. We owned a house. We had a dog. People looked up to us. Second, even though it was a huge ego boost to have a hot wife and a hot girlfriend while I was getting As at school and working a job, it was exhausting. But, if I'm telling the truth, the reason I was able to turn away from Virginia was because a new girl had just turned my head. Another straight girl.

I redevoted myself to my primary relationship because the second I met Maisy, I was terrified. I knew the instant I saw her I would end up destroying my relationship for her. I wanted to deny that fate, like I'm good at that or something.

I met her at a coffee shop in Powderhorn that is special to the lesbians and progressive puppet people of that neighborhood. Benny worked there, so I spent countless hours, writing papers and being close to Benny. Maisy came to visit Benny one day. She worked at the co-op where Benny held a second job.

She had witchy, sexy green eyes. She had one of those Kathleen Turner voices and the sensuality to match. Meeting her was one of those moments that makes me ponder the plausibility of fate or past-life connections, but then I also wonder if those theologies actually just stem from a common mental illness. However it works, I instantly knew I was about to make a mistake I'd made before and repeatedly, in every former life, since the beginning of time.

My next step down the path of self-immolation was asking Benny if she could get me a job at the co-op. I started a couple weeks later. Over the next year and a half, I would occupy that creepy mental funhouse of unobtainable girl torture only butch dykes and nerdy teenage boys can understand.

I've spent countless hours analyzing my straight-girl problem. Is it a lifelong, unsatisfied desire to win? I was so much better at being a boy than all the other boys. It should've been enough to guarantee the mate and success of my choice. Perhaps, my sense of justice was frustrated so consistently that I developed the compulsion to win a straight girl to transform my thwarted identity as a boy. I don't know if my subconscious has always wanted to be a boy as much as wanting my rightful place in the herd as king.

It never takes me long to figure out what a girl's lifelong desires and insecurities are and perfect my affectation of what she's always secretly/obviously wanted in a man. This is exactly as psychotic as it sounds. But in all of my experiences with straight girls, except for with Gillian Anderson, it has never been a solely one-sided enchantment, no matter how often the girl acts like she can't remember my name.

In her head, the fact that you weren't born with a penis alternates with the suspicion you're her preordained soulmate. She willingly engages in the suspense, the uncanny tension of potential destiny. She saves her most intimate confessions for her time with you, because you're the only one who understands. You're different than the other boys. You both have little scars in the same places. She can't believe how easy it is to talk to you . . . and the next day, you're the mumbly guy who just got on the bus and she's avoiding your gaze so you won't sit next to her. She ignores you. She goes out of her way to mention her crush on some beta boy within earshot. For the next several days, she is cold.

You spend every second away from her analyzing details of something she said or a way she looked at you. You're either obsessively confirming her secret love for you or convincing yourself that she hates you. The second you decide to give up on her for good, a parapsychological alarm goes off in her head. She finds you immediately and asks you to coffee and sits too close to you. Her eye contact is too sincere. She will be yours any day now, until she gets scared and doesn't talk to you for a week.

This humiliating cycle can continue for some time. I set a record with Maisy. For over a year, I flailed between making her mixtapes and lifting heavy things in front of her to privately lighting candles, praying to the goddess to take the obsession away.

I didn't want this to be happening. Patricia saw it clearly and told me that I didn't need to do it. She told me I was past it. I prayed that she was right. I went camping by myself to meditate on it. I did light bloodletting rituals to alter my course. I exercised harder than I ever had, trying to manufacture discipline, resistance.

That was a hard year. It was painful for both of us. By spring, I was lobbying for an open relationship. Patricia didn't mind that at all, but her only restriction was Maisy, who was my only reason for wanting it. Living through the slow death of a relationship that you truly value is one of the most painful things life offers. The fact that I wasn't strong enough to combat my own insufficiencies was brutal to face. What the hell was wrong with me? Was I a horrible person? Was my whole identity a mistake? Is there anything of substance about me? Has this all been a hoax? Was I meant to be a girl all along, but I couldn't compete with my mother, so I became a hollow boy instead? I used to want to be like Cher. I had long hair. I used to fuck boys. Had I wasted all of this time to become an unlovable, unsympathetic catastrophe? Why isn't being queer ever good enough?

I spent a lot of time on our front porch unable to enter the house, praying for the apocalypse. I didn't know anyone was listening.

# CHAPTER TWENTY-NINE

# FIRESTARTER

Oddly, I was growing more charming when I wasn't feeling suicidal. Depression is often the flip side of charisma. My body was morphing toward something suitable with new muscles and smaller hips. An outside observer might suggest I was in a manic phase. A revolution was sloshing about in my belly. When I wasn't feeling nihilistic, I could sense the rising power in my capabilities. I didn't know that something had begun.

I started my final semester at the U. I took "Dissident Sexualities in US History" taught by a smart gay boy named Kevin. The last class section covered alternative lesbian sexualities in San Francisco in the nineties. It was 2006. It occurred to me that what I'd been a part of was special and didn't exist anymore. I realized music for the past five years, except for Gossip, had really sucked. I looked around and saw nobody angry about anything that felt important to me. 2006 was probably the year most Gen Xers started getting crotchety.

People started talking about gay marriage. The rich gays and conservative Republicans started talking about that a lot. Initially, I had unquestioning faith in the Holy Gay Agenda. But it didn't take long for me to connect this seemingly innocuous campaign to the death of rock 'n' roll. It was part of a larger Log Cabin Cock Crusader plot to tone down our shitty, tacky, fabulous culture. I started to wonder aloud what the gays were doing. I began to proselytize about San Francisco, the nineties, and the subsequent demise of queer style.

That was the me I was at school. That was the me I was with Patricia. Then there was the me who was trying to destroy my loving, queer relationship to win the straight girl and, by sheer assimilation magic, transform into the normal adult man I would never be. Yes, I was aware of the irony.

The fight for the girl was going along as feared. In February of 2006, I was invited to a queer hipster birthday party in a warehouse space. The attendees were all encouraged to bring a bit of performance to share. Performance isn't normally in an old-school butch's skill set. But Maisy was going to be at this party. The party was for a rival butch that we worked with who also had the hots for Maisy. Challenge accepted.

I wrote a poem called "Ode to a Butch." It was pretty good. I knew it would be a hit with the arty, hipster crowd, especially if I could get Benny to read it with me. Nothing is cuter than butch buddies doing something in public that makes them uncomfortable.

Benny refused. Then I made her read it, and she agreed to do it. We spent half the party that night in a stairwell, rehearsing. We were the very last to perform. The poem was a hit. Everybody cheered. I had included a couple lines about butches and straight girls everybody found hilarious but also wounded and impressed Maisy in exactly the right amounts. I handed the poem to the rival butch as Benny and I greeted our fans.

This was the night I stirred my watchers at last. They'd been watching me slowly destroy my life while preaching against the milquetoasting of queers for over a year. This tiny offering of boldness and potential struck the magic frequency. They whispered a secret in my ear that I could not hear that night, but it lodged in the coals of my brain.

School was nearly done. I could finally visualize the graduation party I'd been wanting for my parents for almost twenty years. Being on a college campus for a couple years also reminded me of my forgotten duty to change the world. As an easily identifiable queer, I was often enlisted as a pundit concerning the ongoing spectacle of gay marriage. I refined my sermon warning of the dangers of making heteronormative assimilation the denouement of our queer history.

In April of 2006, I happened to read some letters to the editors of *Advocate*, the oldest gay newspaper in America. They were from some bitchy old gays throwing a tantrum over the upcoming Pride season. They suggested that parade organizers around the country not allow drag queens or leather daddies to participate in the parades, that their presences might jeopardize the chances of gay marriage legislation by scaring the straight people. Then, the only Twin Cities gay bar with a successful weekly lesbian night put a security guard outside their men's room door to check IDs to determine the birth sex of anyone who wanted to use the toilet. Dykes were just starting to transition with growing frequency in the queerscape. The gays were turning their backs on their own freaky family. The promise of mainstream entitlements was leading them to remarginalize the more eclectic members of our community, a predictable dick move made by older social justice movements.

I got drunk with Patricia at home one night and started ranting about how the gays had forgotten how fabulous it was to be queer. "I have not been fighting with my mother" —and by metaphorical extension the entire evil empire of normativity—"my entire life just so I can now fight to be just like everyone else." *Are our own bars going to segregate us? A sanctuary is necessary. We need a place for the weirdos and the warriors. If I am to find and radicalize the Island of Misfit Queers, I must build it myself.*

The dormant whisper in my head was set ablaze. My actual life had become more than I could bear. The boring gays and lesbians were out to destroy the only beauty I'd ever cared about. It was up to me to save it. My fantasy world met my mental illness in real time that night.

I would build it. That had always been my destiny. I told Patricia I was going to open a dyke bar. She encouraged me as she always had, but she didn't fully grasp that night that my ties to the practical necessities of my crumbling reality had been irrevocably cut.

I went to stock shelves with Benny at 6:00 a.m. the next morning. She would wait until I got close to her to fart on me, a typical morning. Then I told her about the night before. Benny was a butch dyke from a small town and Catholic parents. She understood the importance of finding the gays to young queers. What would happen if the little weirdos from small towns never found the big weirdos in the big city? What would happen if the sissy boys and the tough girls came looking for the world they heard existed, that they might have a chance to be happy in, and all they found was Rainbow Day at Crate and Barrel? We had a duty to do something.

"Benny, I'm going to open a dyke bar and I want you to be my bar manager."

"Okay," she replied.

I had my first disciple and the only dyke in Minneapolis with the right pseudomilitaristic sense of honor and classic butch skill set to accomplish what was to come.

# CHAPTER THIRTY

# SPIDER-MAN

So, what's the first step when you decide to open the gay bar of your dreams? What's the first logical thing you do to set this phantasmagoria in motion on the physical plane? Opening a dyke bar isn't an uncommon fantasy among queers born with vaginas. All clusters of outcasts want a special place for their own celebrations and awkward ceremonies safely outside the gaze of dominant culture. It's a modified apocalyptic fantasy, where everyone else doesn't exist inside the boundaries of just one space and your own spunky crew sets the rules for utopia. At the time, there was no dyke bar in the Twin Cities, and there hadn't been one in Minneapolis in living memory. We all wanted the fort. How do you make it happen?

When embarking on any impossible quest or attempting to resurrect a dying paradigm, it is important to have some kind of psychotic break. It should be severe enough to completely disable your ability to participate meaningfully in any relationship in your life. Next, embrace the murky but persistent suspicion in your head that you possess magical powers. I always suspected I was a wizard, but I was now certain I was also a pirate action hero, charged by the watchers of history to build this enchanted hideaway. The weirdos had always been my people. I had seen the burning bush. Benny had thrown down her nets.

The next necessary incantation for manifestation of visions is transcription. The vision appeared complete in my head, like the ark. But it's important to say it out loud and, preferably, write it down. The sacred vehicle I chose for this purpose was a spiral-bound Spider-Man notebook serendipitously purchased from a Walgreens on the way to my first "meeting" about the bar. "Meeting" needs ironic quotes at this stage because having a secret meeting about opening a bar while making twelve dollars an hour stocking shelves feels roughly like strategizing a trap for the tooth fairy.

Benny and I accomplished three things at this first session: I roughed out a sketch of the space I was imagining, we made a long list of the items and services we imagined a bar would require, and we decided on a name.

The first page of my notebook recalls the imagination of the bar's physical space. It includes renderings of a stage, dance floor, bar, pool tables, and a quieter area with tables. There are three restrooms, with one set aside as gender inclusive. The resemblance of this drawing to the as-yet-unmet building that eventually housed the bar feels a bit supernatural.

People who learn of my interest in theology often assume I must be religious or spiritual in some way. This is inaccurate except in the most intimate and cryptic sense. More precisely, I am superstitious. I've always sensed unseen voyeurs watching me as if my life were a movie. This is likely a delusional psychological projection channeling my lifelong desire to have something take an interest in my more secret, authentic potential. Or perhaps it's a subconscious perception of an alternative reality where underdogs prevail and all you need to access aid from this morally attuned dark matter is earnestness of heart and a narcissistic disdain for commercial practicality. Whichever it is, the universe / a lifetime of squandered potential wanted me to open this dyke bar. The Hobbit quest that followed that day can only now be comprehended as fairy tale, complete with fortuitous fairy encounters, chance treasure finds, and the obligatory gauntlet of trials of faith.

The next several pages of my Spider-Man scripture were filled with a long, subdivided list of all the things we could think of that this space might require. My favorite passage can be found on page 1, category 2, under the heading "Building." Under it was the simple instruction: "Buying." I do not recall why the gerund form was used.

I do remember when we decided on a name. We fumbled with increasingly ridiculous suggestions, but we both felt the magic of Pi when it appeared at the table. We knew we had guessed the right name and in uttering it together, we conjured the specter of its future.

Many have asked me about the name, and even more think they know why we called the place Pi. Some know I used to be a math geek. More know I turned into a philosophy nerd with a special love for translating ancient Greek. In math, Pi is the constant no matter how big the circle gets—an apt metaphor for our endeavor. In philosophy, the concept of Pi has been used to hypothesize the existence of order in an ostensibly chaotic existence. Pretty deep, kinda cool, a bit esoteric for commercial application. There's also the double entendre created by American slang. Pie is a word for pussy. Belly up to the pussy bar. Get it? All boys, including the gay ones, assumed this to be the implied allusion and thought it amusing, which it was. Lesbians always acted like they'd never heard of that euphemism. Whatever, lesbians. The name Pi, in addition to being all of those things as a bonus, was my nickname for my partner, Patricia.

Patricia, as usual, was being supportive of this new direction. I don't think she expected me to succeed, but she never let me know that. She'd meant everything to me for nine years, and I knew I was in the process of wrecking our relationship. I was also denying that our relationship was drawing to an end. The name was a form of homage to one of my very favorite people from whom I was distancing myself and trying to deal with the pain that caused us both.

I left our secret meeting with a transcendent sense of resolve. I couldn't even think about my personal catastrophes or my useless philosophy degree. Neither Benny nor I had any substantial experience working in a bar. I thought that I could treat the bar like a research paper. I headed to the public library.

The only nightclubs and gay bars in Minneapolis were all downtown, which was financially prohibitive for my imagination. Plus, lesbians won't pay for parking. Any business that sold liquor outside of downtown were restaurants. Most only sold beer and wine. I was going to open a nightclub, with dancing and booze. I needed to find out how.

On the fourth floor of the Minneapolis Central Library, I found the entire collection of Municipal Codes and Ordinances for Minneapolis. I read the entire tome devoted to Liquor Codes. I found that Minneapolis required establishments that sell alcohol to make 60 percent of their revenue from food and nonalcoholic beverage sales. My heart sank. That wouldn't work. I read further and came to a tiny ordinance subsection put there just for me. Any new liquor license granted south of downtown would only be given to a restaurant, hotel, or fraternal organization. It would be held to the 60/40 rule unless the building was in an area zoned for commercial use, in a seven-acre contiguous plot, and five hundred feet away from the nearest residential zone. There it was. The tiniest opening, the slightest hope. At that moment, in the library, holding the biggest three-ring binder I'd ever seen, I was one of the Goonies and I'd discovered a long-lost treasure map. I would have to be a "restaurant," but I could sell booze like a gay bar if I could just find the right building.

I returned home to Patricia. We had a graduation party to plan. My parents would be visiting in a few weeks. I was finishing finals. I was training for a triathlon. I still needed to carve out time to obsess over Maisy.

Mom and Dad came in May. The party was at our house, a place my parents had refused to enter on a few of their visits. Like my clothes, it was sometimes too much for my mom. I invited everyone I knew. Normally, I start panicking about my parents' visits a couple weeks before they arrive. At the last minute, I usually buy a new shirt and maybe some hand towels for the bathroom, as if these small tokens might distract my mother from the terrarium of weird I live in. This time, I wore what I normally wore. Jeans, white T-shirt with the sleeves rolled up, tattoos showing. I told Patricia to wear what she wanted, even though she'd collected a small, less provocative wardrobe for my mother over the years. I decided we should give it a try.

I'd always known that I should try "being myself" with my mother. This was my first semisuccessful attempt, but it was my dad for the win. He rarely came with my mom for visits. He cried at my graduation ceremony. I'd never seen him do that.

The morning after the party, as we smoked together on my back deck, he asked, "Did you build this deck?"

"Yeah," I answered.

"And the fence, and the garage? Did you make that archway in your living room? Where did you learn how to do those things? Where did you meet all those people? I didn't know you had so many friends. They're smart. I liked them. I just can't figure out why they don't make more money." I smiled. "Well, why don't you and Patricia take the day off. Good job, kid." He patted my back.

I went in and told Patricia, "I think my dad likes me."

I didn't tell my folks about my dyke bar prophecy. I keep my visions to myself when my parents are around. I also didn't want to ruin the moment. If my dad likes me, he tells my mom, then she's prompted to agree. I'd earned a day of approval.

After they left and school was over, I could really focus on my fantasy life. My next mission was to a bureaucratic catch-all office called "One Stop." It was the first place I was going to have to talk to a representative from the government-capitalist complex I was trying to infiltrate, a grown-up in the real world. I was Frodo in the Big City. No one else knew the gravity of my quest. I had to act like I wasn't a sneaksy Hobbit out to steal legitimacy and thwart the evil powers of assimilation. And I wasn't the asshole I normally felt like. I was caught between worlds as I rode up the escalator, the real and the wizard. Those escalator rides became dear to me and something of a ritual. As long as I was standing there, nothing else existed. I met my first fairy at One Stop. He seemed gay, but I am also thematically referring to his charmed role in my tale. I tried to sound sane as I explained why I was there.

I wanted to open a bar. I recited the necessary geopolitical details for the exemption I required. I asked if he knew of any areas of South Minneapolis that met those criteria. He looked at me for a moment, taking in my appearance, which was butch dyke in sweaty cutoff T-shirt and Dickies. A widening grin crept across his face. It was the face he reserved for people who wanted to build a straw-bale garage or add a moat to their property. Regardless, he pulled up a zoning map and turned the screen so I could see it too. We discerned that the only possible area in South Minneapolis that met my needs was an awkward, semi-industrial area southwest of the neoliberal Seward residential neighborhood. I was confident, looking at that screen, that the treasure was hidden there.

The "One Stop" fairy informed me I would have to find a building in my nonexistent price range, in the middle of that small area of old warehouses, that used to be a restaurant or a bar. I would need a location to even start my liquor license application.

All I heard was that there was an area of South Minneapolis where the exemption could be met. I found the cipher, and he showed me my treasure map.

I was sure my benevolent invisible forces were watching me walk out of that office in slow motion that day, to face insurmountable odds. As I stepped back onto the escalator, seventies power chords began to lay the mood. "Back in Black," maybe.

Benny and I started blabbing about our plans. By the end of June, the hipster queers were talking about it at parties. We were creating a venue for them. They believed us. They believed in us. My personal delusion was crossing the bridge into collective hope.

July was particularly painful for Patricia and me. Maisy had started to acknowledge her feelings for me. I was winning, and I didn't know what to do about that.

I went to Yellowstone with my mother in July. I was in the best shape of my life and my father had just discovered that he liked me, so conditions were optimal. My mom informed me that she and my father had inherited fifty thousand dollars from my Grandpa Buddy, who had died the summer before. My father wanted me to have it for my future, since they were relatively financially secure.

My parents have always wanted me to succeed professionally. Coming from their generation, they still believed that if you got a college degree, you would be successful. Though I have never grasped what their visions for me have been, I'm positive they didn't include a queer nightclub. While hiking into the mountains one day, while my mother was isolated, I told her about my plan. As a business owner, the risky plan made her uncomfortable. But the entrepreneur in her allowed the vision. She would have to talk to my father, but she unexpectedly encouraged my impulse. They both owned their own businesses. I probably should too. We talked like business people, which is how I should always talk to my mother. She gave me the money the next month.

In addition to this unexpected seed money, Patricia and I had a home equity line for an additional forty-five thousand dollars on our cheap, smelly house.

Then a woman I didn't know who was good friends with an acquaintance of mine heard about the bar and asked to meet with us about investing. My vision had sent out tentacles.

Patricia and I met with her, and she was all-in. She was kind of a stoner but not super vulnerable. She wanted to be Sam Malone from *Cheers* except in a dyke bar. It seemed benign and easily accommodated. She wasn't interested in shaping the vision, just showing up when it was time to impress the ladies. She'd come into her money through a divorce. She wanted to be a part of what we were creating.

So, just like that, money unexpectedly appeared. I set an appointment with a commercial real estate broker. We needed a building to get an application for a liquor license. A day before our meeting, I rode my bike through the magic zone on the treasure map. On a side street, I passed an enormous, low-slung, brick building. A decaying American Legion sign clung to the top corner of the building, obscured by an overgrown evergreen. The prairie growing in the parking lot suggested it had been abandoned for some time. A For Sale sign had partially fallen out of the front window. I called the number on the yellowing sign and got a voicemail for some software company. I thought I'd gotten a wrong number, but left a message anyway, expressing my interest in the property.

I met the real estate agent for coffee the next day. I listened as he explained that most aspiring bar owners could expect to search for up to two years to find the perfect property. He wasn't privy to my otherworldly timeline. I became increasingly aware that he wasn't part of this adventure. I nodded politely to expedite the dead-end conversation. I even muted an incoming call so I wouldn't appear rude. I thanked him and told him I'd be in touch.

When I was safely on the sidewalk, I checked my message. It was the owner of the building I'd called about, wondering if I had any free time to look at it the next day.

Soundtrack changes to *Flashdance*. "What a Feeling." My watchers had sent me a portent of their intentions. I obediently hit redial on my flip phone.

# CHAPTER THIRTY-ONE

# MY LOW-HANGING DISCO BALLS

I met the owner in front of the building the next afternoon. I already knew this was the place.

During the showing, I wedged a rock into the jamb of an inconspicuous side exit. I came back some hours later so the building and I could become better acquainted in private. The ruins of this brotherhood of veterans had summoned me. As I stepped inside, somebody's shadowy nostalgia, stuck to the old school cafeteria tile, was reanimated with my footsteps. The mold, the standing water, the rotten carpet, the smell, all faded from perception as I saw what was to occur here and as what had happened here came out to meet me. The decay was meant to obscure the magic from the unworthy. The building had been waiting for me.

There's something special about the feeling of refuge that bars create for the loyal misfits who assemble to form clots in them. That warm, tangy aroma of stale cigarettes and old beer gets pulled over your damage like a fuzzy blanket when you open the front door. It smells like a secret that belongs to you. Bars are relatively safe places for the more intense versions of yourself that feel vulnerable in the daylight. I believe in a kinship of consciousness that exists between the bold outskirts of an individual's bar persona and the audacity necessary for true social transformation. I'm intentionally ignoring the many fantastically destructive scenarios that also occur at bars because, occasionally, rare moments of humanity's dangerous beauty are birthed only in the alchemic orgy of desperation, dance, sweat, and alcohol. Bars briefly become Dionysian temples. These shared experiences create unique tribes, bound by special initiation.

As I walked through the building for the first time, I felt its hope. The invisible interactions of past and present revealed their machinations to the corner of my eye. I was negotiating a promise as I sifted through remaining artifacts and made note of smooth, shiny irregularities of wear. I projected my desires onto the remains of another clan's ceremonial hall. The wreckage granted me permission and gave me a caved-in mirrored disco ball as a housewarming gift.

It was the only building in Minneapolis that met my obscure geographical criteria, and it was within our shaky financial reach. The building needed to feel like an underdog too. We found each other.

We bought it the next week, contract for deed. As soon as our check for the down payment cleared, the owner handed us the keys to a building we couldn't afford. We had two years to create a successful business and convince a bank to give us a regular mortgage. If we were unsuccessful, we would have to give the building back.

My entire inheritance and half of my investor's money went to the down payment. I didn't know how I would make the monthly interest payments. I hadn't started my business plan yet. This was the point of no return. But I was in a movie where improbable things happen to and for the protagonist toward the climactic achievement of a lofty dream. My leap of faith would be rewarded.

That was August 2006, four months after deciding to open a bar. I quit my job the next week. The week after that, I ran a triathlon. The following week, Maisy and I started having an affair. A week later, Patricia told me she couldn't do it anymore. I had failed her and myself. She moved out the next week. Failure and regret dusted every surface in my house, the dream I insisted on the last time.

I wanted to break up with Maisy the day Patricia left, but I couldn't face hurting her too. It wasn't her fault I was a monster. I couldn't process the grief of my divorce in front of her. I had to pretend like I'd meant it to happen.

I lost our friends in the divorce, as I should have. Only Benny and Christa would still talk to me. I couldn't go to the second floor of our house, where our bedroom had been. Patricia's *New York Times* started piling up. Our dog, Ingrid, looked disappointed in me. Bell still tolerated me.

At least I had an impossibly large project to focus on. My only source of income was our home equity line. With this, I paid my mortgage and bills and the interest payment on the building. In another two weeks, I started paying my best friend to keep me company at the bar. Thankfully, I had pretty much quit eating. There was no other money in sight. I had little understanding of how much money it would take to rehabilitate this derelict shell into a permissible business. I had a laptop, a cell phone, and an old phone book I found in the building. Because of the divorce, some people tried to talk me down. But I'd already spent the money. My only choice was to move forward. I told them that I had been called by god to open a dyke bar. The part of my brain that could not face my real-life grief and self-hatred made anything practical taste terrible.

Had I been seeing a therapist, they might've locked me up. It was hard to contain that much sadness, self-hatred, and stress and look like I knew what I was doing. I allowed myself to cry in solitary fits of self-pity on the short commutes to and from the bar. But I couldn't have accomplished what I did at that time while maintaining personal stability. Traditional psychology is not inclined to encourage uncommon states of consciousness in an otherwise functional cultural participant. The correlation to dangerous outcomes is too unnerving. The only version of myself that I liked was the one opening the bar. That guy was alarmingly charismatic and my only hope for redemption.

The liquor license and business plan needed immediate attention, but on the first day in my new broken-down, moldy temple, it was just me and Benny. I don't know where the fuck Gandalf was. It was impossible to know where to start. My instinct was to let the building know it had a responsible new caretaker. I also knew we would have to win over our new neighborhood of functioning businesses. We would need formal approval from the Seward Neighborhood Group to advance our liquor license application. My endless teenage hours spent mowing, raking, and detailing my parents' yard unearthed my father's wax-on, wax-off karate wisdom. The first thing we did on this leg of our journey was clean the yard.

Pi had a big parking lot and a patch of grass out front. The parking lot was full of cracks, through which a prairie had been trying to emerge for the last several years. We spent an entire Minnesota August day clearing weeds, mowing the lawn, and trimming the bushes. Benny and I joked about our yard work as it seemed inconsequential against the tidal wave that was our to-do list. But, if there's anything that growing up in suburbia teaches you, it is that the maintenance of your yard is the foremost indicator of your sense of responsibility as a neighbor.

After our sunny triumph over the weeds, there was the following day, and another one, and another one. The building was in such a state of disrepair and decay that it wasn't worth listing potential renovations at this time. It seemed reasonable to focus on removing things that smelled or were potentially hazardous. When opening a business, a good portion of time is spent deciding what the next step should be. Many prospective restaurant owners hire people for this very task. Lack of money was my only project manager. We assessed our inventory of discarded treasures. We found a twenty-foot shuffleboard game, an impressive air pistol under an old couch, a bonanza of furniture carts and dollies, various crutches and wheelchairs, and a framed picture of an old Legion member with a beaver on his hat we named Vern.

Benny took charge of the demolition and crap removal department and independently assumed the responsibility of bringing me turkey sandwiches every day since I became unable to feed myself.

It was my job to go talk to some grown-ups. Lacking any plan or experience, it felt awkward to assume I had legitimate access to the gatekeepers of capitalism. For a lifestyle underachiever, it felt like a private club that my parents belonged to, and my only glimpse of the protocols had been from a lifetime kiddie table at holiday events. But I'd been to those events, and I grew up around my parents' businessy superpowers, and I'm white. I instinctively knew my privilege would aid me.

I didn't understand how complicated it was to obtain permission to sell alcohol in Minneapolis. On the morning of my appointment with business licensing at City Hall, I wore my usual summer uniform, Dickie's cutoffs and a black T-shirt. I grabbed a canvas tote that contained my Spider-Man notebook, date book, and the remains of a bag of sunflower seeds that had spilled and got on my trusty mountain bike. My mother would've been appalled by my wardrobe, but the intimidation I felt demanded I make my otherness public. I was an envoy for the misfit masses. My outfit provided the resolve to face the faces of authority.

At City Hall, I passed through the clusters of people who stride everywhere and checked in at the correct plexiglass. I was ushered into a small office and seated at a small conference table. Three large older white men in nice suits with impressive briefcases came in. They were followed by a slightly scruffy, compact man in a short-sleeved button-up and khakis, Phil.

Phil sat next to me and began his spiel, carefully distributing professional respect around the table. When he noticed my Spider-Man notebook, he told me about his twin two-year-old boys who loved Spider-Man everything. When the 60/40 requirements came up, one of the lawyers said their corporation was seeking a "nightclub" exemption. I told Phil that since the "nightclub" exemption was only possible downtown, I obtained a location that met the geographical criteria necessary for the other exemption. Phil said he wasn't aware of such an exemption, so I recited the pertinent code and offered the reference number.

The smile he offered me then told me I had found a magic ally to my quest. One of the businessmen chuckled and offered me a job. The contrast of my antagonistic appearance with my casual eloquence was playing well in this tiny room. I had passed through a gate. I left the meeting with a thirty-page application and the confidence of an underdog who hadn't been comprehensively dismissed.

The next step was writing a magic report that makes banks give you money. Mom Fedexed me three different books on business plans. I looked for templates on the internet. This research mostly yielded tips on how to make your plan "pop." I hate that word used in that context. I needed practical step-by-step consultation. I heard about Women Works, a nonprofit that helped female entrepreneurs find funding for their projects. They'd been featured on Oprah, who donated boots to help women getting into the construction industry. I went to an introductory meeting that cost thirty-five dollars. Surrounded by images of Oprah, they wasted an hour of my time encouraging me to indulge in one of their spa retreats for some me time and networking opportunities. Not one useful word was uttered. Afterwards, I cornered the facilitator, asking if they had people who could help me write a business plan or if they could talk to me about bank requirements. She seemed overwhelmed by my determination to open my own business, which confused and angered me further. She helped me make an appointment for individual consultation, which yielded nothing but a "good job, you seem to be on the right track" and cost an additional eighty dollars.

This was the first in a substantial list of bewildering experiences where a woman-centered company or individual stunned me with disinterest, disorganization, and self-importance. I was a butch woman opening a dyke bar. How much more vagina cred did I require for your assistance and solidarity? Sometimes, being a lesbian or a groovy liberal feminist doesn't make you interesting or brave or insightful. Sometimes it just makes you an unimaginative, condescending, self-aggrandizing turd.

As I left the building, wondering what I was going to do next, I noticed a small office with its door open. The sign on the door said Small Business Administration. I sort of knew what that was. I peeked in and saw an older man with distractingly bushy eyebrows watching *The Price Is Right* on a small portable TV. I asked him what they did, and turns out, in the same building as Women Works, the SBA created a small satellite office whose sole purpose was to help people write business plans. They had free computers with business plan–writing software. A retired business owner would help you through the process, then read your completed plan and provide thoughtful feedback for free. Tom. Tom would also give you free coffee and sometimes doughnuts.

Suck it, Women Works. And Oprah too. Just kidding, Oprah. I'm scared of you like a Catholic schoolgirl is scared of Jesus making her pregnant.

I hung out with Tom for endless hours the next month and a half. I crafted mission statements and projected revenues. I pretended I knew what repairs to the building would cost and how much we would need for bar stuff. Tom told me that it was all just guesswork anyway. I'm good at making shit up.

Benny maintained her other jobs but would come to the bar whenever she wasn't working. We were a long way from having a bar to manage. But the money and the building appeared just when we needed them. And I gained the favor of two unlikely straight white male demi-wizards with conventional entrepreneurial powers. We came to cautiously expect Pi miracles.

# CHAPTER THIRTY-TWO

# THE PI PROGRAM

A mere day or two after acquiring my liquor license application, I received an unsettling call from our emerging ally, Elena.

Elena was a regular at the coffee shop where Benny worked. She was an insider in municipal politics and thought we were cute. We'd always been friendly, but with the initiation of the Pi Project, she gladly made herself our own City Hall mole.

Elena called to inform us that a prominent city councilman had already heard about our bar and said he would never allow us to get our license. This news was confusing because he not only was openly gay but also represented a ward dominated by middle-aged lesbian feminists who now held various respected community leadership positions. Nobody wanted to piss them off. Pi was in another ward, but it still seemed like a big deal that a city fucking councilman already hated us.

I freaked out a bit. I called his office to try to talk to him but was rejected. So I was sitting on Benny's stoop, asking her whether I should continue trying to open this bar or run away to Hawaii with my new girlfriend and live in a hut on the beach. Then I looked at that fucking Benny face.

It made me want to be brave. It made me want to be not disappointing. My life turned into a cartoon that day with the appearance of a mustachio-twirling villain. I had no idea that important people might take me seriously. Thanks, Councilman Old Twink. You made me want to win.

People knew what I was doing. There was more at stake than my personal need for redemption. Obsession is melodramatic. One end of the line distinguishing the poetic from the creepy is clenched in the teeth of the obsessed, the other is held by the people you imagine are watching you. The plausibility of real-world benefit from your compulsive visions is determined by the quality of your hustle. I had serious game just then. I made myself mayor of the Island of Misfit Queers, and people were starting to encourage me in real life. It was like those kids running behind Rocky in *Rocky II*.

Benny and I attended National Night Out in the residential neighborhood closest to Pi. Some of these people attended the next assembly of the Seward Neighborhood Group. They remembered the old bars that had once dominated that area. They didn't want a resurgence of drunken hooligans who trampled their hostas and urinated on their driveways. They were also worried about our inexperience. Some architect with a perm and an earring suggested we think about a smaller venue. I thanked him for his advice and didn't stab him.

I secured a couple of bids from lesbian contractors. We wanted this to be a family endeavor. The contractor said she could resurface one of our walls for twenty thousand dollars. Benny had already torn out the moldy drywall with a dust mask and a crowbar. Benny said, "They are obviously not on the Pi Program." I opened our outdated Yellow Pages and called the commercial contractor with the biggest ad.

The next day, Big Marv and his brother Ron walked into our family, a couple of giant farm boys from Southern Minnesota who'd been helping restaurants and bars open for twenty years. They had a loyal army of subcontractors and knew every city official and inspector in town. Ron was the quiet craftsman. Big Marv was the magic man.

He walked through the building with me and talked to me like I was a grown-up opening a business who also enjoyed dirty jokes. I told him about my dream, that I wanted to open a space for my community. I tried not to let on how much money I didn't have. He said, "I've always wanted to be an honorary lesbian. I do love pussy." He said it with such warmth that I knew he was my kind of lesbian. When I told him about the lesbian bid for our north wall, he just laughed and said, "You know how to paint, don'tcha?"

He worked up a bid for the repairs we'd need to pass our inspections and have a functioning bar and restaurant. It was extensive. I didn't tell him I had none of that money. He would let Benny and me do everything he thought we could to save money. "I like what you're doing here. I'll help you. We'll get this bar open."

Even though I now had Marv as a potential ally, I still needed money to pay him and his subcontractors. The second half of my investor's money went to a new roof and scraping the tile off the main floor. Jeff, the floor guy, chipped up about seven thousand square feet of school cafeteria tile by hand, then sanded it while smoking Marlboro Lights and drinking Mountain Dew. I had half of my home equity line left, which was earmarked to pay the mortgage on the building and my house for three more months.

It was the end of September when Tom and I made the final edits on my business plan. I donated twenty dollars to print ten copies of my business plan. I thanked Tom and told him to come by the bar for a drink. He wished me luck, and I never saw him again.

There's no businesswear department for butch dykes. You either wear men's suits or women's suits. Benny and I looked terrible in both. We settled on long-sleeved button-up shirts and clean pants and took time away from the bar to cold call on banks. This is an activity where you walk into a bank, un-announced, and ask a stranger to loan you $280,000, based on the merit of the "plan" you pretend you have.

It's hard to keep a straight face when engaging in this task. You don't have any money or experience. You need more money than you've ever conceived of dealing with in your life. Your dream will die a horrible death if you don't con-vince someone to give it to you, and you're wearing the same shirt you wear every time your mother visits. Benny's was paisley. We went to six or seven banks over the course of a week and were rejected. The list of banks was growing short and I was running out of copies of my business plan. Then we went to the Private Bank. I'm not making that name up. It was on a high floor in a skyscraper, downtown. We had to pay for parking. Everyone we passed was in suits and taller than us. When we got onto the elevator with an extraordinarily well-dressed and attractive woman, we both started panick-ing and blabbering.

"What the hell are we doing here? We can't talk to these people. They'll have us arrested. Maybe they'll have us killed." Benny chuckled.

"I don't know, but we already paid for parking," I said. "Who gives a shit? We can say we were rejected by really classy people. Maybe they like lesbians. It'll be fun." When we finally got off just shy of the penthouse, the attractive woman got off with us. She smiled and disappeared behind a polished oak door. "Oh perfect," I said. We approached the stern-looking woman at the front desk with a fierce bun and no upper lip. I held up a copy of my business plan and ex-plained why we were there. She informed us that everyone at the Private Bank was very busy, but she would inquire on our behalf. We sat down, giggling with terror.

Then the woman from the elevator emerged and handed

us a folder with promotional materials and a complimentary bottle of water. She was the assistant to the vice president. She said she'd spoken to her boss, who would have time soon if we cared to wait. I assured her we'd be happy to wait and thanked her. Power Bun looked indignant. Fifteen minutes later, I was sitting at the head of the largest conference table ever created explaining my dyke bar vision to a warm, intelligent woman who financed stadiums and skyscrapers for a living. She gently explained that the Private Bank usually serviced much larger loans. She did, however, have a friend at Wells Fargo she thought would love to hear about our plan. She called him right there and set an appointment.

The next day, we met John at Wells Fargo. A week later, Wells Fargo gave us a letter of commitment. If we could successfully jump through the next eight dozen hoops to make a commercial loan close, we could get money by November and start the buildout process. Another Pi miracle. This was exciting news considering that I would be out of money by October.

The pace quickened. This annoyed my investor. She'd stop by the building and see things getting done and feel left out. She was uninterested in the details or doing anything helpful but angry we weren't including her. I tried to give her things to do. I told her I needed a provisional menu for our imaginary restaurant for our liquor license. She came back a week later with a handwritten list of smoothie flavors.

"Um, thank you. Is there more?" I asked.

"Well, that's just a start," she replied.

"Okay great. I don't know if we're going to have smoothies though."

She became irate and left. Benny and I stared at the "menu."

"Did she get stoned with her friends and say, 'You know what really sounds good right now? A smoothie. Oh my god, the bar should totally have smoothies.'"

"Does she have any idea what we're doing? How are we going to handle this?"

Luckily, she didn't show up that often.

We came to the point where there was little more Benny could do before the contractors came. I retrieved our Yellow Pages and told her to call some liquor distributors. A magical thing happens when you tell salespeople you're opening a business. They assume you know what you're doing and treat you like a potential customer. One, Suzy, even took us to lunch and brought us bottles of wine as samples. It was the first decent meal I'd had in months.

When salespeople figure out you're not normal customers, but a couple of earnest dreamers, they start to care about you, because the rest of their customers are creepy douchebags. What you are doing touches the part of their soul they thought was dead. Suzy started to stop by whenever she was in the neighborhood to check on our progress and confide in Benny.

When Benny and I went to the next Seward Neighborhood Group meeting, we got a unanimous vote of support from the neighborhood and a standing ovation. Benny called Suzy. I called Elena. They both met us at Pi. We ordered pizza and Suzy brought bottle after bottle of expensive wine in from the trunk of her car. We had a dance party, the very first at Pi.

Halloween was approaching, the most important holiday. An aspiring DJ had recently materialized and offered to help. The first time I'd met DJ Bucky a few years earlier, she instantly annoyed me. She talked to Patricia and me like she didn't know how cool we were. "Well, there's somebody I never want to spend more than two minutes with ever again," I whispered to Patricia as we walked away.

Five years later, DJ Bucky heard about our bar. She found us and told us she could be our DJ and organize shows. This time, her overblown bravado was exactly what I needed. This job would be an extension of her ego, so she wouldn't let it fail. I saw she had been waiting for this opportunity. Our relationship would be mutually beneficial. She would have a unique platform for self-promotion, and I would have a devoted diva. Benny and I knew how to work twenty hours a day. We didn't know how to make this bar cool.

The building still didn't have any heat or a PA system. We strung twinkly lights and hung our magic disco ball. I rented an industrial heater and DJ Bucky borrowed a portable PA. It would be her second DJ gig ever. She MySpaced the event to her fan base.

I dressed in drag. I wore six-inch heels and a sleazy black dress. This was a habit I'd started in the nineties. I always dressed in drag for Halloween. It was a ritualistic tribute to a tiny, distant part of myself I still owed. That bitch always emerged when I put my heels on. She gave me temporary access to the dominance and indifference my boy self could never manage. I needed a little domme for the first public viewing of my dream.

Around a hundred and fifty people turned out. It was the place to be that Halloween if you were a dyke in the know. A venue was being imagined for them, for their talents and energy and desires. The cold night buzzed with the potential of its reality in our world. Nobody cared that the toilets were dark or that they were dancing on an unfinished concrete floor. I spent almost every last cent I had on a keg, some wine, and T-shirts commemorating the event. It was the building's first sprinkling of our fairy dust.

I spent most of November on the phone with assistants in the loan department of Wells Fargo. I purchased a cheap fax/scanner/copier and turned on phone service at the bar solely for this activity. Closing a commercial loan involves endless hours of locating and copying every receipt, bank statement, and tax document your life has ever produced. Every day I received a call from the bank requiring some fresh piece of evidence. They still hauled us all in near our scheduled closing date to tell us there was a new problem. While reviewing our investor's financial documents, they discovered she had enough cash to collateralize the entire loan. Because of that, they required she put the entire amount in an inaccessible account or put something else up against the loan. She'd been growing more antagonistic with me, but her initial investment was already gone. She chose to put her house up as collateral, which made everyone incredibly uncomfortable. But at this point, there was no turning back for any of us.

# CHAPTER THIRTY-THREE

# I GOT THIS

The loan closed the next week. Big Marv showed up with a dozen subcontractors the next day. Teams of giant men with skills filled my delusion with the terror of real-life evidence of its materialization. It was happening. Efficiently, and competently. Big Marv made sure we were treated like family.

I was now officially over a million dollars in debt, which feels very much like jumping out of an airplane. Your brain has no innate frame of reference for the unlikely event of falling from that distance. You're not sure how terrified you should be. Once you're out of the plane, it's too late. You must make it work or lose everything.

One of my business partners was my ex-wife, whose presence gutted me with pain and guilt. My other business partner clearly hated me for every decision I made yet avoided helping me make them. My girlfriend was becoming increasingly sad because I spent most of every day at the bar and it had become the love of my life. My dog looked at me with disappointment every time I came home.

If you ever wonder why people have heart attacks in their thirties, it's stress. I didn't have time to exercise or sleep. I lived on Benny's turkey sandwiches and contractor's leftover tater tots. I ran a triathlon in August. By Thanksgiving, I couldn't complete the charity 5k I tried to run with Benny. Sometimes I blacked out and fell on the floor for a second. Nothing was going to stop this dyke bar from happening, except the different stupid thing that happened every day that required me to revise my wish list or lower my expectations.

I was spinning webs of credit like Spider-Man. For a shining, golden month after the loans closed, my credit was a theophany. Not only did Wells Fargo throw in a couple of credit cards for bonus debt, but I got credit lines at Home Depot, Fleet Farm, and Menard's. I bought our entire sound and entertainment system on credit at a tiny store in Minneapolis. The rest of my home equity line was already earmarked for the mortgage payments on the building and my house and would be completely tapped by February. I probably had less than a hundred dollars in my bank account and no income.

My dad called one night. He rarely called me. He'd had a few. He was hanging out with his friend Walt. They'd decided I needed a big truck if I was going to own a bar, and they'd just got me one. My parents drove a shiny red pickup all the way from California for me. My dad seemed happy about the bar, like it was something he wished he could've done. I think he liked that I had found my balls. He wanted to help.

He drilled me on the money and the plan relentlessly. He liked Big Marv and Ron, and they liked him. He and Mom tolerated meeting Maisy so they could see the bar and talk business. They didn't understand my personal reasons for opening the bar, but that didn't matter. Mom didn't bother me about my outfit for the span of a whole visit. Just kidding, she offered to buy me new clothes to wear to the bank.

After they left, I turned my focus to finishing our liquor license. Everyone told me there was no way we would be able to get our liquor license on the first try. Since I would be out of money in two months, failing to get my license on the first try wasn't an option I could afford.

Lacking money for an architect, I created schematics for our interior and parking lot using a protractor, an Exacto knife, a glue stick, and a copier. I obtained a parking agreement with the business across the street. I got safety plans approved by our local police and fire precincts. I produced financial reports accounting for every dollar borrowed and spent.

It had taken me three months to assemble my application. When I gave it to Phil, he said, "You're only the third person I've worked with who wrote their own liquor license."

"Who normally writes them?"

"People hire lawyers for that."

"You could've told me that three months ago, Phil."

He smiled and told me that it looked like we had everything we needed. The city council vote would take place in the middle of January. The council usually approves Neighborhood Group recommendations, but any councilman can single out any agenda item for debate.

I thought about my city council nemesis. Elena hadn't reported any new developments. I had no idea if he was still plotting against me.

Then two weeks after I'd turned my application in, Phil called me.

"Hey Tara. Say, do you happen to have a copy of your application?"

"What? Um, no Phil. It was kind of a one-of-a-kind document."

"Well, do you think you could get it together again?"

"Phil. You got my original drawings. Six of those documents need to be notarized. I need to get both of my partners' signatures on everything, which is nearly impossible and incredibly uncomfortable. It's near Christmas. Nobody is around. What the hell happened?"

"It's missing."

"What do you mean, it's missing. What happened to it?"

"Honestly, I don't know. It was on my desk, then it was gone. My assistant and I have been looking everywhere."

I went out onto our future dance floor. Marv and Ron and Benny were chatting. I was smoking and panicking. "Phil just called. He asked me if I had a copy of our application. He lost ours."

"Do you have a copy?" Benny asked.

"Of course I don't have a copy. I'm a fucking idiot . . . okay. Okay. This will be okay. I'm gonna smoke this cigarette, then I'll just start over. I think I have most of the documents."

I started furiously reassembling things. I called the bank to set up a time to get their stuff. I called the police department and the fire department to tell them they'd have to sign off on another safety plan. I called Patricia and my investor to tell them what happened. Then I got another call from Phil.

"We found it."

"Oh my god. Where was it?"

"Well. For some reason it was on the desk of an aide to a city councilman. Do you know Councilman Bitter Queen?"

"Yes. Yes, I do. I don't know why he would have it. I'm glad you found it. Thanks, Phil."

This didn't bode well for our chances. I just filed it in my superstition vault containing all the unuttered reasons we probably wouldn't open in time. A week later, Phil called again to tell me that Pi's city councilman wanted to meet with me to discuss the exemption I had exploited.

Benny and I put on our button-ups again and headed to City Hall. We were seated in the private chambers of the city councilman for Pi's ward. In attendance were his aide, the head of business licensing, the head of liquor licensing, and Phil. The councilman had figured out that we were trying to open a dyke bar in his neighborhood. The heads of the other departments had figured out that I had discovered a loophole they'd never heard of. The issue in question, the only one they *could* question, was whether or not we intended to be a "restaurant." They also suspected we were trying to open a dyke bar.

As the powerful men began to tease apart our intentions, Phil spoke up. He said, "I, for one, have read their menu, and I can't wait to eat there."

Benny looked confused. I kicked her under the table.

Phil said, "As far as I have seen, these ladies are trying to open a restaurant. There might be some dancing on the weekends, but a restaurant is what they see their community lacking."

Benny and I exchanged a brief glance. The councilman looked at me and chuckled, "Well, I guess that's all we needed to hear."

Benny and I were dismissed. We went directly to the restroom and panicked.

"Do we have a menu?" Benny asked.

"Yeah, don't you remember that smoothie menu? . . . No, we don't have a fucking menu. I turned in some bullshit I made up with our application. A city official just lied to a city councilman on our behalf."

"Should we offer to suck his dick?"

"Probably. I'd blow them all right now if they gave us our liquor license, multiple times."

Benny and I returned to the bar feeling our growing pirate mojo.

We were halfway through build-out. Benny and I painted the ceiling and the floor. Ron salvaged the tip of the old horseshoe bar and transformed it into the DJ booth. We started to pick out light fixtures and paint colors.

My investor came in one day to ask me where the smoking

patio would be. She told me she wouldn't allow the bar to open unless her girlfriend had a place to smoke.

I said, "Do you understand how precarious our standing is with city hall? I can't ask for a special variance for an outdoor patio. Plus, we can't afford it."

"I'm not letting this place open without a patio for my girlfriend. You never let me make any decisions. I don't have control over anything."

"What would you like control over? Is there anything you want to do?"

"Well, nobody's done anything to the coat-check room. Can that be mine? I'll pay for it all myself, but I want to do it all."

"Of course you can. That sounds great. I haven't even thought of that room yet."

Pi had a small front office with an opening facing the front door. It would make a perfect coat check and security room. It was the least of my concerns.

My investor hired two lesbian contractors who were her friends. I'd encountered them while attempting to get bids early on. They immediately took a combative posture toward Marv and Ron, and us.

I really had wanted our project to be one big, happy Towanda treehouse. I would've been thrilled by an affordable platoon of strapping, competent big-boned gals. Sadly, the women I encountered at first were underqualified and over-priced, and they didn't care about our vision or that we were spunky. They weren't nice. Maybe they didn't have that lux-ury in an industry completely dominated by white men. But it ended up being the well-connected straight white guys who donated dozens of hours of labor, who lied to get us a liquor license, who believed in our idea and got us funding.

Benny and I had just finished peeling the old grass cloth

wallpaper off the hallway near the entryway. It would be our rotating art gallery for local queer artists. The glue had left a splotchy texture on the wall. Benny and I were wondering what to do about it. One of the lesbian contractors came out of the coat check room to gratuitously consult. She was just telling us that we'd have to take off all the drywall when Big Marv rounded the corner.

"Marv, do we have to take this drywall down? Couldn't we sand it down or something?" I asked.

"Shit no, just paint it," Marv said.

The lesbian contractor was aghast. "You can't paint it. It won't stick to the old glue. It'll all chip off."

"You can paint a turd if it's dry," Marv answered.

You sure can, Marv. A week later, I found a dog turd from Benny's new boxer puppy, Blu, who spent most of her days at the bar, dried up next to the couch in the storage room. I took a can of silver spray paint and proved it. I taped it to a piece of paper and wrote our new motto under it and hung it in the office. Marv would occasionally spy on their progress in the coat-check room. He told me, "She's putting the coat racks directly into aluminum studs. Coats are heavy. They'll rip right outta those walls."

"I'm sure you're right, Marv, but I'm not saying a fucking thing to any of them."

The second week of January rolled around and it was time for the vote, the one that would decide our fate. Benny, Elena, Patricia, our investor, and I all went down to city hall. We sat in the hallway waiting. I was on the floor with my back against the wall when the door gusted open. It took me a second to recognize the man striding toward me as the mayor of Minneapolis. I barely had time to stand before he was shaking my hand.

"Good to meet you. Hey, good luck today. I have a good feeling about the vote," he said.

"Uh. Thank you so much. It's an honor to meet you," I said. And then he was gone.

I turned to Benny, "Wasn't that the mayor? How the hell does he know who I am? What just happened?" I still have no idea how he knew who I was.

We walked into the chambers. There was hardly anyone else in the public seating area. I was terrified. This project had depended on the circumstantial luck of a hundred different long shots, and this was the longest. We needed everything we had, but we needed this most of all. We all sat. I held Benny's hand. We faced the full council, sitting on elevated chairs in a semicircle looking down on us. My adversarial gay was seated to the far left. After some formalities, the agenda turned to the Neighborhood Group recommendations. Pi was in Ward 2, so we wouldn't have to wait long. And then another miracle occurred. My cartoon foe got up and left the room. The vote for Ward 2's recommendations was approved without incident. He abstained from the vote. That was it. We got our liquor license.

Shit was getting real. It was time to find a staff.

# CHAPTER THIRTY-FOUR

# LIKE FLIES TO A MAGIC PAINTED TURD

I received a call from an acquaintance of mine I'd once spent a charming evening flirting with at a show. "Hi Tara, it's Tif. You remember me. Say, I heard you were opening a bar and I thought I'd do you a favor and work for you. I'll tend bar."

I did remember Tif. She was not easily forgotten. She had long, curly red hair and eyes like Hart's. Her wit was always a little quicker. She could talk faster than anyone in Minnesota and spends every moment in an improv skit.

A friend of a friend walked into the bar another day, asking if we had anyone to run our kitchen. She was a normal-looking butch who introduced herself as Sammy the Chef. She'd just finished helping another restaurant open and was running their kitchen, but she would leave for the right offer.

I had less than a month until I hoped to open the doors. I had been so focused on obtaining equipment and getting the old dishwasher and vent hood working, I hadn't spent any time planning what I was going to do with the kitchen once it was operational. I still didn't have a menu. The salary Sammy suggested was substantially more than what I'd planned on paying Benny, DJ Bucky, and myself. Plus, I had to pay her to set it all up before we were open. My budget was nearly gone.

She seemed nice enough. It was just one more gamble out

of a Gatling gun of gambles. I hired her on the spot, relieved somebody else would make us a restaurant.

I hired Kim as my art coordinator. She and Chamindika started painting a mural in the pool room and on the wall of the kitchen that faced the dance floor. I didn't have the resources to pay for a mural, but local, queer art was part of my vision.

To get the rest of the staff that it suddenly appeared we might need, DJ Bucky organized a job fair. Benny and I came in early one morning to find there were already people waiting to attend. The first people through the door were Carrie and Toni Stanton.

Carrie and Toni were a couple with two kids. Carrie was tall with short, bleached blond hair, lots of tattoos, and heavy eyeliner. Though she addressed Benny and me with professional deference, there was no doubt she could demolish both of us in a bar fight. She explained she was mostly a housewife but wanted to waitress to get out of the house and have a little fun. Toni's head was shaved smooth. On the back of it were bullhorns tattooed over the breadth of her skull. Under that, in loopy cursive, were the words, *Big Daddy*.

And that she was. She was about three hundred pounds and moved with exuberance and grace. She was quick-witted and casually eloquent. She explained to me that she'd run security at a strip club in East St. Paul and had a loyal crew at her disposal. She was very excited about a new dyke bar. She was wondering what my plans were for security.

Again, I hadn't made plans. I hadn't planned on making it this far. I hadn't wanted my hubris to jinx anything. I saw no reason I shouldn't defer to Big Daddy's expertise on this issue. That day I gained my own private mafia with a smile and a handshake.

After hiring Toni, Benny and I emerged from the office to

find that other people had shown up. Lots of people. "I guess we should pretend like we know what we're doing and talk to them," I said.

Benny and I spotted someone who looked familiar. She was a petite, stunning brunette with excellent fashion. It took a minute for us to remember we'd seen her in a burlesque performance we'd been to. She was the one who stripped while hula-hooping.

"She wants to work here?" I said. "She's way too cool for us. Holy shit, she's coming over here."

Tawnya approached us and handed us her resume. She even seemed a little nervous. She wanted to be a server. She said everyone called her Sweet Pea. She relaxed a little when we admitted that we'd seen her show. "Maybe we could perform here sometime," she said.

"That would be amazing," I replied.

A friend of Sammy's approached us. Shandell. She was ridiculously beautiful. Curly blond hair, big, flawless smile. She explained that she used to bartend for a long-established monthly lesbian night and that the customers loved her.

"I'll bet they do," I said.

A regular of Benny's from the coffee shop came. Ruth was a tall, exotic ginger with dramatic model features. She'd been bartending at First Ave downtown since she was nineteen.

DJ Bucky's girlfriend, Stevie, had also been a server. She was another stunning, petite brunette but an entirely different creature than Sweet Pea. Stevie was all rock 'n' roll. She was smart and quick to laugh. We had already casually hired her after the Halloween party, but she came to the job fair anyway.

We had a share of friends who'd already asked for a job. Benny's girlfriend, Roxanne, was on the roster. She'd worked in the service industry since she was fourteen. She rounded out our trio of hot, petite brunettes. She brought along a couple of her coworkers from Chiang Mai Thai. She introduced Heather as the most competent, hardworking server she'd ever worked with. And she brought Corey, a tall, sweet straight boy who could bartend. Roxy's best friend's husband, Grover, also needed a job. He was one of those stoners you can't help but adore because he'd do anything for you.

I hired another server, Melissa, who'd been serving me and Patricia at a pizza joint for years. And the Gailor needed a job. Everybody called her Gailor because she had been in the navy and she was gay. I hired my friend Lea to barback. She was part of the gayborhood and a hot butch folk singer. An old friend of mine from the Wedge, Spencer, came sniffing around. Spencer was one of my pretty straight boy friends. He was disappointed I'd hired someone else to run security, but I told him he could work security when he had time. I also gave his wife, Cole, a serving job.

We'd hired Kate the carpenter at the Halloween party and named her Junior. Sweet Pea convinced me to hire her girlfriend, Mea, a very stylish soft butch. They would both be barbacks.

Sammy assembled her own crew for the kitchen. Klinkert, boy Cole, and Ran had all been friends since high school, which hadn't been that long before. Klinkert and Ran were both dykes, and Cole was an affable werewolf. Kitchen Carrie was a young, enthusiastic hippie dyke who hadn't even come out yet but somehow found us anyway. I didn't want to interfere with Sammy, but I asked to make a couple of additions.

The staff I gained from the job fair were noticeably homogenous. That hadn't been my intention, but I hadn't done any outreach to prevent that. Mea was the only person of color that we'd hired. I hired the only Black person who came to the job fair. Aubrey was a cocky young butch with no experience. She said she could start out doing dishes. I asked Sammy to let her.

At the end of the day, DJ Bucky said, "You know who you should totally get? Marie La Rosa."

I knew she was right. I'd met Marie at a couple of back-yard fires and been acquainted with the legend of her over my time in Minneapolis. She was locally revered as a queen to the punks and the queers and the odd ducks who were plentiful in this town. Marie was a fierce, Sicilian hard femme with a gentle, undeniable significance within the space she occupied. We had enough butches. We needed a matriarch, like Wendy and the Lost Boys.

Sammy bristled when she met Marie. Marie is not easily bossed. I made Sammy find a place for her in the kitchen anyway.

I had been gifted the most talented, resilient, capable, and attractive staff of any dyke bar in the history of dyke bars. I was suddenly the leader of a hot, outlaw service industry gang. They had heard the calling. That's the sound that's made when you pull a queer bar out of your ass nine months after deciding to open one. This was going to happen. And it was going to be good.

# CHAPTER THIRTY-FIVE

# OVERTURE TO QUEER GLORY

The last two weeks were spent tending to smaller and smaller details. Ruth's boyfriend was a hipster tech nerd, so he wired us for internet, which we would need to run credit cards. DJ Bucky spent her time rolling around the building in one of the wheelchairs the Legion left us, drinking PBRs. Ron spent almost all his off-time making sure we'd be ready. He showed Benny how to tile. Benny painted every door frame in the building.

I was now at the bar twenty hours every day. I spent no time trying to be a good boyfriend. Maisy came to the bar occasionally. People tried to encourage her, but she was a nice straight girl from Wisconsin. She didn't know what to do with a pirate ship. I didn't have time to help. I was the one who ran to Home Depot for more CAT 5 wire or to a suburban restaurant graveyard for an old sink. I needed this bar to open on schedule. I didn't have enough money to pay the March mortgage or enough to keep the people I was paying to stay for one more week past the middle of February.

My investor stopped by one day to check on my progress. She brought a snippy gay man for support. She learned that I'd chosen a graphic for Pi's promotional materials. Kim had created several, and I had chosen a simple circle with an ellipsis after our name. My investor and her wingman cornered me and started attacking me about the logo. I said I hadn't cared much about it. It was just one of a thousand tiny decisions I'd made that week. They escalated their derision to screaming at me.

When I got up to leave, they followed me into the pool room. My investor was now physically challenging me to engage her. I don't know what that triggered. Adrenaline, I guess. Perhaps the mounting stress and sleep deprivation finally reached a tipping point. I collapsed on the floor. I started hyperventilating and twitching. My investor loomed above me, screaming that she hoped I died. Then she started laughing at me.

I felt shame at my inability to get up. I couldn't speak. Kim, who was working on the mural in the pool room, went to get Ron, who stormed in and placed himself between me and my investor. Benny rushed in a second later and was the only reason Ron didn't kill her. Her antagonism turned a corner. I was embarrassed I had allowed her to win a fight, but I still felt deep responsibility toward her investment. She didn't seem to understand that we both needed this bar to open as soon as possible. I no longer knew how to meet her expectations.

A few days later, I received a call from Pally. We only talked every few months, but I knew she'd been doing well. She'd bought a house in Oakland with Mike. She and Rina had broken up, but Pally had stopped using junk. She was dating someone new she was really into. The story she told me that day isn't mine to tell, but it was sufficiently tragic and sudden that Patricia and I pooled our remaining resources to buy her a plane ticket to Minneapolis. Pally was coming to stay with me. I told her she could probably work security if she wanted. She could stay as long as she liked. I knew Ingrid would like her. She would arrive the morning after Pi was scheduled to open.

We were going to open on a Friday. We had less than a week. Then we had a day. The morning of our opening day arrived. I left Benny in charge while I ran last minute errands.

While at Menard's picking up walkie-talkies for our security staff, I received a phone call from Benny. "The fire marshal is here. Sammy was cooking chicken when he got here, and he made her stop. He got really mad about it. Then, the trip switch for our sound system if there's an emergency alarm isn't working. He gave us twenty minutes to fix it or he won't let us open."

"That sounds about right," I said. "There's not much I can do about it from here. I'm going to pretend like everything is going to be okay. You're doing a great job."

"You're an asshole."

"I love you too."

I continued to Fleet Farm to pick up some black Dickies short sleeves. I would not allow even a droplet of negativity to escape my consciousness. I knew my watchers would come through for me. If I didn't open tonight, if I did not have a positive cash flow starting that night, I wouldn't last another week. And what would they do then? Crushing depression makes shitty TV. When I got to Wells Fargo, I got a call from Benny. "Ron fixed it. The fire marshal actually shook my hand and wished me luck. Sammy's cooking chicken again. I'm going to shit myself. Where are you?"

"I'm at the bank. I'll be there soon."

One of the many details I had overlooked was the fact that I had no change. I also had no money. I had not a cent of actual cash to put in the tills to start the night. I approached that teller with a smile that channeled the collective superpowers of the entire dominant paradigm. That smile was my inheritance from the most gifted salespeople in Earth's history, my parents. I felt their power as I approached, along with the confidence of a legion of invisible fairy godmothers who'd been watching me my whole life and were now willing my success into the mortal realm. They had decided it was finally my day and I had dreamt the right dream.

I had a fat stack of tired credit cards. I had no idea if there was any money left on any of them, or if the woman behind the counter would actually give me cash against a credit card.

"Well, good afternoon. How are you? I'm opening a bar tonight. I'm very excited about it. I got a business loan from you, from John there just down the hall. Say, I really need some fives and ones to open tonight. I have these credit cards. I was wondering if you could help me out."

"It is not standard procedure to give cash against credit cards."

"Oh, I see . . ." Smile flickers, deep breath.

"What's the name of your bar?"

"It's called Pi." Chin up. Sparkle eyes.

"Do you serve pie?"

Cock head and posture, affect a slight southern accent. "Do you remember those deep-fried pies at McDonald's that used to burn your mouth and they were fried in lard?"

She looked at me and smiled back for the first time, as if she could taste them. "Gimme your cards."

I left the bank with $1,200 in fives and ones. Two hours before opening the doors, I had officially maxed out every line of credit I had access to, and I had less than ten dollars in my personal checking account.

Today was the day. I shaved my head back into a mohawk for the occasion.

I returned to the bar to find my platoon readying our fortress for battle. My only dress code for the front of the house was no nip. They all looked like the perfect outlaw deities I had imagined: tattoos, cleavage, unnatural hair colors, and the shine. Security suited up in black and put in their earpieces. The kitchen was up and running, and it smelled like a restaurant.

There were already people waiting outside to get in. We opened the doors at 4:00 p.m., February 9, 2007. The first dyke bar in Minneapolis was ready to remind them how beautiful they were . . .

# CHAPTER THIRTY-SIX

# WE ARE THE CHAMPIONS

4:00 a.m. Saturday morning, February 10, 2007. I was sitting on a blue beanbag chair in a closet missing most of its walls, next to an open floor safe. I'd spent the past hour improvising a system of paper clips and rubber bands to make the money real.

Benny came in and stood over me with a look on her face you only get when you've just been abducted by aliens, really loud, drunk aliens. We stared at each other, struggling to find a memory of what had just happened that would tether us to time as we had understood it before. We know it would happen again in just hours. The need to strategize those hours suddenly hit us both. "Can we do this?" Benny asked me.

"Come here and hold out your hands," I said.

She sat on the floor in front of me and held out her hands. In each, I placed a clipped and banded loaf of twenties. "That's ten thousand dollars, Benson. We're gangster rappers now."

The laugh we laughed then had become one of our spontaneous rituals that sanctified that time and transformed our bond and changed us both. It was a laugh that simultaneously expressed "Holy shit, look what we did," "Oh shit, what did we do?" "Shit, what are we going to do?" and "Let's do this shit." We alone were adepts of this laugh. We could do with our guts what Tuvan throat singers can do with their vocal chords. The laugh went on for some time. We were the only two that could have done this, made this happen . . . a fact that still makes us laugh.

The only reason I can remember anything that happened that night is because I've told the story so many times. Over a thousand people showed up: our official capacity was around four hundred. I was out of ones and fives in twenty minutes. I thrust five hundred dollars into the hands of a friend of mine (not an employee) and told her to go get as much change as she could. Then the credit card machines went down. I was behind the front bar on one cell phone with Wells Fargo tech support and another with Ruth's boyfriend while "The Electric Slide" blared and the lesbians were five deep at the bar.

February in Minneapolis means coats. As predicted, within hours of opening, the coat racks ripped from the walls, spilling hundreds of winter coats and numbered tags into an indecipherable heap on the floor. My investor was running the coat check that night, showcasing her contribution.

We had a local lesbian folk band do a set on our tiny stage. We had ripped all the drywall off the wall behind the stage during remodeling; lacking the money to replace it, we had simply painted the concrete. That wall now bounced sound waves back toward our new PA system, causing endless, painful, screeching feedback. We assembled a legion of allied customers behind the band, creating a human sound curtain. The band played, the crowd cheered.

A toilet in the back women's restroom caved under the new workload. Water gushing through the bottom quickly flooded the whole bathroom. As I turned the shutoff valve behind the toilet, it came off in my hand. Water shot out of the decapitated valve into my face. I scrambled up a ladder in the back room to the crawl space above the toilets and closed the main valve. Resorting to this cut off water to both back bathrooms. We taped off the entrances to both bathrooms with caution tape. Within minutes, this tape was ignored. The unflushable toilets were used by hundreds.

Cars were towed. Complaints and critique were absorbed. We ran out of beer. Nothing stopped the people from coming. Nothing stopped them from dancing and drinking. Nothing stopped them from being happy and grateful for what was born in that space that night. They were on our side that night. They rooted for us, for the chance we took for them. Then, mercifully, they finally left. The wreckage, the piles of sticky money, the broken glasses, the bottles, the vomit were all welcomed as a new and well-defined task. Everything up to that point had been new, but nothing had been well-defined.

After our 4:00 a.m. sacramental laugh, Benny and I sorted out our tasks for the next twelve hours. That was a Friday night. We opened at 4:00 p.m. to start Saturday night, our second night, busier than the first. Benny drove to Wisconsin to get beer and stopped at Restaurant Depot for more pint glasses. I drove to the airport at 6:30 a.m. to collect my best friend from the nineties to come and live with me. Then I hired an emergency plumber, purchased rolling coat racks from a church, and got black comforters from Target to hang behind our stage. Someone cleaned the toilets. Pi opened for its second night. We were pirates now.

I took Pally back to my house and showed her the bedroom upstairs. I was still living downstairs in the dark, cramped cubby behind the dining room. My house was now the part of my soul that died when I failed Patricia and our happy queer life together. I wanted little to do with it. Pally's grief newly occupied a forgotten room, farthest away from mine. There was plenty of empty space for both.

Maisy was still holding onto the hope that we could be a

happy couple. She had tidied the house a bit, but she too was a reminder of my failure. My home was just the place where I tried to hold new enthusiasm for her over old sorrow in the same face until I could go to bed or back to work. Sleep was almost all I did at home.

Pi was winning. I was the patriarch, the dad who won. I wasn't just everything I'd always tried to be, but more than I'd dreamt I could be. Even my parents were impressed. I had done it my way, and something good came out of that for the first time. That first weekend rained down money like the good lord Freddie Mercury's own divine validation. It was the correct order to the world. The staff and Benny and I formed a family by the end of that first weekend. We had gone into battle together. We'd created our own utopia, and the world outside our doors didn't exist. If it did, it was wrong and unimportant.

If I hadn't had the staff I was lucky enough to employ, the lesbians would've rioted and burned the bar to the ground. At the top of the list of modern efficiencies that most restaurants don't open without, but I couldn't afford, was a computer point-of-sale system. Those things cost like five thousand dollars apiece. We didn't have food runners or bussers. The cash registers I bought for the bars were one step above Fisher-Price. This meant we ran a modern nightclub like a fifties diner, with paper tickets. The servers had to "buy" their drinks from the bar to separate liquor sales. The first night, Tif lovingly trained me how to do a "checkout" for servers and bartenders and added that if I wanted the money from the credit card sales, I had to tell the machines to give it to me. I recorded what I thought was pertinent sales data in an old-school bookkeeping pad.

But it happened. I overcame considerable adversity and made a dream come true. My fantasy life arrived in the real world with the aid of my manic compulsion. I found the extent of my capabilities, and I was a little impressed with myself. I had been so overwhelmed with the success and difficulty of the first two nights that I had failed to anticipate that the adversity would continue.

We opened for our third night. The next day, I was served. My investor was suing me and would continue for the duration of the business. At the initial meeting, I offered to start paying back her investment, with interest. She didn't want the money, she wanted the job, the prestige. But no one wanted to work with her. Everyone thought she was unstable and mean, which wasn't inaccurate. We were at an impasse. Patricia was required to attend all these meetings, which just made them more uncomfortable. We gained a lesbian lawyer for these meetings. She believed in Pi and was willing to help us pro bono, which was good because we didn't make enough money to get sued.

Also, lesbians are exhausting. I'd made myself completely accessible to our patrons, for their critiques and desires. They took full advantage of this offer. The lesbians who were five to ten years older than me mustered the first sortie. As early as the second night, they overwhelmed me with wistful nostalgia, mourning the last full-time dyke bar in the Cities, the Metro, which had closed some years prior. The music at Pi wasn't as good and there were too many babies. It just wasn't the same.

*Of course it's not the same. Your twenties are over, as well as the nineties. We're all sad about it.*

Almost as aggressively, I heard from the stylish twenty-somethings whining about the presence of so many older women and too much tired disco music.

*They are your elders, and this is your legacy. Suck it up and show some respect.*

I also heard from some suburban-looking dykes who were put off by all the tattoos and progressive hairstyles that our staff and some of our patrons had. "Is this a punker bar or something?"

*Oh boy.*

Conversely, the hipster gayborhood, my friends, complained about the draw of hockey moms and softball dykes and wondered if I was encouraging them.

*See fam, this is why we can't have nice things.*

They were all really happy that Pi was open; it just wasn't quite the clubhouse that they'd imagined. They were all full of helpful suggestions so I could tailor it to their own specific needs.

*Oh precious naked Xena and Gabrielle, can they really not see the portal I opened for them? Do they not understand the Divinely Ordained challenge to the dominant paradigm I have manifested for them? It has always been my destiny to be a cult leader (in a good way) and lead them all out of the darkness of normativity, past the expectations of society and their parents, into a righteous apocalypse. Is it too much to ask that they talk to someone they don't already know?*

I listened patiently to many who thought they were merely going to a dyke bar and could not see it was the fulfillment of an ancient prophecy. The more I listened, the more they talked. Nevertheless, the magic that accompanies projects at this level of devotion, risk, and luck began to reveal itself through the cracks of factious whining.

After a couple of weeks of establishing routines and mastering our new domain, the original staff of Pi became a tribe. We were a new people. We relied on each other's love and mutual respect. We knew why we were there. We were safe to be who we wanted to be, and we got the family who encouraged and supported us. It didn't matter if any of our staff were straight. Everyone who was drawn to Pi had a story of isolation, loss, or betrayal. Everyone who understood Pi was on the Pi Program. We knew people could do better.

During build-out, when I was paying Benny with my home equity line, I'd developed the habit of writing "Pi Love" in the memo line of her checks. On the proud day I received my first envelope of payroll checks, I maintained this habit. They had come for the love, and I got to pay them for it.

Those first two months of Pi, paying the bills was easy and pleasurable. The lesbians and other queers who had no home at the gay bars found us and kept coming back. We covered our expenses with Friday and Saturday night, and the rest was a bonus. I didn't worry that we were slow on weekdays, because I wanted to be there for anyone who needed us. We were open seven days a week from 4:00 p.m. to 2:00 a.m.

The magic started with the staff. The younger butches on staff, Ran, Klinkert, and Aubrey in the kitchen and Junior behind the bar, started to discover that acceptance and attractiveness were possible under these conditions, just like I had twenty years before. They began to display signs of confidence and trust.

Shandell and Ruth, both mythical, timeless chimeras with pretty faces and long histories of emotional injury, dated men who liked to date pretty women. Their boyfriends were forced to be on their best behavior if they wanted to come to Pi. The circus of judgement awaited them if they were less than deferential to our princesses. You might get drunkenly body slammed if you were cocky. Another server eventually left her abusive husband because she didn't need him anymore.

Tif just knew we were the circus she'd been waiting to join. Toni brought in her cousin, big Mike, and their buddy Joey to round out the core security staff. And there were always more Stantons if the occasion called for them. Pally was welcomed, as I knew she would be. Everyone liked Pal. Nobody seemed to notice or care she'd started doing junk again. Nobody is more functional on drugs than Pally. She's the one who broke up Pi's first fight, which was between Toni's younger sister, Tracy, and her girlfriend. Pal had Tracy on the ground in a chokehold in seconds, whispering, "Don't make me choke you. I like it." This endeared Pally to the Stanton clan. Mike and Joey started to fix things around the bar.

Most of the staff started spending much of their off-time at the bar. During business hours, we had a smoking lounge in the back of the building, where we kept paint and did the bar's laundry. We had a couch and some chairs and ashtrays. Select customers were allowed access. It became a shitty VIP lounge. After-hours drinking took place in the office where all the managers had desks and we kept our liquor inventory. Everybody put cash in a coffee can and had to leave when the sun came up. Pi was a bar. We were bar people. We spent our downtime drinking, laughing, or crying. Our parties were more fun than yours.

Despite the complaints, Pi drew regulars from all factions. Lesbian lawyers were an unexpected demographic. We had the lesbians over sixty-five group, who had monthly dinners. They told me not to try too hard to make the forty-five-year-olds happy because they were just going to whine anyway; also, our menus were too hard to read. Some real punks found our free pool room in the afternoon. You could smell them when you came through the door. And we sponsored the Octopussies. They were terrible softball players but loyal, loving drinkers.

Older transwomen found Pi, and that is the squishiest part of my reminiscence. In 2007, transmen were just emerging as a significant and seen political and social presence in Urban Queer America. I understood their struggles more personally and had opened with a gender-inclusive bathroom with us all in mind, but transwomen have always occupied their own softly lit dressing room in my heart. The staggering complexities of their vulnerability and strength in the mirror or in the grocery store swell my chest like a southern drum line. Lots of transwomen found a place at Pi to socialize and relax without the threat of unwanted attention that often accompanied their experience at gay bars. Lorna was our regular. Lorna used to be a steelworker. She had steelworker arms and three sons who treated her like shit. She used to drink rusty nails at our bar until, sometimes, her clothes fell off. Then she would drink rusty nails at our bar in her lingerie.

We started to fill our weekdays to attract more people after dinner. On Mondays, I would show queer movies that everyone should have come to but hardly anyone did. On Tuesdays, we somehow got actual celebrities to spin actual records. Venus DeMars and Lori Barbero alternated weeks. Venus had headed up Minneapolis-based transgender glammetal band All the Pretty Horses. She has an immense soul as an artist and a person. Lori, in case you didn't know, was the drummer for Babes in Toyland and once told Courtney Love she couldn't play with her band. I was completely starstruck by both of them and a little dumbfounded they wanted to spin records at my bar for seventy-five dollars and a bar tab. What was even more unbelievable was that none of the hipster gays I knew seemed to care about the cool points they were missing out on because they never showed up. At least I got to drink martinis with Lori and listen to her laugh. She's got a fantastic laugh.

DJ Bucky's girlfriend Stevie, in addition to serving, started a successful karaoke night on Wednesdays, which expanded our list of regulars. Thursday nights were close enough to the weekend that people might be tempted to stay up past their bedtimes for the right event or theme. It was a suggestion box night. We were still getting used to our new roles as event planners. I began to realize opening our doors and playing music wasn't quite enough to cover labor costs.

Thursdays and Sundays are good days for live music at a gay bar. Friday and Saturday nights are about dancing and trying to find someone to have sex with. You don't want to complicate these cash cows with cultural experiences. We had art openings on Thursdays. We tried a funk night. We had a few local bands. We had our first Latina night in April. I organized it with a group of Latina regulars from our Saturday nights. I was happy that they wanted to make a night. It became a monthly event.

I'd also just had what I thought was a productive exchange with a young Latina lesbian about how Pi could attract more people of color. The next day, I was alerted to lively chatter on MySpace about how I was the Man, the condescending Big Bossman who was uninterested in the more marginalized voices in the queer community. I was angry and hurt, but this proved to be a valuable lesson. Even though your heart wants everyone to feel welcome, you should send out invitations anyway. I realized that my position as owner and general manager of this special little island was public and precarious and important. My good intentions made me a target and a leader. I didn't want to let anyone down. Pi was my idea of how people should be treated. My responsibilities felt sacred. Pi wasn't a normal bar. The possibilities were unfolding.

Tif bartended Thursday nights. After the dinner "rush," she would come into the office to drink and brainstorm with me. A queer theater group had just approached Pi to host a meat raffle. (Meat raffles are a thing in the Midwest. If you don't know what one is, it's exactly what it sounds like.) We cackled about lesbians attending a meat raffle; "Should they have a couple rounds for tofu? You know, they should really raffle dildos instead. Oooh, they should play Bingo for dildos. DILDO BINGO!"

We said it at the same time. We knew we had just invented something. We ran through the bar shouting "Dildo Bingo," giddy with our own brilliance. We hammered out the details. Tif would host, obviously. The money we raised from card sales would be given to a different small local nonprofit of our choice every month. Anyone we knew who didn't work in the service industry worked for a small nonprofit, so we had plenty to choose from. I could rent cards from a party supply store and sell and collect them between rounds.

The next day, I called our local woman-owned feminist sex toy store to ask if I could buy sex toys at a discount for our charity event. The owner of the store volunteered to donate sex toys in exchange for promotion during the event and on flyers. When I called the city to inquire about any permits I might need, they informed me that bingo was a highly regulated form of gambling, and I couldn't do it. Oh, Minneapolis, sometimes you're such a square. I just skipped the part where I asked for permission. We decided to hold the first ever Dildo Bingo in early June. Pride month.

# CHAPTER THIRTY-SEVEN

# INTO THE DESERT

Sadly, it was still the end of April. We'd been making money for two and a half months. And then the sun came out. The end of winter is normally a cause for jubilation in Minnesota. I didn't see the sun anymore, so I hardly noticed. All spring meant to me now was a nosedive in revenue. Any bar in Minnesota that doesn't have a sweet patio for summer can expect to lose business. Vitamin D deficiency trumps lesbian solidarity. I hadn't anticipated this.

I hastily filled a thirty-foot section of scrub between Pi and the adjacent warehouse with cheap concrete pavers, and Ron came down and fenced it in. It was a patio, but it looked a lot like the yard that people in solitary use for an hour a day.

It doesn't take long to run out of money when you're running a business. The money left over in my checking account after paying myself a "salary" for the first two months went right back into the business to meet a payroll. Then an old 401k went to another. I started laying the bills out in an evil, judgmental rainbow around my chair in the office, so I could prioritize who to pay and who to put off. Work schedules had to be adjusted. Everybody had to cut back. The stress of imminent doom crept in.

Every day I drank and laughed with my Pi family. That made everything worth it, until I had to go home. Things with Maisy were strained. People at work asked me daily if I'd broken up with her yet. She and Pally didn't get along. Out of my many fantastically dysfunctional relationships, I'd never maintained one that was so wholly disconnected from everything that was important to me.

One day, Maisy called me at work to tattle on Pally. She said there were people at the house who scared her. She thought that they were casing the place, and she was afraid to leave our room.

I was annoyed but left work and came home. The people had left. Pally told me my girl was tripping. They were friends of Pally she met wherever Pally did the things that she never talked to me about. Maisy said she didn't want them in the house again. I wasn't home often enough to be the boss there. I needed them to make it work and take care of shit. They couldn't. When I said to Maisy that maybe it would be a good idea if she got her own place, she said, "Why does the junkie get to stay?" And that was that. Some people in your life always get to stay.

It was good that I broke up with Maisy when I did. My sacred duty as Pi patriarch had largely suppressed the historical shortcomings of my ego. But it would have been implausible for my character to surround itself with hot queer women and not eventually take a romantic interest in one of them. I'd already been giving Marie rides home, and we'd been having long conversations.

Our first Dildo Bingo was an emotional success, and it was lucrative for a Thursday. The Legion had left us an abundance of folding banquet tables and chairs to encourage events like Dildo Bingo. I took an empty beer box and strung rope through the corners to hang from my shoulders and donned a red bistro apron so I looked like a vendor at a baseball game. Music played between rounds while I collected and resold cards and flirted. Tif was brilliant. An instant local icon. And even though I almost lost half my service staff because two hundred people all wanted table service at the same time, Dildo Bingo was born.

It wasn't enough to float us to the end of June, when Gay Christmas happens. I needed our Pride celebration to be huge. I needed it to generate enough money to catch up on everything so we could hobble back into fall. Minneapolis has one of the biggest Prides between the coasts. Even though Pi's location was far from the main festivities, I was confident most of the lesbians from the upper Midwest would show up.

We planned events for all three nights. For Saturday and Sunday, I got permits to have an outdoor festival in our parking lot. We would have live music, fire spinners, and female break-dancers. Kim lined up female graffiti artists from around the country to paint the entire side of our huge building live all weekend. I bought spray paint, had T-shirts made, and beefed up our inventory. I rented a flatbed truck and entered us into the Pride Parade. Sweet Pea got some of her burlesque friends to dance on the back of it while I drove. Toni gathered her extended family to augment security. Sammy planned an outside food tent. We had a beer truck and two extra bars in the parking lot.

Leading up to this weekend, I avoided paying bills more intentionally. Thankfully, you don't have to pay for rental equipment until you return it. Five months after opening, I again extended myself to my financial limit, gambling that my community would show up.

Everyone pitched in to help set up. Patricia volunteered to run the beer truck. Christa volunteered to barback. My staff dressed to accentuate their own assets and encourage tipping. Most of the planning went into Saturday and Sunday, because we were certain that Friday would be busy because we were the only dyke bar in town.

Pride Friday was dead. It was the worst Friday night revenue since we opened. The long-running monthly lesbian night had their annual Pride Friday event downtown, and that's where the lesbians went. I wasn't just sad, I was terrified. If Saturday night wasn't fucking epic, it would mean the immediate end of Pi. I wouldn't even have enough cash to pay the performers or security so I would also have to run away.

Benny and I spent much of the night cleaning up and preparing for the following day. We both fell asleep on an air mattress on the office floor, spooning each other. That's exactly how the woman who cleaned Pi in the morning found us three hours later.

In the morning, somebody gave me some Adderall and we put up tents and bars and scaffolding. Artists started showing up around noon. The sound and light guys and the guys who set up the stage came.

Big Mike came in and handed me six cartons of cigarettes. "I thought we could probably sell these tonight, Boss."

"Thanks Mike. Do you mind if I pay you for these tonight?" I pretended like I was busy, but I didn't have $130 in the safe.

Benny's father decided this would be a good weekend to get married, so Benny had to go do that. And we were ready for Saturday.

We opened at two. I wanted to maximize revenue potential. Everybody looked ready. Everybody looked pretty. We had two entrances, one into the parking lot and one into the building. They were connected through a side door that was normally a fire exit. Artists started painting. Performances started at three. A few people trickled in. I knew it wouldn't get busy right away. I kept my chin up. By five, there still wasn't more than a hundred people between the bar and the parking lot. There were almost as many performers and staff. Patricia and her beer truck crew were getting drunk. Around eight, I started to panic, but held out hope. It could still be okay. Benny returned from the wedding and tried to reassure me. At nine, Sammy came up to me and asked if she could shut down the food tent and start drinking. I resisted the urge to break her nose and told her to give it another hour.

Marie suggested we take a walk around the block. I trusted Marie. We'd already made out a couple times, and I liked her near me. We started walking down the alley and around the block. She told me how much Pi meant to her and to a lot of other people. She said it might not happen that night, but if it didn't, Pi still meant something, and I should be proud to go down in a blaze of glory. I was crying softly and laughing gently as we rounded the corner back into the alley toward the back of the stage.

One of the security guards ran to meet me. She grabbed my hand and said, "Boss, you have to come see this."

She pulled me to the front of the parking lot, where Pally was collecting cover. The line of people waiting to get in went down the driveway, down the sidewalk, and around the corner. The line waiting to get in the front door was even longer.

They came.

I ran to find Benny. I didn't see her again for the next four hours. For the rest of the night, we ran from bar to bar to bar, removing wads of twenties and making change from the tip jars, as fast as we could.

Then we lost the softball dykes. At 2:00 a.m., the task of herding five thousand drunk lesbians out the door became unnecessarily controversial. Everyone felt battleworn. The security staff had been harassed and ignored throughout the day. I was sitting on my bean bag chair next to the safe, trying to make sense of the sweaty cash globs so I could pay the people who needed it right away.

The yelling started before I had a chance to look up. When I did, Big Daddy Toni, the head of my security familia, and

GoGo Pimp Tif, who I was fucking right then, loomed over me, arguing why Big Mike should or should not be fired immediately. Apparently, while Mike was ushering people out the door, a wee lesbian resisted by smashing her freshly purchased French fries into Mike's face. Mike reacted as we all might; he pushed her away. Unfortunately, due to Mike's size relative to the small fry shover, this looked more like Mike throwing a woman against a wall. The queen of the St. Paul softball dykes witnessed the incident and was now outside calling the cops and yelling that our staff hated women.

Mike stood behind Toni practically in tears, offering to quit. Toni told me she would take her entire team away if Mike was fired. Tif said we had to fire Mike or we'd lose all of our customers.

*Oh shit, I think I'm the boss right now.*

It's hard to know what's right at moments like this, and if what's right is the same thing as good for a business with good intentions. But a decision was immediately necessary. So I said, "Mike is family, and he isn't going anywhere. Tif, this is none of your business, and I really need you to help shut down the bar and count your money. Toni, keep Mike in here and send someone nice outside to make sure that woman is okay and talk to the cops when they get here."

The woman was okay. Everybody went back to work. The softball dykes largely boycotted us, which was kinda okay even though it wasn't. Everybody forgave Mike and me eventually, but Pride wasn't even close to over. It took me until seven in the morning to sort and count the money. We'd just sold thirty thousand dollars in less than four hours. That day was not our day to die.

Pally and Junior slept on the stage that night to guard the equipment. Tif helped me count the money and fell asleep on my lap with her head on my chest. That's how the cleaning woman found us two hours later.

At nine, I loaded Pally, Sweet Pea, and Mea into the rental truck and drove downtown. We took our place in the parade lineup, and I fell asleep with my head out the window. Sometime later, I was gently roused by a pair of false eyelashes upon bedazzled lids looking down onto my face, imploring me to start the truck. The truck now sported a mylar fringe, and Pi T-shirts had been affixed to both doors with duct tape. Despite our hasty preparations, we were a hit. To be sure, the credit for that went to the barely clad, talented performers, dancing and flirting all the way down Hennepin Avenue on the back of our rented flatbed. But the crowd knew who we were. We were the new promise in town. Our "float" was a perfect metaphor for our bar: cheap and tacky and sexy and perfect. They loved us. We won the award for crowd favorite that year.

By the time we got back to the bar, it was time for Pride again. We had an uncomplicated and profitable Pride Sunday. Then it was time to break it all down and clean up. Marie stayed with me Sunday night. The cleaning woman found us sleeping on the air mattress when she came in.

The rental equipment that wasn't picked up Monday morning had to be returned. I used the truck to take back the scaffolding, made an enormous cash deposit, and then returned the truck. My investor called me during my errands to scream about me sleeping with all my staff and how the lawyers were going to hear about it. Her friend the cleaning woman had told on me. She was uninterested in the fact that I hadn't actually had sex with anyone that weekend, because I'd been working for seventy-two hours straight. She couldn't care less that her investment had survived another week.

I couldn't care less that she was yelling at me. I hung up

on her. I was atwitter with the euphoria of exhaustion and salvation.

A week before Pride, Ruth had suggested we close Pi on Monday and all go tubing. That sounded like the best idea ever. I reserved a party bus to take the whole staff. I made sure we could drink and smoke on that bus.

The only things in the history of the world that have ever kept the zombie apocalypse at bay are tiny, momentary triumphs of devoted bands of underdogs fighting the good fight. Solidarity, altruism, and swagger occasionally win. We survived another battle. Ruth said the lesbians clawing for Mich Golden Light were like orcs attacking at Helm's Deep. Nobody worked for Pi because it was easy and lucrative.

These victories demand celebration. The cosmic watchers of human history are especially charmed when these celebrations involve a herd of vampire pirates descending upon a small town on the Minnesota-Wisconsin border to float down a river on inner tubes with as much alcohol as they can keep track of.

Everyone was half canned by the time we got there. Just the right mixture of exhaustion and alcohol is a glorious high. About forty of us spilled out of a flat black party bus, trailing smoke and mirth. Unwarned onlookers froze as they took in the tattoos and gender functional swim apparel. After repeated exhortations from the proprietors that this was a "family" river, I ascended atop the nearest picnic table to rally the troops. I thanked everyone individually. I thanked the platoon. "You went to war for me, and we won. Pi Love!"

By the time we returned, I had lost my shirt, my bra, my hat, my sunglasses, and a shoe. But I was still smoking a dry cigarette. Boy Cole, from the kitchen, gave me the shirt off his back. I spotted Big Mike bringing up the rear of our flotilla, carrying Benny's girlfriend, Roxanne, who was half-frozen and passed out. He was wearing one of our server's floppy sun hats that had been lost earlier that day. I was glad he was still with us, that we were still whole.

With the money we earned from that first Pride, I was able to pay for that weekend and catch up on some more aggressive outstanding debts. But then, we were in the same financial situation as before. August and September were bleak. I did use this period to get rid of Sammy. I already had to talk with her about how there was no yelling at Pi. When I asked Sammy to take a substantial pay cut and make what the other managers made, she offered to run the whole kitchen herself and fire the rest of the staff. I assured her it would be better if she left. I gave everyone else in the kitchen a raise, and we started running it cooperatively.

It was during this time that Marie and I started having an affair. She was a force I couldn't resist. It was also probably the only pairing the family would've accepted. I was the dad and she was the mom. She happened to also need a place to live. She started off with her own room in my house, but when people who live together start banging each other, boundaries blur. Pally liked Marie, which was enough for me. Marie brought air and color back to my house. She also made Pally soup and got me to come back upstairs.

# CHAPTER THIRTY-EIGHT

# KEEPING UP WITH QUEER AND THE MAN

I got a citation from the city for having graffiti on my building. They'd received a complaint about the murals that were created during Pride. The city said I had two weeks to paint the entire building, or they'd send someone to do it at our expense. I brought the offending document to the bar, where Benny was bartending. I was bitching when a tattered boy I hadn't noticed, sipping on a tropical cocktail, chimed in, "You can get a mural exemption from the city for your side wall, and I can help you with the back. It's why I came in, actually. I can get a crew here tomorrow, probably by noon, to fill your back wall with murals too. It'll only take a couple of days, if that."

I took in his appearance and considered his bravado.

"How much?" I replied.

"Oh, they'll paint for free. Can you get us some paint?"

"There's tons of it left over from Pride. Really? You know people?"

"I know everybody."

I didn't really expect much, but what could it hurt to show up at noon on the off chance he wasn't full of shit? I came in the next day to a crew of skinny hipsters waiting for me. I opened the back door, where the paint and ladders were. They went right to work and remained well into the night.

Over the next couple of months, random dudes would show up at random times to paint our walls. The murals started wrapping all the way around our building to our smoking patio in the back. Marie made them hot cocoa and quesadillas, and I brought them beer. We got our exemption from the city, and our building became the coolest in town.

The temperatures mercifully dropped, and the snow started to fall in October. The lesbians abandoned their backyards and came back to Pi on the weekends. We had our second Halloween party. It fell on a Saturday that year. I dressed in my traditional slut drag. I let Sweet Pea do my makeup so I looked exactly like Elizabeth Taylor as Cleopatra, if she was also old Elizabeth Taylor going through chemo.

We had a kids' Halloween party. Lesbians and hipsters from all over the Twin Cities were thrilled to bring their children to a bar and let them run around while they drank. We hung decorations and bought candy. DJ Bucky put Disney movies on the big screen and even took music requests from children, who have the same taste in music as lesbians. Some lesbian moms approached me, objecting to Disney movies because of their traditional gender portrayals, and suggesting healthier snack alternatives for little IzzyAbbyStellaOlive, who doesn't eat refined sugar and is lactose intolerant. "This is a bar. Can I buy you a drink?" I responded.

Then Pi was accused of being racist. A couple of color came in for dinner and got shitty service from a server who was a little shitty at her job. I was horrified. A new regular of ours who ran a listserv for queer women of color alerted me to the criticism. Ann was white, but her partner was Black, and they'd been figures in the QPOC community for years. DJ Bucky invited Rox Anderson, a respected and talented QPOC community leader, to join our team as a consultant.

Rox initially started a soul night on Thursdays with her friend and DJ, Carla.

Ann sent out questionnaires to her list and set up round-table discussions for me. I spent weeks answering questions and addressing concerns. We all started planning a more high-profile night catering to the queer Black community in Minnesota. We enlisted two other DJs. DJ Naughty Boy already spun for us most weekends and had also been a regular DJ for house parties. Ann and her partner, Susan, introduced us to Lady L, an elder and iconic local DJ whose partner happened to be a stud.

And then we met the queen. Miss Eva had been doing the cooking for house parties for years. She and her partner, Barbara, were respected elders. Miss Eva agreed to come in and run our kitchen one night a month if our staff would follow her direction. Her cooking alone was enough to legitimize our endeavor.

We had our first First Friday in December. Our work payed off. Some people even came from Chicago for the occasion. There was a VIP section for elders. My job was to buy the studs of this crew tequila shots and make them laugh. I was good at that job, and I loved my work. Marie learned how to make proper macaroni and cheese and shared her weed with Miss Eva. I received many head nods that night that were of the "not a bad job" variety. Pi's circumference got a little bigger.

The kink community also found Pi, especially in the hours before we were open. It was mostly queer, but whatever. A bondage club had ropes demonstrations on some Saturday mornings. A gay leather organization had a brunch on a Sunday, then their minions cleaned up in an extraordinarily efficient manner. The Bizarre Bazaar was held at Pi one Saturday before Christmas. This was an event that combined a local artisan craft fair with a play party. There were flogging demonstrations on stage. The promise of a full body latex vacuum suit was revealed on the floor of our pool room. There was a woman restrained on all fours in a large dog kennel while a dildo attached to a roto hammer entertained her from behind. The bar was filled with moans, whimpers, and cracks for four glorious hours while Marie and I sold her biscuits and gravy through the Pi Hole.

Since most directors of queer community social justice and advocacy groups are lesbians, they all came to Pi to network as well as pick up the ladies. Many of them saw the potential in Pi's large space, kitchen, and audio/visual capabilities and started asking to hold events there. I guilted many more of them by pointing out that holding fundraisers and banquets at the Hilton downtown didn't support our community. We were still barely paying the bills, and I needed to piece together any activities that would get more people through our door. We diversified our offerings out of financial necessity, but that ended up pulling more people into our circle. Pi became more of a community center.

Our new regulars, Reverend Laurie and her partner, Neecie, organized a Bible study series. We had a drag Purim celebration put on by a local queer Jewish organization. The Twin Cities queer chamber of commerce had their young entrepreneurs' mixers. Our local female roller derby team organized an arm-wrestling and football-toss fundraiser with our local female football team. A representative from the Minnesota Lynx started running small promotions on dance nights. Some of the Lynx also showed up.

The HRC and Logo sponsored *The L Word* season premiere at Pi. One of the national directors of the Human Rights Campaign liked to come to Pi and drink martinis and demand audiences with me. She was a butch professional who used to be in the military. She told me once that after she got out, she sold land mines for a living. "Mother Teresa was my main competitor," she used to chuckle. She liked to talk to me about business, and she loved arguing with me about politics. It was right then that the Equality and Non-Discrimination Act was up for debate before Congress. The HRC had lobbied hard to get it there. It was a piece of legislation that would make it a federal crime to discriminate against the LGBT community. The only way they could get enough votes to pass it, however, would be to take the *T* out of LGBT, and the HRC had signed off on the altered bill.

She told me that incremental change is the only way to get things done. I reminded her that she was full of shit and that the movement she capitalized on was created by those in our community who were most often beaten, murdered, or harassed by the cops. *That would be the T, Linda. Did you miss Queer History 101?* Since this was the exact kind of horseshit that led me to open Pi in the first place, I was always happy to debate such an influential leader in our community and spread my gospel. She seemed to enjoy herself and want me to approve of her work. She even took me to Washington, DC, for twenty-four hours for National HRC Lobby Day. I was the only woman in a man's suit and the only person with a mohawk. I took pictures with both of our senators that day, but I didn't bother sending them to my mother.

Another lesbian lawyer walked into my life. This one would stay. Joni was big, loud, and Italian, as well as a very fancy lawyer. She had two kids from her former marriage, a boy and a girl. Joni used to bring them in for happy hour to play pool. We all thought the boy was a girl and the girl was a boy, which was consistent with our theme. The girl was younger, about seven, and she hadn't made up her mind yet whether she was going to be a girl or a boy. She loved Pi. And she really loved Benny. One day, she walked right up to the bar and climbed on a stool. She stared right at Benny and asked, "Are you a girl-boy or a boy-girl?"

Benny's life changed again. She started researching how to transition into a man that night. He couldn't wait to get his boobs cut off. Our barback, Junior, had already begun his transition and had moved away from Pi. Transitioning was becoming a thing our community was doing with increasing frequency and visibility, like cheesy pinup tattoos in the mid-nineties. When questioned about my personal inclinations toward the process, I would say, "I want muscles and facial hair, but I wanna keep my tits. I wanna be the king of the weirdos."

Spring happened again. It was just as terrible as the spring before, except we didn't have nearly the cushion we'd had. I didn't have any more 401ks. I started bouncing checks with regularity. Wells Fargo had this nifty policy of rearranging the order of debits against my account so that they were processed largest to smallest amount instead of chronologically. They did this so they could maximize overdraft charges. This policy has since been outlawed, and Wells Fargo has been sued and fined. I'm still waiting for my check. I know not having enough money is also an irresponsible practice, but anyone who's ever been in my position or poor would understand. I ended up with about $15,000 in overdraft charges.

We did more special events trying to bridge the abyss until Pride. Tif and I invented queer speed dating, more accurately "Queer Speed Dating Is Hard." Between lesbian identity sensitivities and social inelegance, it really is hard. We came up with dozens of conversation prompts having to do with kitties and puppies. We made up the Pi-cathlon with bar games. We had art openings every month.

Dildo Bingo continued to increase in popularity. It started to draw some grown straight women, like Big Marv's wife and daughter and my Aunt Sonya from Owatonna. I started overhearing conversations about sex toys and masturbation from some ladies who had shown up to support the monthly charity but were coming back next month to win the big dick.

We held more fundraisers, for nearly everybody who needed them. It was a win-win for a bar. We wanted to help people, but it's okay that people also bought food and drinks and that helped us. These occasions endeared Pi to all who attended and refined our reputation as a community resource. We had a fundraiser for a Minneapolis punk who lost her eye. The Eye Ball. There was one for a hip-hop dancer who developed breast cancer. We had one for Lorna, so she could get her vagina. Shandell got the West Nile virus and was in the hospital. We had a butch auction for her. They had to auction me off twice. There was one for a family in the neighborhood who lost their house to fire. And we had to have one when we heard that Ron was diagnosed with pancreatic cancer. That one was hard. Ron made it though, and Benny still has the grill he bought from the silent auction.

Pi was nominated for community awards and named the best place to pick up lesbians. People in this town started to really get us. Our calendar fleshed out with events. We added Trivia to Tuesdays. Shanny Mac organized a drag show. I'd wanted one since we opened, but my liquor license didn't allow "cabaret." We figured out a way around it by having the performers sing live instead of lip sync. She produced "Live, Nude, Drag" at Pi, and it was the best drag show in town. It still wasn't enough to pay all the bills. I just did the best I could. Pride was coming up again. We knew what we were doing this time. And my mother was coming. I wanted her to see it. She also loaned me some money for change when she got there.

I planned another outdoor festival for Saturday and

Sunday nights. This time we would have four outside bars, plus the beer truck. We also had a couple beer tubs inside the building. Nothing was going to clog my revenue stream. Everybody knew who we were now. Lesbians from all over the upper Midwest had made pilgrimages to Pi for the past year. We planned Pride editions of Dildo Bingo and First Friday. My mother was finally going to witness undeniable proof that I was sort of famous and kind of in charge in a world of my own creation.

My mother was treated like a celebrity. Everybody loves a mother at a queer function when she is there to support her queer offspring. Plus, she's just so good-looking and charismatic. She got a standing ovation at Dildo Bingo when Tif introduced her. Several studs at First Friday were enthusiastic about dancing with her, which she enjoyed. The entire staff was deferential and flattering and brought her snacks. Customers approached her with testimonials about the magic of Pi and my dedication as a community leader.

My mother has a fundamental aversion to flattery and sycophancy. She finds the sentiment tedious and time-consuming. It distracts from hard work and satisfying difficulty. She's never wanted me to get a big head, especially if it involves my way of doing things or reliance on my bizarre secret skill set. If there was ever a circumstance where my mother could've finally grasped my secret magic, it would've been this weekend. But Pi's financial challenges, which she was aware of, though not to their dire extent, negated the possibility that she would allow the magic to move her fully. She had a little fun, but her focus was on achieving maximum profit from that weekend.

She was unstoppable on Saturday. During set up, if she decided we were running short on extension cords or twinkly lights or garbage bags, she would speed off to Target and return with carloads of anything we might need. During the actual events of that night, she hauled trash like a boss. We sold almost twice as much as the year before and it was comparatively effortless. Tif, who worked the front bar from open to close, sold over $5,300 at her till. That would remain the standing sales record for Pi. I began calling her Agent 53.

Sunday, Mom rode with me in the burlesque truck in the parade while the crowds cheered even louder than the year before. She left Sunday evening and told me to get that building refinanced. "I got it under control, Ma."

I didn't really, but that would have to wait until Tuesday. Post-Pride Monday was for tubing and drinking. I managed to keep my shirt this year. I basked in the triumphant respite of not worrying about money for one whole afternoon. The party bus had karaoke this year. The Pi Love Tribe had fought together and laughed together and loved each other for more than a year now. We knew we were special.

I'd spent most of my life fantasizing that an alternative reality might really exist. I'd always dreamed of that place where everyone is seen and cared for and nobody gets to be a dick. I never understood why people choose to be mean. Pi came out of me fully formed as the grand, desperate hope my imagination demanded. It was perceived and reflected by people and cosmic forces alike. It is possible for a mortal to conjure fairy bubbles, but they take constant feeding and affirmation and luck to survive.

# CHAPTER THIRTY-NINE

# SUPERHERO ANEMIA

Unfortunately, the forces of darkness are attracted to spontaneous joy and unscripted solidarity. My investor was still suing me. She had my financial records subpoenaed. Against the advice of my patient and generous lawyer, I invited her lawyers to the bar and opened the books for them. I would've been thrilled had they found the money my investor was so certain I was hiding. I've never been gangster clever like that.

After the euphoria of the second Pi Pride, my body and my shine were showing signs of fatigue. I'd gotten fat again. I drank every day and lived on tater tots. My skin developed a slight greenish hue. The stress of never having quite enough money was starting to chip away at my soul and stunt my adrenal glands. We were just getting good. There must be a way for this to be sustainable, to grow what we had become.

The Republican National Convention was coming to the Twin Cities at the end of August. I was shocked to learn that most of the larger venues in Minneapolis had been bought out for special events for Republicans. Minneapolis is not normally a conservative-friendly town. What do I know about running a viable business? Pi had not been approached. We decided to throw an anti-RNC event and raise money for organizers protesting at the convention, The Flaming Carnival of Deviance.

Two weeks before the event, Pi got a special present from the Republicans. The Republicans had printed guidebooks for delegates highlighting entertainment offerings in the Twin Cities. A brief national controversy arose when all of them were recalled and destroyed because it was discovered that a gay and lesbian section was included. At the top of the list of the offensive festivities highlighted in this section, as quoted by a senator's aide during a real press conference, was Dildo Bingo! He actually said "dildo" on national television. Tif and I were beside ourselves with pride. We cost the Republicans money, and we were famous for the span of half a national news cycle.

For the carnival, we partnered with Bedlam Theatre. They were a Minneapolis alternative performance institution, headed by a talented, unyieldingly brilliant band of rebel freaks. Even if some of them weren't queer, they were queer as Pi defined it—someone who doesn't suck and is some kind of awesome. They organized a freedom-of-expression cabaret and a fire show by Rah, one of their queens. We scheduled a burlesque troop, not caring about violating our liquor license. We would also have live music well past our official cutoff time and Lori Barbero would DJ. I rented a dunk tank and one of those hammer-ding games. Kelly Brazil, our extraordinarily overqualified dishwasher, made a ring toss game from some old dildos. This night would become my favorite event at Pi.

We were going to do it our way. The increasing financial instability of Pi had emboldened us to take greater risks and make more vocal political declarations about what we stood for. We were fighting a larger darkness now. The staff had largely stopped calling Pi a dyke bar by this time. We were a queer bar now. You could still be a dyke at Pi, you just couldn't be a dick anymore. The Pi Love Tribe would not tolerate judgement. Our looming demise had consecrated our sanctuary.

Everyone dressed as whatever they thought their embodiment of a carney looked like. I used the clippings from my freshly shorn head to form big chops and a porn stache. I borrowed one of Marie's bustiers but donned my usual black Carhart's and steel toes. I would be in charge of the hammerding attraction. One of our regulars, Cindy, better known as Tits McGee because of her unlesbianish fake tits and brash demeanor, volunteered to be the barker in our dunk tank. Nobody knows how to antagonize someone into spending money to shut her up better than McGee. Even Benny wore a kilt.

Everything about the night was perfect. The warm, orangey glow of Midwestern summer streetlights delineated the borders of the electric fairy world manifested in a once weedy, semi-industrial parking lot. Everyone we loved came and nobody else did. Together, we laughed that laugh of moral certitude, pirate magnetism, and defiance that everyone there shared. It went on all night. The Republicans were over in St. Paul, preaching their restrictions on the world. We were in a completely different universe, celebrating everything they would never have.

The next day was the first day of September. My contract for deed on the building was due to expire the last day of September. We needed to find traditional financing to buy the building or lose it. It was the middle of 2008. The biggest financial crisis since the Great Depression was underway and had left everybody who wasn't a bank thoroughly fucked. Big banks' questionable banking practices were about to be rewarded with bailouts and bonuses, while Wells Fargo told me that Pi's revenue forecasts fell just shy of their threshold for financing. I went to bank after bank. Even when it was a smaller bank that seemed more sympathetic, they would always end the conversation by reminding me that even if Pi was more solvent, my business partner was suing me and no bank would take on that additional liability.

I tried to call the owners of the building to renegotiate our contract. I explained that even if they got the building back, no one else would be able to open a business in it. The banks weren't going to loan money to any new restaurant or bar. But they were too excited by the thought of repossessing a turnkey business. After all, I'd put about $300,000 worth of improvements into it.

A couple of my regulars told me they'd always wanted to own a bar and wished they could be a part of this one. They came to a couple of banks with me. One of the banks even agreed to loan us some money. It was just $200,000 shy of what we needed. My new friends then offered to invest $100,000 of their savings and put up their house as collateral for the rest. The bank agreed to the new terms. I said I needed to think about it.

I went back to the bar and spent all night thinking about it, smoking and playing Bejeweled by myself. I could tell they were earnest, just like I had been. They were willing to risk everything because they believed our community needed to keep a place like Pi, just like I did. Unlike me, they were both schoolteachers and foster parents with real stability and children who needed them.

I couldn't do it. I couldn't pull two more dreamers into the risk of Pi, because I knew its success hinged upon my crumbling ability to change the world. I could see no way to save Pi. I had to concede. We weren't going to make it.

I told Benny first. He was sad, but I could tell he was a little relieved. He'd given all he could to this dream and worked harder than anyone to make it happen. He never would've abandoned me had I made the decision to continue. But Pi had revealed the promise of a new life for him. I couldn't blame him for wanting to live it.

I called an all-staff meeting to tell the rest of the family. They weren't surprised, but it was devastating. I told them we would stop paying the mortgage after September, and it would take two months for the owner to evict us. We would close in the middle of November. We had a party, an early wake. We resolved to make the most of our remaining time together and go out in style.

Pi was no longer my project for personal redemption. It hadn't been for some time. It had become more special and farther reaching than I had anticipated. We had succeeded in pulling in people from divergent backgrounds and cultural affiliations and getting them to see each other. Bridges had been built. Strange alliances had been forged. Pi, for many, was a refuge of acceptance and care. Lesbians from small towns and suburbs had found the possibilities I had intended.

My cat, Bell, died at the end of the first week of September. My friend, Christa, came over to my house to put her down. Christa had been my only touchstone to the reality outside of Pi. She saw what I would have to face once I'd lost it, things my brain wouldn't allow me to see yet. Bell had been my faithful companion through all of my grown-up darkness. She wouldn't be there when I came home from Pi for the last time. I hadn't been around much for her the last two years of her life. Christa stroked my head while I clutched my dead friend for well over an hour and sobbed.

I crafted a letter for our customers that I hung near the entrance honoring the staff and the community that had made my dream come true. I expressed my gratitude for getting to be a part of it. It announced our closing date, November 15, 2008.

When everybody learned Pi was closing, they realized

what was being lost. Our last two and a half months of business were busier than our first. Everyone came. Every day began and ended with tears and stories and wine. There was an uncommon magic in that time of ongoing grief. The community, the staff, the regulars started to draw even closer together. Everyone was on their best behavior and old grudges and superficial judgements were temporarily suspended. Something special and complicated was about to die. It wasn't a time for blasphemy.

Even the softball dykes came back for one more event. They asked to hold their annual beer bust at Pi. After going through nine kegs of Mich Golden Light in three hours, I was passing through the dance floor when "The Electric Slide" started playing. The organizer of the event was attempting this line dance with all the natural rhythm of a softball dyke. I approached her from behind, grabbed her hips, and began to lead her through the steps I had learned so long ago. This spectacle drew a crowd and raucous approval from her fellow jocks. After the song, I was behind the front bar. She approached me and reached across the bar. She stared into my eyes as she caressed the side of my shaved head and said, "This doesn't matter. We're the same. You and I are the same."

*Well, you do have a Bush/Cheney bumper sticker on your truck, but of course we are. We always were.*

Pally moved home to Oakland before Pi closed. She had healed enough to return. Marie and I were making a home together. Or mostly, Marie was preparing a home for us that would sustain us through upcoming catastrophe.

In early October, Kate Bornstein, the author of *Gender Outlaw* and kind of a big deal, came to Pi to give a talk. A queer organization had paid for her appearance in Minneapolis and decided to have the event at Pi. The house was packed. We had recently hired Zealot to work in our kitchen. Zealot was an African American Satanist genderqueer just coming into their own possibilities as a true transgressive force in the world. They wore understated eye makeup, big boobs, and little devil horns to work every day. Zealot was very excited to meet Kate. After their joyful acquaintance, Kate invited Zealot back to our hastily constructed "green room" that took up a corner of our enormous storage room. I learned later that she had asked Zealot to help her put on her corset for her performance. We were not able to keep Zealot in our kitchen for the duration of Pi, but Facebook tells me they went on to be a noted queer performance figure and they've found their voice.

Pi's third Halloween was the most successful. We'd gotten good at not giving a shit as a collective. Kelly Brazil ended the night by riding her purple Harley through the crowded dance floor with Sweet Pea on the back. I ended the night by being carted home by Marie's visiting Aunt while puking into a plastic pumpkin head. "If you drink like a pirate, you puke like a pirate," she said.

By the time November rolled around, I had been drunk for two months. Every time I resolved to go into work and not drink, some customer or employee would start to reminisce, then cry. My soul was caving in like that old disco ball I'd found in the building a couple lifetimes ago. On the first Tuesday in November, Barack Obama was elected to his first term as President. A couple hundred people came to Pi to witness the event. After his victory was announced, and chants of "Yes We Can" echoed through the bar, my friend Joni, the lawyer, got up on stage to make an impromptu speech. Obama's election had given the room hope. And while that's the last fucking thing I wanted right then, there it was. Joni started revving the crowd up about saving Pi. The community could find the money. We could all be partners in our own salvation.

Some more regulars got onto the stage with Joni and started offering their own testimonials and getting out their checkbooks, while election coverage was still going on behind them on the big screen. I sat in a chair, watching, unable to grasp what was happening. Did I want this? I was unsure I did. But I couldn't help getting caught up in the warmth of the moment. They all urged me onto the stage. When I finally relented, I got the same cheers Obama had just gotten moments before. I couldn't resist the hope. It crept in.

Over the next week, I received over $40,000 in small donations, often accompanied by a heartfelt note of encouragement and love. We technically had until the end of November to come up with the money, but I knew we wouldn't make it. I kept our closing date firm. I knew I wouldn't be able to withstand another leap of faith. I would have missed. I was barely hanging on as it was. Nothing was going to forestall the financial disaster that was about to overtake me, my ex-wife, and my investor.

DJ Bucky became increasingly antagonistic during this period. She promoted events she scheduled at other venues after Pi's demise, neglecting to promote our closing events. She pissed off Marie in the kitchen by demanding her food be prepared before customers' food. She amplified her derision toward security staff while giving them longer guest lists for people she wanted to impress for her own self-promotion. She yelled at Tif for not comping drinks for some dippy hipsters she was schmoozing. You can't talk to a ginger like that. Tif informed DJ Bucky that she wouldn't be giving her or her friends any more drinks for free and she would inform the rest of the bar staff of the new policy. The fight spilled out onto the dance floor, where they found me mumbling back to the office.

I took DJ Bucky into the storage room. I knew what she

was doing. I'd been watching it happen for weeks. I knew how much Pi and the family she'd found there meant to her. Like many of us, the way she protected herself was to be a complete dick and push everyone away. I knew that was what she was doing, and I couldn't let her do it anymore.

"DJ Bucky, I know somewhere inside you, you love this place and everyone in it. I know you're hurting, but everybody else is too. You're fucking up our last week together. I see no reason that you should come back for our last two nights."

That did it. DJ Bucky broke down. I relented. "You can be here, of course I want you to be here, you were a part of making this all happen. But you can't be the only one hurting. Everybody is too sad right now, and we have to pull together." She said okay and that she was sorry.

We held the last Dildo Bingo as a fundraiser for ourselves. I had largely given up the notion of a miracle that would save Pi, but I still had to make our last payroll. I also had to pay our liquor distributor. They were the only purveyor I cared about. Suzi, our liquor rep, who had helped us with our initial order, had personally guaranteed to her bosses that we would pay our last bill. It is normal procedure for suppliers to cut off their customers once they learn they are going out of business, but they didn't because of Suzi. Everybody else could go fuck themselves.

The last Dildo Bingo was the most successful. The next night, our last Friday, was huge. Then the longest, hardest day of my life began.

# CHAPTER FORTY

# WHO'S GOT THE KOOL-AID?

Somebody from the fire department called me personally that afternoon to assure me that nobody would be coming by for a surprise inspection. Mourners started arriving as soon as we opened the doors. I hid bottles of wine in various locations around the building so they would never be far from me. Some of the peripheral Stantons who weren't working security that night came in and asked what booze I thought we wouldn't be able to sell that night. I sold them some cognac and apple pucker and they disappeared toward the smoking lounge at the back of the building.

I prepared a speech to give at the end of the night. I grabbed a fistful of wristbands. We were certainly going to have an afterparty tonight. All the staff were invited, but there were so many regulars who should come as well. As I encountered them throughout the evening, I would hand them the coveted wristbands, indicating their invitation.

Pi quickly filled. We were way beyond capacity. Cocktail variety was increasingly limited, but no one complained. At some point, we completely ran out of beer. Benny and Shandell's boyfriend went up the street to the Eagle Lodge and came back with most of the contents of their beer cooler. Nobody cared that our entire beer menu suddenly shifted to whatever can of crappy domestic the bartender was closest to.

I have no memory of the hundreds of touching moments I'm sure occurred over the next few hours. I don't remember anything more until it all started to go wrong.

Toward the end of the night, in the kitchen, Patricia approached me and asked for some extra wristbands for her new girlfriend's friends. Like a wounded dumbass, I said, "Well, if Eve doesn't have any friends that already have wristbands, maybe she doesn't belong here." At this moment Patricia finally decided to process her anger over our divorce and the countless ongoing sacrifices she had made for the business. She yelled at me for the first time. She had every right to do it, but it was more than I could stand. I ran out the back door and cowered in between some recycling bins.

I crouched there crying and snotting all over myself. The snow was falling gently in front of an alley streetlight, and it was so quiet. I wanted to go home and hide. I didn't want to shoulder Pi for even another hour, which was all that remained of our official life. I didn't want to face Patricia or the staff or the music anymore. I didn't want to be a superhero anymore. I didn't want to be a leader anymore. I wanted to disappear.

But the culmination of my entire life was against my back. I couldn't stand up and make myself leave. As I sat there, having an existential movie moment with myself, one of our security guards spotted me while she was smoking outside. She went and got Marie.

Marie picked me up and brought me back inside. She held me as I cried myself out. Patricia was off to the side, mouthing, "I'm sorry," to Marie. She thought I couldn't see, but I saw you. I'm the one who is sorry. You can't possibly know how much.

And then it was time for the eulogy. I made my way to the stage. I grabbed a mic and started preaching. "Look at you beautiful motherfuckers. I fucking love every one of you fucking freaks. Thank you so much for coming to the last night of Pi Bar. I want you to take a look around and see what you've done. See what this community, no matter who you are, see what this community can do. Remember to work for this. Remember to be this. I fucking love you."

Benny was on my right in that goddamn paisley shirt. Marie was on my left, looking fierce and beautiful. The stage was filled with staff and family behind me. After I attempted to list every last person I wanted to thank for helping to make this happen, DJ Bucky started the last song.

We had chosen the Righteous Brothers' "(I've Had) The Time of My Life." Really what other song would've been appropriate? It's emotive. Everyone knows the words. And who doesn't have a sentimental attachment to *Dirty Dancing*? DJ Bucky even muted the music during the refrain so the voices of the crowd carried the song. Everyone was dancing and singing and crying. Often, they were singing directly to me on the stage.

For me, from my view, from the window of my history and my visions, this was the moment I'd been dreading for the last couple months and the one I'd been waiting for my whole life. For the space of a song, I achieved the Rainbow Connection that Kermit the Frog had once promised me as a child. It was only in the moment of Pi's death that the secret dream of human history was temporarily revealed and came true. I transcended common human suffering, my own suffering, and saw the true face of potential and beauty. Not every human gets to be a witness to this phenomenon. I knew enough about what I was experiencing to remain humble and grateful.

I barely noticed when Toni approached the stage and demanded I come with her. Marie cared enough about what I was experiencing to decide she didn't give a shit if the building was on fire, this song was not to be interrupted for me for any reason. She handed off my humming, sobbing body to Kat, an appropriate guardian, and left with Toni.

The song ended, the lights went up. Everything turned to shit.

During the last half of the last song, DJ Bucky left her booth and was walking through the storage room to the back bar for another martini when she encountered the extended Stanton clan, who had been drinking cognac and apple pucker back there since we opened. Tracy, the youngest of the Stantons, took it upon herself in that moment to stand up for her family's honor and the legacy of Pi. Benny came upon the standoff, which is fortunate because it was about to get physical and DJ Bucky was about to lose. He reflexively told Tracy and the rest of her crew to get the fuck out, now.

So now it was Benny and DJ Bucky against the Stantons, and I was to be the deciding vote. I was to make my allegiances clear. Before that could happen, security had to empty the bar of drunk sad people, which is actually quite difficult. During this process, one of our minor regulars started a fight in the front bathroom, adjacent to the corridor through which everyone was being herded. She became so violent and upset that she had to be restrained. Security put cuffs on her as she was splayed on the hallway floor and hundreds of people were forced to step around her.

Whenever you handcuff someone for security reasons, you have to call the cops. When the front bar staff realized the cops were on the way, they started yelling to the remaining regulars, "The cops are coming. I don't give a shit who you are or if you have a fucking wristband. If you don't work here, get the fuck out. Now!"

I returned to the office, where Tracy was with her father, who was working security that night. DJ Bucky and Benny were there too. Three of them were yelling at me, and the Stanton patriarch was looking at me with gentle sympathy. I still didn't understand the full story. The only thing I knew was that Tracy had to leave, and I wanted that to happen in a way that her family felt sufficiently supported so that they could stay. We'd all been through too much, and tonight was the end. I tried to reason with Tracy. This process took longer than Benny and DJ Bucky could tolerate. They thought I was taking the Stantons' side and betraying them. *Goddamn, you fucking babies. Why am I even in this position right now? This is my fucking night.*

DJ Bucky stormed out. Shortly after that, Tracy's father led her out of the building. DJ Bucky's car broke down, so she came back but wouldn't speak to me. Benny sequestered himself behind the kitchen with a folding table and proclaimed that nobody else could sit there unless he approved it. The rest of the staff started taking sides or just experiencing their last night together in various places around the building without any knowledge of what had occurred.

I spent the next several hours sitting alone on my treadmill in the storage room, sobbing and feeling sorry for myself. My last night with my greatest achievement, was taken from me by petty bullshit. All I wanted was for the family to spend one more night together. I made this. I wanted a few head pets and a little gratitude. This would be the second temper tantrum of my life. I was helpless to stop it and so was anybody who came to get me until about five in the morning.

When I emerged, the mood was much softer. Many didn't know what had happened. Many were asleep. Marie started making everybody breakfast. At some point, everybody went home. I still couldn't leave.

If you're ever considering becoming a cult leader, you should know it is dangerous. If you fail to deliver the promised vision or if the compound is compromised, before you become famous enough for somebody to assassinate you, people turn on you. It doesn't matter if it was your fault or not. People are mad at you because you got their hopes up, and that is your fucking fault. You will lose everything you built. You will lose the family you brought together. And that doesn't even include what it has done to your health and your soul.

I had two weeks to tie up loose ends and say good bye to the building. Kat and V came by to help me dismantle the sound system and put it in my truck. V had been working in our kitchen for months, and his girlfriend Kat spent almost as much time there. They were loving, gifted, apocalyptic fairies. I spent just as much time at the bar those last two weeks as I would have had we been open. People would come by. Some would bring snacks and stay to talk or offer help. We started cutting chunks of the murals out of the walls. People came by and left with their piece of Pi.

I called Wells Fargo to tell them that I would be defaulting on their business loans. It took forty-five minutes for the auctioneers to show up. They're like undertakers for small businesses. It was a husband-and-wife team. The husband was the soothing, sympathetic front man. His wife was the one who prepared the body. Several days later, I watched as everything was claimed and taken away.

The night before I was to be evicted, we had one last party. It wasn't very big. Kat and V came by with home movies they'd been shooting for the past few months. Benny came. We made up. He hadn't been around because he needed some space. We smashed some blocks of concrete leftover from our ATM machine, then used the chunks to break bottles set in various places. We started throwing them through the drywall in the pool room along with some rotten citrus we found in the walk-in. At some point, I simply fell asleep in the recliner Marv gave me, which I'd dragged into the pool room.

When I awoke, it was to the sight of a teddy bear, perched atop a child's bicycle, smashed halfway through the wall nearest me. As I walked into the storage space to look at the other side of the bike, I saw the lemons and concrete chunks had been augmented by our remaining spray paint. There was a giant, dripping cock freshly covering our green room wall. The other walls were used for more abstract emotional release.

Joni, the lawyer, showed up with her girlfriend and a trailer. They helped me dismantle and load the pergola on the patio, along with some other odds and ends. Then the building owner came to change the locks. Joni intercepted him, so I didn't have to talk to him.

And then it was done. His handyman changed the last lock. I was on the outside when it happened. It was the door I had wedged open on the first day I went inside the building. I said good-bye and went home.

I spent the first two weeks sleeping fifteen hours a day. In my awake time, I returned every donation check I'd received with a personalized note and a Pi sticker. I then wrote everybody who had ever worked at Pi a letter. I never sent those. After that, a sadness settled in unlike any depression I recognized. It was like my chest was filled with cement. I couldn't feel anything. It was too much to process, so I didn't.

Poor Marie. She was more like my nurse than my girlfriend during this time. She made sure I ate. She entertained herself while I played Zuma in my office and smoked. Nobody called me. She told me nobody knew what to say. It took me a few weeks to adopt that narrative. I didn't want to be angry and hurt about my family while I was also angry and hurt about the world. I wanted to be happy for my family wherever they were not calling me.

One day, Marie came into my office and broke my computer game. It was time to leave the house. It was time to move on.

# CHAPTER FORTY-ONE

# DAYLIGHT HURTS MY EYES

Shandell's boyfriend was general manager at a busy downtown restaurant. He took Benny on as his bar manager and gave a few more Pi staff bartending jobs. Benny offered me a job barbacking. I did that for a couple months, but it was too soon for my shattered ego.

Kat got me a job at a liquor store downtown. This was easier on my inner atonement compulsion. It was easier to not be around Benny right then, and it was easier for him to not be around me. We'd been through too much together and needed to establish independent existences before it didn't hurt so bad to be close.

Marie's friend got me an additional job working overnights at a transitional housing facility for at-risk youth. That felt substantive and useful. I worked with kids who were facing far more adversity than I ever had. It put things into some perspective.

Both Patricia and I had to declare bankruptcy. Our investor lost her house. I am still sorry about that. Even though I think she spent most of the rest of her trust obsessively litigating my downfall, I never wanted that to happen. Patricia, in keeping with her optimistic demeanor, assured me that bankruptcy was positive for her since she'd racked up shopping debt since our breakup.

I didn't talk to my parents often during this transition depression. I'd also lost their money. I'd failed at showing them what a big deal I was. I had not convinced them that I could be successful my way. I lost the lifelong philosophical conflict yet again. But they did have a concessional respect for my effort. Opening a bar wasn't a lazy or unambitious thing to do. They could sense how fragile I was. That made them too uncomfortable to talk to me much. My father, who in the last few months of Pi had instituted weekly drill sessions over the phone, with profit-and-loss pop quizzes and combative cost-cutting calisthenics, just told me to keep my chin up. My mother told me she should have never let me buy such a big building, and she'd be happy to get me some new clothes for interviews.

In the first summer without Pi, I was approached about doing a Dildo Bingo at another location. They wanted me to sell tickets like I used to. I still had the box and the apron. They'd enlisted Tif to reprise her starring role. I agreed.

I had a lot of anxiety leading up to the event. Would people accuse me of being a has-been? Would they think it was just sad? Was I ready to face my legacy? Was I ready to face DJ Bucky? The faces of my regulars?

When I did Dildo Bingo before, my signature cocktail had been vodka Red Bulls. I don't know why—they are disgusting—but superstition is important. Leftover from Pi, I had a case of sugar-free Red Bulls and several bottles of promotional grape vodka. Do not try this at home. This combination should only be attempted by the profoundly broken. I had three or four before we left and a roadie for the trip.

People recognized me as I strolled in. The bartender slid a complimentary vodka Red Bull across the bar as homage when I asked for it. The charity running the event explained the modified procedures they required to my obviously intoxicated and combative face. *Don't tell me how to run a Dildo Bingo. I invented this shit.*

I spotted DJ Bucky at the bar with Stevie. As I sidled up to her to receive my next cocktail, I asked, "So are you ever gonna hike up your skirt and talk to me?"

DJ Bucky spun on her heels and returned to her perch to DJ. I began to sell cards and dance and flirt. Anyone paying attention could've sensed the train wreck approaching the station.

Halfway through the rounds, a performance piece was scheduled. One of our regulars, Nader, was doing her Engelbert Humperdinck drag with a can of Cheez Whiz. I was standing by the stage, where Tif was emceeing. Nader approached me with her aerosol cheese and I naturally demurred to her showmanship. As I straightened again, mouth agape with processed cheese food, my eyes landed on Tif's calf.

There, tattooed on her leg, was something like a county fair ribbon, with "Barmaid" as the prize title. In the middle circle, the place that would designate her showing in a competition, was the number 53. My Agent 53. Here I thought nobody gave a shit anymore. After I spat Cheez Whiz all over Tif's leg, I sped back to the bar.

As I received another complimentary cocktail from the bartender, Marie recognized the very specific and dangerous table-flipping gleam in my eye. I had gotten into that glorious habit at Pi whenever the occasion called for celebratory destruction. But this wasn't my bar, and these weren't my tables.

"Let's go have a smoke, Bo Bear."

"No! These people know nothing!"

Right before I actually started flipping tables and right after I started having a public rock-'n'-roll meltdown, Marie got me out of there with the help of some trusted allies. It was too soon, apparently.

By fall, enough time had passed that I organized a Pi Family Reunion one year after its death. Kat and V helped me promote it. Ruth, Tif, and Shandell agreed to bartend. Naughty Boy agreed to DJ. I reached out to DJ Bucky but received no response. A shady nightclub owner who bought my old sound system gave me a family discount on his space. It was an unused space on the third floor of his building with a stage and a couple bars. Its shabbiness and unfinished charm recalled the DIY heart of Pi. I was the greeter at the door all night. Everybody was happy to see each other again and I got a small do-over for my shitty last night.

Shortly after this, as I was working a quiet overnight and scrolling through Facebook, I was assaulted by promotions for the upcoming First Friday. This announcement punched me right in the dick. No one had even given me a heads-up. I was irritated it was being done in a hipster straight bar in a neighborhood not known for its friendliness toward African Americans. I was irritated Marie and I were the only representatives from Pi at Miss Eva's funeral a few months after Pi closed. And I was especially annoyed it was being promoted by DJ Bucky. I spent the rest of the night crafting a brilliant Facebook rant. But by the time the sun came up, I realized I'd ridden the crazy train far enough and was grateful for whatever supernatural force that had restrained me from posting any of it.

# CHAPTER FORTY-TWO

# PLAN B, WIZARD SCHOOL

I needed to accomplish something new, something big. It's the only activity that makes me feel okay. I didn't want to be bitter anymore. I didn't even want to be mad at DJ Bucky anymore. I needed a new dream.

I happened to have one dream left, hidden away for just such an occasion. While I was still in the classics department at the U, a recruiter from Harvard Divinity School had come to give a presentation one day. I had attended with four other nerds, chuckling to myself at the ridiculous notion I could ever attend Harvard.

A lot had happened since that day. I'd gained a little more confidence in my magic powers. I'd rolled the dice as a real tough girl, with mixed results. I probably wasn't going to make it as a professional athlete. Perhaps the mystic in me could be salvaged.

When my mother called one day to gently suggest another career, location, shirt style, and haircut, I preempted the full menu with news I planned on going to grad school. Harvard specifically.

"Well, you have to take the GRE. Do you need me to send you a study guide?"

"Nah. Thanks, Ma. I'm scheduled to take it on Tuesday."

"What other schools are you thinking of? Shouldn't you apply to some more schools?"

"I don't think so. Love you, Ma. Call you after my test."

It was fall. Applications were due by the end of the year. I indulged in a trip to Boston to an event for prospective students. I needed to write a brilliant and emotionally manipulative admissions essay, and I wanted to meet my audience.

I knew them instantly. I used to help them find the fresh turmeric at the co-op and take them on Mendocino wine tours in a party bus. Harvard's Divinity School stresses diversity, unique paths. I got this.

I did well enough on my GRE. I collected reference letters from my two favorite professors at the U and Joni, my favorite, fancy lawyer friend. I gathered my various, colorful transcripts. I asked Christa to read my essay, but by the time we met to discuss her many thoughtful notes, I'd already sent it all in. I get very impatient when manifesting visions.

My fortieth birthday came around in January. Marie gathered all the family she could and threw me a party at our house. Benny and I hadn't seen much of each other. We were still working through the enormous, unprocessed shit tangle of emotion that was left in the wake of Pi. We were discussing his transition and how happy he felt when I said something stupid: "Well, it just seems like you're too good for the weirdos now." He might've told me to fuck off or he could've said nothing. He left and wouldn't talk to me anymore.

I had a hysterectomy in February. My uterus had grown a fibroid the size of my uterus. My body has always sent me urgent messages about the state of my subconscious that I ignore. My mom came out to help. That was nice, but she really doesn't like sick people. Marie and I settled into a cozy seclusion while I was waiting to hear about my application. Marie had been born with the soul of a true artist. That beautiful soul had faced adversity far greater than my own. Over the years, she'd found reliable resiliency in caretaking for others. We were sweet to each other. We spent most of our time watching crappy TV and smoking cigarettes and saying nice things. I probably should've never allowed the caustic volatility of my thwarted desires near such a precious and singular presence in the world, but I never would've made it through this time without her near me.

The lifelong compulsion to be something bigger than people expected of me had again, unbidden, begun to ooze its way through the pores in my concrete chest. It called out again.

And again, the call was answered. It had been a smaller personal ambition this time, something to soothe the disappointment of my parents and remind me I was supposed to be special, but I'd secretly known the cry would be heard as soon as I'd sent in my application. I was working another overnight shift at the housing facility in early spring, checking my email. The only one that mattered suddenly stared at me from the screen. It was from the admissions department for Harvard Divinity School.

It took a few minutes to gather the courage to open it. I like to make things dramatic, even when I'm alone. It said what I was certain it was going to say but had never uttered out loud because of jinxes. It began with "Congratulations," and that was all I needed to read. Even though it was a little past ten back in California, I called my mom.

"What's wrong? Are you okay?"

"I just got an email from Harvard."

"Oh my god."

"It's says congratulations. I got into Harvard, Ma."

She started crying and repeated the news to my father next to her. I heard him say, "She got in?"

Mom replied, "Well, she did take all that ancient Greek."

"Our daughter knows how to translate ancient Greek?" Dad responded.

I chuckled to myself. It was a perfect moment I had earned, and I let myself enjoy it.

Marie's response was a little different. I was moving to Boston for two school years, and she was afraid she was going to lose me. Even though I assured her that night, I couldn't deny my lifetime of flinging myself into new existences, desperately hoping to land in one where my skin finally ceased feeling uncomfortable. Was it better to selectively ignore my remarkably reliable intuition, or should I have preemptively fucked everything up?

In the summer before I left, Marie and I went to a queer Fourth of July BBQ. A typical South Minneapolis affair. There was a woman I remembered from Pi. She was one of the female graffiti artists who had contributed to our mural. She'd had an art show at Pi. Katrina was crazy hot. She was tall and lean and smart and different. She had a rare confidence and the most beautiful lips I'd ever seen. She was dating the cute folk singer butch who'd been one of our barbacks, and I was dating Marie.

That didn't stop us from talking to each other all night, but I wasn't ready to fuck everything up just yet.

In the fall, I packed up a rental car and headed east. I was scared and excited. I was unsure about leaving the relative safety I'd created with Marie, but I knew I couldn't heal in Minneapolis. The whole city had become painful, and I didn't know my place in it anymore.

My mother met me in Boston to take me to Bed Bath & Beyond and advise me on my wardrobe. My room was up four flights of stairs, and I shared a bathroom with two men. I could hear the trains running on either side of my building. The lights from Fenway illuminated my dark room on game nights. I had a dorm fridge, toaster oven, and hot plate. My life was necessarily simplified. I had little to remind me of the pain I left behind.

Mom left and it was time for my first day of school, of Harvard school. What the hell does an aging, broken pirate wear to the first day of Harvard? Against my mother's insistent advice, I decided to dress as I had for the past twenty years. My nineties-warehouse wardrobe had become my bar-owner wardrobe and, lacking any alternative, became my Harvard wardrobe. Carhartts, black T-shirts, boots, and Dickie's short-sleeved button-ups. I knew they'd let me in because of my eccentric CV. I trusted that dressing the part would only add to my mystique.

The first day was part of new student orientation, to be followed by numerous opportunities for wine and cheese. The student groups of the Divinity School set up greeting tables all over the main building. When I passed the "Queer Rites" table, it was clear coming out wouldn't be necessary. I was what the kids today had heard dykes used to look like.

Most of my fellow students were in their mid to late twenties. Most of them were thin and good-looking with surprising depth in their unlined eyes. I represented both queer and working-class worldliness. That's double diversity bonus points in neoliberal board games if you're playing along. There was an especially bright-eyed Northern California descendant greeting me from the cleverly named rainbow activity table. You could tell Katie was a good hippie right away. This is a special immortal fairy subsection of the long-dead cliché of the Summer of Love. These magical creatures instantly diffuse anxiety in strangers. She seemed to think that it was obvious that I should join the school's queer student group.

The grand total of my queer accomplishments and

catastrophes reared up in my head like a bitchy queeny dragon—*Bitch please, do you know who I am?* What came out of my mouth was, "Of course I want to join. I love the name. My name's Tara. It's really great to meet you." I was happy someone talked to me.

I'm sure there are people who attend Ivy League schools without an innate terror of being exposed as a fraud, but I suspect they're all douchebags. I was wearing my nineties nostalgia as armor, hoping it would distract people from my lack of experience with this world. Cambridge, and Harvard's campuses specifically, really do evoke the sensation of being at Hogwarts. It can't be helped. I'm not the first to make this analogy. There is an entire intramural Quidditch league at Harvard. Going to classes there makes you feel as if you have been plucked from the muggles and there's a chance there might be something special about you.

This sensation is especially valid for the Divinity School. It's basically magic god camp, where every day, you're asked to ponder the meaning of life, or theorize megacategories like gender or class, or reflect on nuances of consciousness and possibilities of transcendence. You even stumble into the inexplicable and mysticism. These conversations not only spill out into the hallways but continue at cocktail parties. I loved it, but for the first time in my life, I was surrounded by people who were as smart as me. Okay, some weren't as smart, but almost, and some were smarter. Most of them had already gone to a fancy liberal arts college. They had all read Foucault and Butler. I had not.

School was challenging for me for the very first time. I wasn't familiar with this vocabulary. I never received my social theory "word of the day calendar." Most of the time, I didn't understand what anyone said in class. I took five classes that first semester. Thankfully, two of them were language classes, ancient Greek and Coptic. The rest of my class load could also be viewed as language classes, but I was struggling to understand a rarefied dialect of my own native language. It took much more effort to expand my academic, English vocabulary than to understand dead grammar.

# CHAPTER FORTY-THREE

# PLAN B, SUBSECTION: FUCK ME

A couple of weeks into the semester, I was standing with a small group of students behind the Div School's main building. Between us and the labs where the human gene code was being deciphered was a small, high-fenced garden and a couple of opaque greenhouses. Its presence there seemed mysterious to me. I was just quipping about its possible nefarious purposes, staring at my feet, when a voice I had not seen approaching offered, "Oh, that's a replica of the Garden of Eden. Harvard had it installed for us."

When I looked up, I saw the sparkling eyes of assured destruction staring right through me.

*Aw c'mon. You can't be fucking serious. This isn't funny. No, no, no. Oh please, just turn around. Go away. I can't fuck this up. Shit.* That's what I heard from that hardheaded sucker that's been living in my gut my entire life. "Hi, I'm Hope," is what she said. Of course you are. "Rock upon which you are destined to repeatedly dash your soul" is much less poetic.

Hope was beautiful. She was young, elegant, bright, and creative. She'd been damaged just enough by the world's expectations of her to be experiencing a predictable Saturn-return reckoning with her rebellious taste in men. And here I was, in the most unlikely of places, right on time.

There's no reason to recount the details of our personally

humiliating, divinely scripted Lifetime miniseries over the rest of the semester. My fairy god watchers had their fun. I need not reward their mischief. Highlights include agreeing to let her see me naked in a women-only hot tub for our first date; sending her terrible poetry; "breaking up" with her at least thirty times only to text her within an hour, usually with more poetry; and arm wrestling the pretty boy she was destined to marry in front of her mystics club. She didn't deserve all the crazy she got. She couldn't have anticipated the out-of-control rock-'n'-roll semi, overloaded with grief and tornadoes, she was encountering when she made her first clever jest to me. She was just hoping for an escort into the forbidden roadside queer juke joint she hadn't yet had the occasion to see.

There's no logical reason she should've been attracted to me. What do pretty straight girls see when they look at me? They couldn't possibly know what to do with the history of my body. It is a fact that will consume the illusion. I didn't know what I was doing either, but I knew how it would end. Do I have a compulsion for failure? Self-sabotage? Is my masculinity only ever achievable as reflection? Are we actually attracted to one another? None of those things matter in real time. She was twenty-eight and had a yoga body. I was forty, fat, and broken. No matter how many ways we figured out what a terrible idea it was, we always ended up in each other's fairy confessionals, sharing past life memories of our infinity together.

I was more invested in this obsession than she was. She always knew she would move on and be successful and beautiful and loved. I knew that too. I also knew I would be crushed and distracted and risk a complete and public psychological breach. But I couldn't just stroll through Harvard without trying to bring about my own failure. This had been a lifelong cosmic test and I was going to fail it enthusiastically, one more time.

Harvard is hard. My usual amount of academic effort was insufficient by half. My uniqueness and some of my experiential insight were occasionally affirmed, but my work wasn't receiving the acclaim I was accustomed to. The institution itself, being the oldest and snobbiest in the nation, mocked my presence. I started to doubt I had shine enough. You can't completely hustle Harvard.

I started to unravel. The mass in my chest started breaking apart. All of my waking thoughts were in dimensions of destiny and underdog training montages. Alone in my room across the river, I fell back upon AC/DC as I spasmed myself into trances, stretching back for the anger, calling on the powers of defiance to find me in this foreign land. I had packed my copy of *Hedwig and the Angry Inch*, which I started watching nightly. I was a "blow it all to shit" junkie, and I'd finally parked myself in a situation I couldn't allow myself to wreck. I made Hedwig my sponsor and my higher power. *There ain't much of a difference, between a bridge and a wall. Without me right in the middle of it, you would be nothing at all.* Amen.

I was away from the queer bubbles I had lived in for twenty years, cut off from the safety of the fringe. You can't be a pirate when everyone around you finds it an interesting subculture. I called my own bluff. I needed to find the authenticity that had eluded me my whole life by the time finals rolled around.

I called Christa almost every day. I will forever be indebted to her patience and wise insight. She spoke to me in terms I understood. She said I was Frodo and I needed to deliver the Ring. I could not allow the forces of darkness to win. She introduced me to the toddler living in my head who liked to smear shit on the walls whenever he was scared. We named him Jasper. I was to control Jasper in mixed company. Under no circumstances was I to leave Jasper unsupervised. She methodically reminded me of everything I already knew about my doomed dalliance with a princess.

It was only because of Hedwig and Christa that I was able to finish the semester. During finals, Hope and I were unable to resist one last misty stroll through our eternal, gossamer shit puddle. She took a cab to my little room. I made her watch *Hedwig*. We stared into each other's eyes until we could see who we were in former lives. We did it with the lights on. Then she called a cab. I walked her downstairs, and she said something poetic and left. I knew it would never happen again. I knew I would lose. I felt both condescended to and completely disgusted by the inevitability of my character.

I received straight Bs. And those were likely gratuitous. Harvard doesn't want people to fail. It makes them look like they didn't know what they were doing when they admitted you. Between the failings of my intellect and my charm, I felt like I'd been in a bar fight for three months. I could also feel all the injuries I had been sustaining for decades, like Harvard had ripped off all the scabs. I was grateful it was over. I couldn't face another semester like the one I'd just barely made it through. On the plane home for winter break, as I watched the full moon rise beneath my window, I tried to think of something clever to say about this omen that would impress Harvard or Hope. But the moon only reminded me of my failure and fraudulence that night. The moon told me it was time to be a man.

# CHAPTER FORTY-FOUR

# I GOT THE TOASTER, WHERE'S MY DICK?

I'd thought about this before. There's no way I could've avoided the possibility in the world I lived in. I admit, I had occasionally thought it was a bit of a cop out. But I'd seen my friends become happy and calm by transitioning. It might have initially been capitulation for me, though. I could not return to Hogwarts without an additional layer of protection spells. I gave in. I didn't want my presence in the world to be antagonistic and unintelligible any more. I didn't want to be anyone's exotic pit stop ever again. I was thoroughly exhausted by all of it.

To my surprise, at the mere thought of becoming a man, an optimism sprang up to greet me like we had never met before. I was suddenly quite excited by the promise of facial hair and big muscles. I started wondering how soon I could start the process. I became impatient in my airplane seat. About five minutes had elapsed. Time for a whole new life.

When I got home, I felt guilty around Marie. I didn't tell her about Hope. Just one more shitty thing I've done. I knew she'd been right. I was in the process of creating another new existence, but it wasn't time to break everything apart yet. I was relieved to be home, around my family. I still loved her. I told her about my decision right away. Then I told Christa and Patricia. They all suggested that I not rush this decision like they had never met me. They suggested more yoga and a healthier diet.

Then I texted Benny. We still hadn't spoken. I wrote that I'd decided to transition and wanted to learn to be a good man, and I couldn't think of a better man to help me than him. He came to my house, through the front door, and threw his arms around me. "Let's never do that again," he said. I'd missed him terribly. He knew I was making the right decision.

In a month, I was back at Harvard, armed with my shiny new hope, ready to not suck this semester. My transition needed to happen quickly. I knew most protocols involved months of psychotherapy to get a diagnosis of gender fuckery to bring to a doctor so you could access hormones. That is not the speed at which I make life-altering decisions.

I had the best health insurance I'd ever had at Harvard. I simply made an appointment with my primary care physician. I explained to her what I wanted to do. She'd never prescribed testosterone for this purpose. She asked me what dose my friend back in Minneapolis took. I told her what I knew. She looked up the prescription on her computer, then handed it to me.

One should probably not take the DIY approach when altering one's gender, but why should this process be any different than the rest of my life? I just pretend like I know what I'm doing, then catch up with the learning curve at some point. It took me less than an hour to obtain my magic potion and some syringes for the impending ritual.

I returned to campus and enlisted the help of an emerging ally. Sierra had let me drone on about Hope and my academic insecurities for thankless hours during my first semester. She'd shocked me with her youthful wisdom and was among the only people here that could make me laugh about things I fully understood. I'd already shared my new plan with her. I found her as fast as I could and revealed my secret package. I said I wanted to do it right away, but I didn't know how to inject myself.

"Oh I can show you. I used to give myself B12 injections. Come on," she said like it was no big deal. We descended to the basement where the big, individual toilet stalls are and went in together. I giggled as I dropped my drawers and sat on the toilet, and she made some joke about how everything would improve when the rumor of our affair started to circulate. Even though I'd told the doctor Benny took 0.5 milligrams of T, the prescription that she gave me recommended one whole milligram. I don't know who that prescription is for. It's twice the standard dose for trans men who've been on T for some time and about three times the dose normally prescribed for those just embarking on the process. We decided to follow the directions anyway. Sierra put the needle in my thigh, and I was on my way.

That's a lot of testosterone. Over the next few weeks, I began to experience a primal, general lust I hadn't previously understood was possible for humans. My brain flooded with a constant stream of filthy, filthy porn. Bulges in clothing became objects of considerable fixation. It didn't matter if they were boobs, butts, or dicks. They were fascinating. Sometimes, in class, or trying to study, I would be kidnapped by a diabolical humping compulsion in my giant, imaginary schlong. It could not be reasoned with, just distracted by racing to the gym and running faster and longer and lifting more weight than I'd ever mastered in years of trying. You know what's better than menopause? Puberty. Despite all of the distracting side effects, testosterone turned out to be an effective antidepressant and superhero aid for me.

After a month, I suspected I might be overdoing it. There happened to be a gender health clinic about four blocks from my apartment. I walked in one day to see if anyone would answer some questions. The nurse who obliged looked horrified when I confessed my current dosage and how I'd come upon it in the first place. She calmly informed me that Harvard had an entire team devoted to gender transition and gave me their contact information. I was assigned a doctor and a therapist. The doctor was disturbed by my story but continued my prescriptions at a scaled back dosage. The therapist turned out to be a good idea in general. I probably should always have one of those.

After another month, my voice started to crack and my ten chin hairs started to multiply. My mother was coming for a visit, and I would have to tell her. It wasn't a secret I could keep.

Most trans men in the first year of transitioning are fascinated with the minutiae of every hair, every muscle, every tiny alteration to their bodies. I was no exception. Testosterone is cheating. My ass got smaller. My shoulders got broader. I had more energy. I didn't cry every day. And even though I gave myself masturbation blisters, I managed to improve my academic offerings a little, largely due to fresh confidence. I got straight Bs again, but they felt like better Bs. I was learning to unpack freighted discourses like a big boy. I left for summer break with a sense of wonder that I might actually graduate and eventually be okay.

On my drive home, I had a lot of time for daydreaming. There were the usual straw bale home designs and deciding who would survive the apocalypse with me, but I also remembered Katrina from the summer before and decided I would have an affair with her. I still hadn't broken up with Marie, and I completely understood how fucked up my thought process was. But I was returning to Minneapolis with a newly forming identity, and I knew I would upend my life and someone else's one more time.

Hurting Marie is very high on the list of shitty things I've done in my life. She saved my life. She nursed me back into the world. She took care of Pally and my dog and my house. What's the point of saying you regret something when you can't change what you've done? When you hurt someone who trusted you, they don't want you to be sorry. They can see that you're sorry. They want you to have not done it in the first place.

Collecting these trinkets of shame and repeating the narratives of your character flaws is a common human habit. It's a bad habit. Those are hard to break. I have complicated feelings about the idea of "forgiving yourself." I'm leery of meme psychology. I think the process is much more complex and involves wading through the shame, acknowledging that you've done something harmful to someone else, and figuring out a way to allow the harm you've also suffered in your life create a small reservoir of compassion and humble entitlement from which you can begin to enact new, less destructive habits. And sometimes you just cash in another of your precious tokens for a fresh start and try not to be a dick about it.

A couple weeks into the summer break, I found myself trolling Katrina on Facebook. I attended her art opening. A couple weeks later, when Pride rolled around, I ran into her at First Friday, and again at another queer BBQ. When I saw her on Pride Sunday, I ran to catch up to her. I didn't come home until late that night, and I already knew my new path. It took me another week or so to find a way to tell Marie it was time for me to go. Thank you for saving me.

By the end of the summer, Katrina was my girlfriend, even though she wouldn't allow that label yet. I already knew she was the one I could stay with if we could figure out a way to trust each other. She was strong and confident enough to combat my controlling impulses. She was stubborn enough to make me wait for the new vision in my head. I would have to finish the other dream I'd started and return with untarnished commitment before she would allow me to see the miraculous, unfettered alliance she had waiting for me.

As the time for my return to Boston drew near, she was unwavering in her reluctance to cast our relationship as exclusive. We were in love, but she would not admit it yet. We spent countless hours negotiating the terms of our ambiguity and nonmonogamy during my upcoming absence. Vague boundaries and casual faith have never occupied space in my comfort zone. I was awash with fresh anxiety over my deferred destiny. I needed to complete Harvard, while transitioning, with my head filled with delusional nightmares about Katrina's secret inclination toward recreational gang bangs.

I began my third semester as a new entity half-baked. I had some fresh confidence in my academic intellect. I was taking the time to trouble out the intentions of the esoteric tomes I'd always pretended I understood. I found with increasing regularity that I had stored knowledge of lofty psychological and even theological abstractions within the sediments of my own experience. I just hadn't understood the vocabulary with which esteemed philosophers chose to convey their theories—pompous pricks that they all are. What did they know about rock 'n' roll?

My new body was beginning to take shape. I was shedding fat in feminine places and gaining muscle in desirous ways. I was still unsure of my ability to pass, and that seemed to be the unspoken goal. My cohort and my professors were delighting and fretting in the fresh opportunity to be sensitive. I refused to correct or affirm anyone forced to use my name or pronoun. I wanted their discomfort more than their self-congratulating accommodations. I think I was a little mad at Harvard for being so well-adjusted and respectable. I would finish this degree despite this institution's passive design to crush the hubris of the uncommon and insecure. I wanted a win for my parents. The fantasy of their attendance at my graduation kept me going.

Katrina and I split our communications between phone sex, fantasizing about our future, and fighting about my hypocritical delusions of her ongoing infidelity. My obsessive visions of how she was spending her time reached such a point of implausibility and frequency that I finally asked my therapist for some antidepressants. I needed something to help me not destroy my chances of finishing my degree. It was Christa, again, who supplied the rest of my stamina. She listened to my obsessive rantings and soothed the squirrels in my head. She's the only one Jasper listens to.

# CHAPTER FORTY-FIVE

# GLORY FOR STABILITY

Toward the end of my third semester, my mother called me one night. She seemed a bit frantic. "Do you have a recent picture of yourself? A nice one? I can pay to have one taken if you don't."

I had recently taken headshots with my computer to send Katrina, so I was trying to look hot. I knew my mom would like them. Not the naughty ones. "I think I have one, Ma. What do you need it for?"

"I got tickets to *Dancing with the Stars*." I knew this was the season that Chaz Bono was a contestant. "And it's for the night that Cher is going to be there."

Because my mother is magic and she knows it, she assumed she would meet Cher at *Dancing with the Stars* and tell her the Bo story. She wanted a nice picture of me to show Cher so they could have their moment of shared destiny. In the same phone conversation, she also told me that I was better looking than Chaz and a better dancer. God, I love my mother.

I again received straight Bs my third semester. My last semester, I got straight As. Katrina and I had been fucking and fighting over the phone for nine months, and we were finally about to start a life together. She flew out for my graduation. Well, she treated herself to side trips to Toronto and New York during finals and never caved on her insistence on non-monogamy despite my begging for a short reprieve from uncertainty while I was manufacturing academic brilliance so I could finally deliver the ring of power to the flames. But she took the train and bought a new dress for the occasion.

Benny and Roxanne flew out. My parents were there. It was the perfect crew to bring to a perfect day. Did you know that when you graduate from Harvard, you get a floppy wizard hood to wear with your robe that has decorative sleeve extensions just like Gandalf's when he's being formal? Your diploma is also in Latin. Mine reads, "Tara K Yule, ad gradum Studiorum Theologicorum Magistri." I'm a motherfucking wizard now. That's all I ever wanted my parents to know.

Katrina drove home with me. About forty-five minutes into it, she casually said, "I think we should be monogamous now. I just wanted to know that you were coming home."

After a month back in Minneapolis, Katrina moved into my house. Benny got me a job at the restaurant I hadn't been ready to work for right after Pi. It was intended to be temporary while I applied for fancier jobs with my brand-new fancier credentials, so it didn't hurt my ego so much that I would be working security and barbacking again.

During my absence, First Friday had moved to this same restaurant due to DJ Bucky's connection to Shandell's old boyfriend, who was general manager. My first night at work back in my hometown, after graduating from Harvard, was to work security for First Friday. I spent the night picking up plastic cups, checking IDs, corralling drunks, and trying to comprehend the cosmic irony of the lesson my ego was to take from this experience. Many of the regulars I recognized assumed I was part of the nostalgia they were being served. DJ Bucky ignored my presence. Perhaps this was my payback for all the destruction I had wrought. Maybe this was the price to be paid for legitimacy.

For the next nine months, while I sent out hundreds of ignored cover letters and resumes, and my mother doggedly

294 | TY BO YULE

advised my ambition and wardrobe, I steadily ingested the river of shit that smelled exactly like my former ego's aspirations and failures. Toward the end of the last night I would work First Friday, an old regular of mine approached me at my station and asked, "How you doing? How does all this make you feel?"

I turned to her as the last bit of the defiant bitterness fell away and replied, "I don't know. You're the first person to ask me that. Thank you." I told my boss that night, who was also a former server of mine, that I wouldn't work another First Friday. Benny started giving me bartending shifts. Within a month, I had a regular weekly schedule as a bartender and started earning a solidly lower-middle-class income. It was plenty to pay our bills. I eventually stopped sending out resumes.

Three years after Katrina moved in, we got gay married. We'd been planning on it but stepped up our preparations when her father got sick. We invited people from all the various incarnations of our individual lives which created the dazzling community of unicorns that is ours. Benny and Christa were my co-best men. Pally flew out for the occasion. And my parents came. It was a divine day in mid-March Minneapolis that reached seventy degrees just for us. I bought a tux and Katrina found a shiny, purple prom dress. We had our ceremony in a small theater. I came onstage with our wedding party to "For Once in My Life," by Stevie Wonder. Katrina came out with her father to "Purple Rain." This is Minneapolis. Nobody could stop themselves from crying.

A friend of ours performed the ceremony. We read our own vows and asked the audience, the new family we were making, to affirm them. Then our friend Shanny Mac, the one who created Live Nude Drag at Pi, belted out "At Last" by Etta James. It was the greatest wedding in the history of weddings.

My mom told the Bo story at our reception. She had a microphone with a cord. In her left hand, she held a loop of extra cord to give herself some slack. In her right hand, she swished the cord in front of her and changed directions for theatrical effect. This story is how our family conveys warmth to others. It's our break-out-the-good-dishes-for-company family ritual. My nickname is proof that we've been together a long time and have a shared history. It's as fuzzy as we get.

# CHAPTER FORTY-SIX

# PANCAKES, BEARDS, AND RESILIENCE

Chastity and I never wanted to disappoint our mothers. We came out to our moms as teenagers while both having mullets. We got fat and blond together in our early thirties. We both transitioned at similar points later in life. One might hypothesize that these similarities are evidence of some obscure psychological template for awkward little girls raised by strong, beautiful, mythical drag queens, but I believe it simply proves that my family is magic. My parents know we are. We've just made different choices with our powers, even though they never felt like choices to any of us. We all did our best.

It took Katrina and me several years to build the real trust and intimacy I didn't even understand intellectually before this point in my life. We have built something that I haven't had one impulse to destroy. It seems sustainable to me. I'm protective of it, mostly from myself.

After the initial enthusiasm of testosterone dissipated, the novelty of every new hair morphed into contentment with appearing as a short, middle-aged, scruffy working-class man. Due to a lack of concentrated effort, I've achieved a pretty sweet dad bod. My hairline is quickly retreating. I have hair on my shoulders and breasts. I have not changed my name or my gender legally, mainly because I'm lazy, but I also have philosophical conflicts concerning the ritual.

I'm not planning any surgeries. I still like my tits. My nipples are very sensitive, and I think boobs are pretty. So does my wife. I would have bottom surgery if I wasn't completely underwhelmed by Western medicine's lack of motivation for innovation in the procedure. Because who doesn't want a dick? I would prefer a chance encounter with the Cock Genie, who might take my specifications into consideration.

I wish penises were merit based. Men would be better behaved, and Benny and I would get the horse cocks of our dreams. Because butch dykes are better at being men. We always were.

After all I've been through, I'm not sure I know what being a man implies anymore. I'm still quite unsure I was ever intended to embody conventional categories. They have yet to serve me anything but heartbreak. I don't think that the "born this way" slash "born in the wrong body" narrative applies to me. There are a great many people for whom it does, and I see its truth in them. The path to embodying one's gender is complex and personal no matter how many commonalities we can discern. What would I look like if "butch" had been a prized gender norm in my childhood? Would I have disrespected my body in so many ways? Though most women have been a victim of sexual mistreatment at some point in their lives, it's not a requirement for basing one's self-worth in the capacity for objectification. My identity contorted itself painfully in its relentless quest to become an objectifiable object. Its impatient distortions have caused pain and summoned enchantment.

What testosterone has given me mostly is space. There is a small safety zone surrounding me now. When I go to work, I simply strap down my tits and serve pancakes and mimosas. Nobody needs to work to figure out how to treat me. I can gay it up for middle-aged straight women wondering why such a handsome, charismatic gas station attendant isn't more successful. Or I can bro down with the businessmen, who are jealous of my tattoos and my edgy worldliness. None of them need to understand my identity to tip me.

The entitlements of passing are not available to everyone who transitions. My decisions to not have top surgery or change my legal gender are related to my ongoing allegiance to the community I love and admire. I don't want to erase the past that I have earned. I enjoy the privileges of both the assimilated and queer worlds. I deserve both and neither. There are those in both worlds who would prefer to exclude me. I still feel like a butch dyke, but I look like a man. My only credentials are my history and its body.

Testosterone has gifted me with a sustainable sex drive that overcame the lifelong struggles I've had surrounding what I look like when I'm naked. This makes the possibility of a satisfying ongoing intimate life with my partner plausible. Most importantly, testosterone killed my straight-girl problem at long last. It just went away. I don't need their gaze to transform me anymore.

I did develop a fairly distracting urge to touch penises again. Ain't that a bitch? I've heard anecdotally that this is not uncommon for trans men, but I have no desire to alter my identity again to accommodate these impulses. I'm only a little gay. I cannot see myself having a real intimacy with a man. After a few months wondering what fresh hell this compulsion was going to be, I began to recognize that this desire shows up when I'm feeling a little shitty about myself. For me, it's connected to a long-ago coping mechanism that caused me to want to be humiliated and emasculated in wholly obscene ways so I could escape my flesh.

Dicks are more powerful as symbols for me. They never quite deliver the impact of my expectations in real life. That impulse is just an old demon masquerading in my squirrelly head as desire, and I have enough history with my demons to guard my precious contentment against their efforts to collect on an old debt.

The one thing that feels like a sacrifice as I become acquainted with stability and happiness is ready access to my own magic. Sometimes I wonder if it's still there. Sometimes I can feel it but can't find a way to reach it. Is magic only available to those on the edge of madness? Will I ever try to change the world again someday? Have I traded in glory for my own chance at peace? Self-hatred was a productive motivator. But I'm a little tired. What do I have left to offer?

I am a bridge between the second-wave feminist lesbians who fostered the origins of a revolution and the millennial queers who sometimes don't seem to realize their opportunities haven't always existed. I sometimes don't know what to call myself in their presence, but I don't want to discourage new enthusiasm. I think those of us who were young when improvisational transgression defined our efforts for social transformation can sometimes feel resistant to boundaries that demand increasing levels of proficiency and specificity. I fit into any number of queer identities, new and old, but I still believe in misfit alliances. I'm on your side. I love your fancy new queer hair. I think we could find each other if we knew how to look and had a place to come together. How do we find solidarity without rock 'n' roll and dyke bars? I honestly don't know. Ten years later, people still ask me if I would open another Pi. The moment for that place has passed along with my way of changing the world. My body aches from a lifetime of not giving a shit what happened to it. I am sedimented resistance and capitulation. But I am corporeal after a lifetime of faking it. I can still spin illusions for others' comfort and mine. Most often I don't.

I'm a happy husband and a good friend.

Once upon a time, I got to be the hero in a real-life fairy tale. Not many people can say that. I was chosen. I bested adversaries and navigated labyrinths. Human and cosmic forces alike joined to aid my quest. It meant something to those who witnessed it. I believe the portal is always ajar if you can find it. What I have left is a story. It is a good story and that is the best reason to become a pirate.

# ACKNOWLEDGMENTS

This book started out telling the story of Pi and ended up being about me due to my overblown sense of self-importance. There are a thousand stories of love and magic at Pi that aren't in this book. More importantly, there were people who made Pi the wonderland it was whose names aren't in it. That makes me sad. I would like to acknowledge and thank some of them here. Stacey, Dalton, Kimmy, Josh, Desiree, William, Josina, Flo, Monica, ZsuZsi, Joel, and my Pi daughters, Frances and Jackie—thank you all for working at that circus. There were some critical regulars: E, Molly H., Terri the big cop, April, Roya, DJ Particle, Tara, Crystal, Irene, Jennie, Kim, and Michelle, pirate accomplice Nicole A, Anna, and so many more that I will eventually regret forgetting to mention. Oh, and Andrea Jenkins. After drunkenly asking you twice about using your real name, I realized that story got cut. Your poetry and presence in the world are an inspiration. I loved my Pi family so much. It was the best and hardest thing I will ever do.

Love to my second bar family at HK. Thanks for being interesting and funny for the last eight years.

Thank you to the professors who got me into Harvard, Melissa and Kevin. And Joni for being my fancy friend. Thanks to the professors at Harvard who were nice to me: Mark, Karen, Amy, and Stephen.

Thank you to the friends who read this and helped me edit

and encouraged me: Christa, Adrian, Benny, Kylie, Patricia, Judith, and especially Katrina. Thank you to Christa especially for your exceptional council and steadfast support.

A huge thank-you to my editors Anitra, Frank, Patrick, Dara, Graham, and everyone at Wise Ink, but especially to S. E. Fleenor, my friend, editor, and fellow superhero.

I gratuitously thank my wise friend, Teresa. Next book's all about you, babe.

Thank you to friends whose voices and laughter I have lost but can always hear: Miss Eva, Hart, Quij, Rina, Rachel, Sam, Darlene, Jim, Janet, Big Marv, and my protector and friend, GeeGee. Monkey loves you.

Thank you to my Minneapolis family. Goddamn, you're gorgeous. Especially Ran and Katrina. The queer retirement compound is happening.

**TY BO YULE** is a scruffy, middle-aged, retired queer cult leader living in Minneapolis with his amazing wife Katrina, his attack cat Kevin, and Miami the hustler cat. After getting his mother's hopes up by getting a master's of theological studies from Harvard, he is currently a bartender who writes things in his spare time. Chemicallyenhancedbutch.com is where you can find his neglected blog or buy this book and also say stuff to him.